A SAPPER IN THE FORGOTTEN ARMY

A SAPPER IN THE FORGOTTEN ARMY

by
JOHN HENSLOW

with sketches, diagrams and photographs by the author

Published by

JOHN HENSLOW
DURLEIGHMARSH FARM, PETERSFIELD, SUSSEX, GU31 5AX

First Published 1986

DEDICATED TO

HON. CAPT. SURYANARAYANA (Retd.)
(my Jemadar "Suri")
and the *thambis*
of the Q.V.O. Madras Sappers and Miners

©1986 John Henslow
ISBN 0 9511268 0 6

Printed and distributed by
Portia Press Ltd., London Street, Whitchurch, Hants. RG28 7LN.

CONTENTS

Chapter		Page
1	Metamorphosis – Schoolboy to Soldier	1
2	One Pip Up	11
3	From Halifax to Bangalore	16
4	On the Road to Burma	27
5	The Forgotten Army	40
6	Training for Jungle Warfare	51
7	Back to War	67
8	The Battle for Kohima	75
9	The Jap Retreat and Follow-up	86
10	A Battle Trophy	95
11	Down the Kabaw Valley	106
12	In Search of the Missing Link	114
13	The Fatal Change of Plan	133
14	Irrawaddy Assault Crossing – Failure and Success	148
15	Pagan and King Col	162
16	The Advance on the Oilfields	172
17	Rangoon, LIAP and the Bomb	187
18	Bangkok and the Fruits of Victory	196
19	Jap POWs and the Victory Parade	209
20	Fire and Flood	218

21	Social Life and Seasnakes	231
22	Goodbye to Bangkok	238
23	The Unexpected Ambush	247
24	Farewell to the Far East	253
	Glossary of Abbreviations	260

LIST OF ILLUSTRATIONS

Sketches and Diagrams

Author's itinerary	Facing page 1
Penis Park, Burma	34
Battle of Kohima, May 1944	77
The Ethyl Pratts mine	88
The Irrawaddy Crossing	153
Main Assault across the Irradwaddy	174

Photographs between pages 120 and 121

FOREWORD

by

Maj. Gen. (Retd) D.C.T. Swan, C.B., C.B.E.

As one who was born in India, and spent ten years between World War I and World War II with the (then) QVO Madras Sappers and Miners carrying out Engineering work in many parts of India, including four years on the North West Frontier under active service conditions, I am fascinated by John Henslow's account of the time he spent in India and Burma.

I served as CRE 1 Burma Division when it was driven out of Burma by the Japanese in 1942, carrying out demolitions, organising ferry-crossings of the Irrawaddy and Chindwin Rivers, etc. I was lucky enough then to have Madras Sapper units under my control. John Henslow was not in the area at that time, but as our paths crossed during the reconquest of Burma his vivid story of Sapper Works with which he was concerned gives me a personal interest in the narrative.

It is apparent that his love and admiration for the qualities shown by the Madras Sappers under all conditions equals my own.

I later got to know John Henslow well when he joined my staff at HQ BAOR as Intelligence Officer, carrying out reconnaissance and demolition preparations against possible Soviet incursions at the time of the "Berlin Airlift" in 1950/51. He showed then the same qualities that are evident in this story.

I greatly welcome the publication of these Memoirs, with their unique photographs, as they serve both as an invaluable record for historians and as a reminder to the present generations of the tribulations (and also sometimes of the fun!) which some of their grandfathers underwent during World War II.

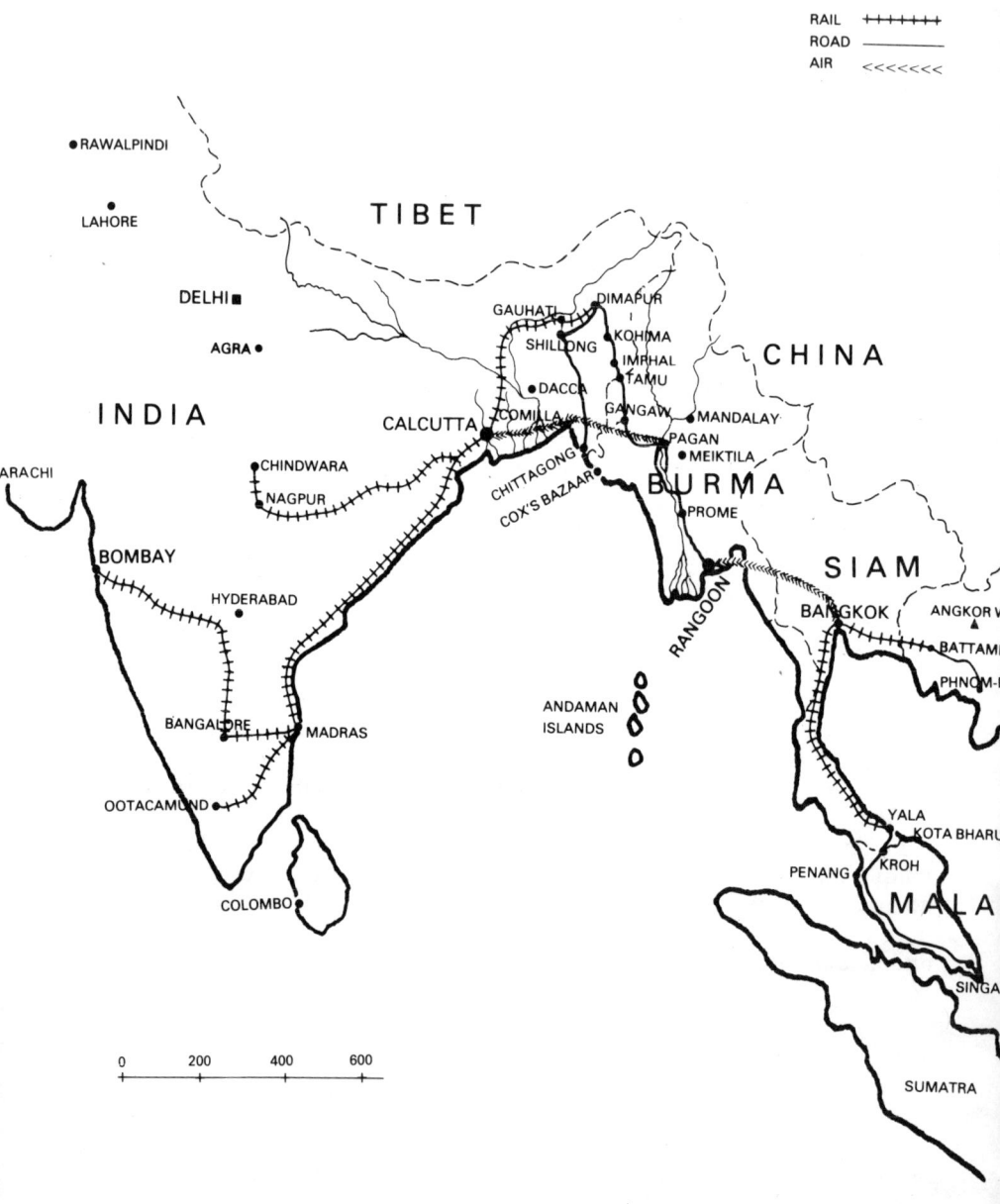

CHAPTER 1

Metamorphosis – Schoolboy to Soldier

It is not so much how to begin as where to begin. The metamorphosis of schoolboy to soldier is part of the story, gradual at first but later accelerated by the demands of the war on Britain's manpower as its commitments spread further across the face of the world.

I had just passed my sixteenth birthday when the clouds of war were gathering. As a schoolboy at Dauntsey's, a small public school in Wiltshire, my chief concern was School Certificate and what came after that, for I was at the age when one has to start thinking about the future. Choosing a profession to follow for the rest of one's life is not easy when one knows so little about the opportunities and careers that exist in the outside world. Careers Officers to advise one were unknown in those days. My interests were numerous but none seemed to fit the pattern of requirements for a good sound career. I had always had a passion for birds, butterflies and all forms of natural history. I loved shooting and fishing. I spent much of my spare time painting. I enjoyed taking part in school plays both acting, singing in operettas and the staging and lighting behind the scenes.

I was a keen rugger player where my fifteen stone and six feet four with a reasonable turn of speed gave me certain physical advantages in the forward line. They also enabled me to achieve some success in field sports such as the shot and discus. Not forgetting that my father was Chief Inspector of Physical Training in the army and gave me every encouragement, and not to mention that he had been instrumental in installing ex-Army School of Physical Training Instructors at both my prep school and my public school, it was hardly surprising that I enjoyed physical training.

However, this diversity of interest did little more than make me a jack of all trades but master of none. I was an enthusiastic member of the art society, the photographic society, the natural history society and half a dozen other societies, not to mention the Scouts – I joined them all, but when it came to choosing a career I was stumped. I would have liked to become a biologist, but in those days the only opening was the Marine Biology Research Station at Plymouth and that was heavily over-subscribed. In the end I plumped for the medical profession; at least in those days it had prospects. Various relations, impressed by my efforts at taxidermy, had told me that I should become a surgeon, though I dread to think what my patients would have thought if they knew that it was my ability to skin and stuff animals and birds that had called me to the profession.

Fortunately, for my future patients, the war altered all this. Munich – peace in our time – and the final declaration of war were exciting times for a schoolboy, a prospect of adventure and excitement that would make life a romantic escapade. I even had a sneaking admiration for Hitler, his boldness and his power over other men was not without appeal to a boy of my age, and British counter-propaganda had as yet to be born.

After listening to that historic broadcast by the Prime Minister of the day, Neville Chamberlain, that contained those unforgettable words; "And a state of war now exists between Great Britain and Germany", I remember expecting them to be immediately followed by the roar of Luftwaffe planes overhead. In fact I had not long to wait before the eerie note of the air raid sirens shattered the peace of the English afternoon with their strange and unfamiliar wail. Whether it was a mistake or a brilliantly conceived false alarm I have never discovered, but it galvanised everyone into action to do something about getting prepared for the realities of war.

My own contribution was to dig an air raid shelter in our garden at Norway Lodge in Fleet. I dug like a badger for two days and the end product was a great pride to me. Steps down at both ends, seven feet deep, with a bench to sit on at the bottom, roofed with corrugated iron mounded over with earth, it even had electric light run off a battery. Unfortunately, my war seemed to have run out of steam. That first air raid warning which I expected to be the forerunner of regular air raids was all we had for the time being. Just as well, for I had overlooked a few structural necessities, drainage for one. The autumn rains filled up my shelter with water which in turn caused the sides to fall in, and make it unusable. I spent the last few days before returning to school filling sandbags to build a blast wall in front of the cottage hospital.

At school, life went on much the same except that we stuck miles of sticky brown paper strips across the window panes to prevent flying glass from bomb blasts. It never got the opportunity of being tested in my time except by a cricket ball. I was standing by the window when it happened and very unjustly got the blame as I collected broken glass from all over the room. I hoped that the brown paper would be more effective against bomb blast than it was against cricket balls.

Time passed slowly during the term as it always does at school and the war became more remote. Even I could see that after the fall of France and the final withdrawal of the British Expeditionary Force through Dunkirk that it either had to be a long war, if we were ever going to win, or we would be invaded and become yet another occupied country under the Nazi jackboot. One did not have to be a defeatist to have such thoughts. At this stage the Axis occupied or controlled the whole of Europe from Norway down to the toe of Italy and as far east as the borders of Russia. The Axis had a firm foothold in North Africa and Britain was left alone to oppose this massive military might that had swamped all our allies in Europe and now lay poised for inevitable invasion only twenty-two miles across the English Channel. An invastion that we seemed ill-equipped to repel.

With these prospects before me I decided not to pursue the five years of study necessary to become a doctor. Better to get myself a front seat in the theatre of war. All my attention from now on was focussed on the army exams. My father, though a regular soldier all his life and now involved in the third war of his career, having served through the Boer War and the First World War, had never tried to influence me in my choice of career. He had once suggested that I might try for the Malayan police, possibly because he had a friend in the police in Malaya who could have helped me. With hindsight it is just as well that nothing came of it. When I told him I had decided to try for a commission in the army he advised me to try for the Royal Engineers. He had been an infantryman in the Wiltshire Regiment before he specialised in physical training and rose to the top post as Chief Inspector, but he told me that if he could have his time over again he would go for the Royal Engineers. "Actual fighting is a very small and unpleasant part of your life in the army. Most of your time is spent training which is both repetitive and boring. My advice to you Johnny is try for the Engineers, you will always be doing something interesting and worthwhile, an infinite variety of jobs and what you will learn from them will always be of use to you in Civvy Street if you decide to come out when it is all over".

It was very sound advice and I was determined to take it but there was one snag; to get into the top thirty of the army exam. The Sappers creamed off the top, followed by the Gunners and the Corps of Signals. These went into the "Shop" at Woolwich. The Infantry and the Cavalry went to Sandhurst. With these regiments, tradition, influence and family connections were what counted, but for the Sappers you had to pass out at the top, and my mathematics were not top class, nor I suspect were my physics and chemistry. However I was determined to have a try and during the following six months I probably worked harder to improve my academic qualifications than I have ever done, and six months was a long time in those days.

If Britain stood alone it was not without its resources. Determined to repel the imminent invasion, the L.D.V. (Local Defence Volunteers) was formed. This was the origin of "Dad's Army".

The L.D.V. was incredible but it was fun. We started with nothing more than arm bands and wooden rifles to drill with and pikes to repel the invaders should they come. Bit by bit our armoury improved which was just as well if the invaders were not to die of laughter. Eventually, the great day came when we were issued with real rifles. Martini single action drop block ·303. They had been requisitioned from the Boy's Brigade and that pattern of rifle had last been used at the Battle of Rorke's Drift in the Zulu war!

We were now ready for action and our job was to do night patrols on the Downs to apprehend and capture any German parachutist. Popular belief at the time was that they could be dressed as nuns. We slept in small tents up on the Downs and patrolled with our Martini rifles and five rounds of ammunition feeling that we were a match for any parachutist. The great day came when we were issued with a further five rounds of ammunition and the original five rounds were to be expended on the local range just to see if we could hit anything.

It was all very solemn and serious. A regular sergeant of advancing years was in charge. Our section lay down in the butts and targets appeared at one hundred yards. Those lethal ·303 rounds slid into the breach and the blocks snapped up behind them. None of us had fired a rifle other than an airgun before in our lives. "On the command target front, line the tip of the foresight in the vee and level with the shoulders of the backsight. On command 'Fire' squeeze the trigger". On the command 'Fire' we squeezed the trigger. There was a click, click, click all the way down the line, but nothing more menacing. The Master Sergeant at Arms blew out his cheeks a little puzzled. "Hand me that rifle boy". Sternly a sharp reload followed by a click, repeated in disbelief several times. Then a closer inspection and finally the profound announcement. "I am sorry gentlemen, but these 'ere rifles have no firing pins. They could not knock the skin off a rice pudding, let alone the guts out of a German".

It transpired that before bequeathing these rifles to the Boys Brigade for drill purposes the authorities had very wisely rendered then unusable knowing what boys are. However, nobody had thought to check their serviceability before issuing them to the L.D.V. We had been patrolling the Downs every night in all weather, convinced that if German parachutists landed we were suitably armed to take them on. If they had I can only hope that they would have been so doubled up with laughter that they would have been unable to raise their Smeitzer automatics and end our embarrassment. By the time this demoralising discovery had been made the L.D.V. had been renamed the Home Guard. Little did we know at the time that its antics would be immortalised by a television programme in the distant future. We felt badly let down over the Martini rifles. The authorities fitted new firing pins and we had another day on the ranges to restore our confidence but our marksmanship did little to restore the confidence of the Sergeant at Arms. "Gentlemen, I think you were more impressive without the firing pins" was his summing up.

Sometime later our erstwhile American allies eased their conscience with 'Lease Lend', a means of disposing of their old outdated destroyers, Liberty ships and, for our benefit, Thomson sub-machine guns – Al Capone vintage – an embarrassment to them and a godsend to us. It was a big step from the Battle of Rorke's Drift to Al Capone as far as armament was concerned. We unpacked these wonderful gifts from America enthralled at their capability. This was the real stuff; we had seen it all at the cinema. Contemporary American heroes spraying their prohibition opponents with a hail of forty-five bullets from a Thomson sub-machine gun. A drum of fifty rounds of ammunition was very impressive to someone who had been dependent on an archaic Martini rifle with five rounds of ammo and no firing pins. It did wonders for our morale even if we were never allowed to fire these fascinating new weapons. There was no military instructor who had any experience in the Thomson sub-machine gun so we just had to read the instructions and hope that when the time came we would be able to remember them.

At this time a spate of new weapons started to arrive, the product of amateur geniuses more than our professional technology. The Spigot mortar, the Blacker Bombard and the sticky bomb. One of these I remember being demonstrated by a self-styled expert. It fired something that looked like a ginger beer bottle but contained a mixture of petrol and phosphorous. When the bottle hit the target and shattered, the phosphorous was exposed to the air and ignited, setting light to the petrol. We were told that it was deadly against tanks – if you could hit them. The demonstrator fired it across the school playing fields, underestimated its range and it crashed onto the roof of the games master's house shattering the tiles, but fortunately it was a dummy round filled with water instead of petrol and phosphorous, so that, much to the disappointment of the spectators, the games master's house did not burst into flames.

At this time also bombing raids were becoming more frequent. Coventry and Bristol were receiving their fair share of treatment, or so we were informed by the 9 o'clock news and the newspapers. Occasionally reality was brought a little closer when a returning German raider jettisoned his remaining bombs on the peaceful Wiltshire countryside and we would hear the crump, crump, crump, of a stick of bombs falling close enough to remind us that the war was for real if you happened to be near the receiving end.

It was about then that I got my first view of the enemy. I was in the school library situated on the first floor and overlooking the gymnasium and the cinder track and field sports ground. I was reading up for the army exam and as was so often the case with me, the outside world was slowly usurping my attention through the window. There was a droning noise, then to my amazement an aeroplane of considerable proportions came over the top of the gym roof clearing it by only a matter of feet. The tip of its wing passed so close to my window that I felt I could have leant out and touched it, but what held me spellbound was not only the German cross on the side of its fuselage, but that for a brief moment I found myself looking straight into the eyes of its pilot. That momentary vision was photographed into my brain and I can see to this day the extraordinary calm expression on the pilot's face as he sailed past my window and was gone, lifting over some trees by the school farm buildings and hedge hopping on towards the Downs, where, we heard later, he crashed his Junker 88 and gave himself up to a local farmer who gave him tea until an army detachment from Imber Tank Ranges arrived to take him prisoner.

We felt cheated out of the glory that should have been ours. If he had only crashed a little sooner he would have been in our territory and our Home Guard section could have gone into action, Thompson submachine guns blazing, and covered ourselves with glory and no doubt souvenirs from the crashed plane. Then I remembered the expression on the pilot's face. Perhaps it was just as well that he was welcomed to British soil by a yeoman farmer and not a bloodthirsty bunch of schoolboys hellbent on proving themselves as worthy members of the armed forces and demonstrating to the world what their section of the Home Guard could do given the chance.

Apart from these odd incidents life was school and holidays, and the war only existed on the wireless and in the newspapers. For most of the time the only direct confrontation of war was rationing of food, clothing, petrol and of course identity cards together with all those posters reminding us that walls had ears, dig for victory, etc. etc. But of all these restrictions food rationing was the most telling imposition to a growing schoolboy. A school in the heart of the Wiltshire countryside with its own farm, produced certain home grown benefits that tempered the severity of rationing, but an unexpected bonus came when a sow on the school farm produced a substantial litter of piglets but no milk to ensure their survival. An opportune word with the farm foreman and three of us had a clandestine piglet apiece which we proceeded to rear on the residue of milk left on the table after school breakfast and tea. The venture was so successful that by the end of term the piglets had grown to a size that could no longer be concealed from the school authorities and had to be transferred home. My parents, who dutifully came down to witness a school play in which I had some small part, found themselves returning with a pig as well as their son in the car.

After the holidays they found themselves, or rather my dear mother found herself, in sole charge of the pig who had to be registered to enable her to buy a ration of pigmeal which, with all the household scraps, kept the pig growing until his ultimate fate was due. The war time rule was that if you reared a pig at home it had to be registered for rations and when it was slaughtered you could only keep half and the other half had to be sold to the butcher to help feed the rest of the nation. However, before our pig's final day of reckoning came he had a better time than most pigs. He was an expert at breaking bounds, and frequently ended up in the foyer of the local cinema. The manager would ring up my mother to inform her that her pig was there again and enquire if he was to be given a ninepenny or a one and sixpenny seat. As my father was nearly always away my mother had to retrieve the pig on her own, but she was a very resourceful person and soon developed a retrieval technique. She would arrive at the cinema with a bucket of swill and once the pig's head was inside she would walk backwards along the main street of Fleet and back to Norway Lodge with the pig following with his head in the swill bucket – great entertainment for the cinema queue, but not much fun for my mother.

The most hilarious occasion was when the manager telephoned her to tell her that the pig was being ridden down the High Street by some rather drunken Canadian soldiers. Nothing daunted she persuaded them to ride him back up the street until he was within swill bucket range when she informed them that she was a personal friend of their commanding officer, which in fact was true and had a momentary sobering impact on them; time enough to get the pig back home the last few yards with his head in the swill bucket. Pig, like all good things came to an end, and I am sure that nothing was wasted from his snout to his trotters, for Mama was a wonderful cook.

At school I had finally taken the army exam. The important thing was to pass out in the top thirty to be sure of getting into the R.E. To my disappointment I passed thirty-eighth from a total of several hundred and was offered the R.A. as a second choice. I was very disappointed as I had set my heart on becoming a sapper. There were more disappointments in store. The Military Academies at Woolwich and Sandhurst were closed down and all my hard work for the army exam was in vain. No more regular commissions would be granted for the duration of the war! Instead future officers would be trained at Officer Cadet Training Units, OCTU's, and would on passing out receive Emergency Commissions. Those who were qualified to be accepted into the technical branches of the army would be sent to a University for six months prior to OCTU.

I did not have long to dwell on my disappointment before things started happening. I received instructions to enlist at the nearest recruiting office and then report to the Artillery Training Barracks at Topsham, near Exeter. Next day my father took me to Aldershot to be enlisted and sign my attestation papers. As my father was a full colonel in uniform and well known in Aldershot Command I received prompt and courteous service at the recruiting office, V.I.P. treatment that was to be in sharp contrast to my first taste of being the lowest form of army life at Topsham Barracks a few days later.

On 20th August, 1941, I arrived at 16 Field Training Regt. R.A. Topsham Barracks, Exeter, to start a course of six weeks in the ranks designed to turn schoolboys into soldiers and let them know what it was all about. There were 150 of us and we were divided into eight sections. My section, H section, consisted of the minority of boys whose school had no OTC or Cadet Corps, a sort of awkward squad. The first day we had a nice polite sergeant in charge who explained that he was there to help us and that all we had heard in the music halls about sergeant majors was a thing of the past. The following day we were in for a nasty shock. The battery commander had decided that we needed someone special in charge to make up for our lack of Corps training at school and he had found someone very special for the job. Sergeant Sessford had spent a lot of his military career in India. In his absence abroad he reckoned that the British Army had gone soft. In his day, you cursed and swore your way to the rank of sergeant and if anyone let you down you tied him to a gun wheel and had him flogged. To be put in charge of a section of schoolboys was bad enough, but when he discovered he had been landed with the awkward squad who might make a fool of him in front of his fellow sergeants, it was as much as he could stand. He was a big man and his short cropped sandy hair bristled right up the back of his thick neck. He was also not unaware that this miserable bunch of public schoolboys were destined to be officers within a year and then he would have to stand to attention in our presence and take our orders. In the meantime we had to be licked into shape and Sergeant Sessford was the man to do it.

He was going to show us what the real army was like. He swore and cursed us. He made us do everything at the double. When we failed to meet his standards we ended up with our packs filled with sand in full marching order jumping across the square at full knees bend. It was a gruelling initiation and only fit schoolboys could have stood the pace. I was a keen rugger player and had kept myself fit for the game but by the time Sergeant Sessford had finished with me I was only fit to crawl into bed and hope that I could survive another day. It was a challenge which I was determined not to fail. One or two could not stand the pace but the majority survived, for the young have great reserves of which they are unaware until put to the test. We had no previous experience of army life. His language was crude and colourful to our young ears. "Stand still boy, stand still, if anyone moves I'll knock seven colours of shit out of him". "You, boy, chest out, stomach in, you look like a pregnant penguin – if you call that standing to attention then my prick's a bloater – come here boy – double halt – stand to attention – you wasn't born boy, you was scraped off the sheets with a spoon – back to your squad – about turn – double – Left – Right – Left – Right – Left – Right". And so it went on from reveille to last post.

In those days the bugle calls ruled your life in the army. They woke you in the morning, told you when to eat, when to get on parade, when to report for defaulters, when the flag was being lowered at sunset and when to turn your lights out and go to sleep. Once you learnt them you never forgot them.

They were very expressive of the order that they conveyed from the awakening call of reveille which ended in "get out of beeed, get out of beeed". The expectancy of 'Come to the cook house door, boys – Come to the cook house doooor' to the more peremptory 'Fall in, Fall in A, Fall in B, Fall in all the company'. The lingering nostalgia of last post as the flag was lowered and finally 'Lights Out, Lights Ouuuut' at the end of a gruelling day. There were many more calls, such as the officers'mess call: 'Officers wives have puddings and pies, Soldiers wives have skilly'. They seem unknown in the post-war army and more's the pity because they were a part of military heritage that was well worth retaining and were practical, for wherever you were you heard the bugle, you were tuned in so to speak, and always got the message.

Eventually we progressed from endless drilling and marching on the barrack square to gun drill. This, we were assured, was the real thing that we should all be looking forward to – particularly as it was all done at the double. Under Sergeant Sessford it consisted of doubling round a large field carrying two forty-five pounder shells to remind us of the mistake we had just made. Sergeant Sessford assured us that however much of a bastard he might be on parade, he was a hell of a nice chap off parade. This we had to take his word for as we never seemed to be off parade. There was the great day when we had our T.A.B., tetanus and cholera inoculations which under army regulations entitled us to

24 hours off duty to recover from the 'flu like effects and stiffening of the arm injected. However, Sergeant Sessford assured us that the best cure for the after-effects was to scrub the barrack room floor until it shone like a mirror. The only person foolish enough to point out that we were entitled to a day's rest to recover from the after-effects ended up cleaning all the latrines with a toothbrush.

Towards the end of our six weeks' training we did have an official dance with late passes all round and an opportunity for Sergeant Sessford to demonstrate just how nice he could be off parade. Unfortunately, one of our squad called Shilston actually danced with Mrs. Sessford and in a naive moment expressed surprise that she was there as he had just posted a parcel to a Mrs. Sessford in Glasgow the night before at the request of Sergeant Sessford. That night after the dance Sergeant Sessford came into our barrack room after poor Shilston's blood. It appeared amongst other things he was also a bigamist with a wife in Glasgow as well as Exeter and poor Shilston had let the cat out of the bag. There was no enquiry, Shilston got thumped good and proper, on the spot for what he had said in all innocence!

Our six weeks were running out. Soon we would be demobilised and sent to a university for six months. We gathered it would be a choice of Glasgow, Durham or Aberdeen. In my letter home I said I did not mind which as long as it was not Glasgow. Needless to say I was assigned to Glasgow. As it turned out it was a good choice, not that we had any choice, but Glasgow University was not what I had imagined it to be. All one knew of Glasgow from hearsay was the squalor of the Gorbles but the University was a rather fine building in an impressive setting overlooking Kelvin Park and its traditions in the faculty of engineering were well founded. Such was the pace of wartime necessity that we had to metamorphose from soldiers to civilians overnight. We finished our training at 16 FTR R.A. on one evening and next morning we were entrained to Glasgow as civilians but without civvy clothes. These our parents had to rail up to us at various university destinations to enable us to complete our official metamorphosis at the other end.

CHAPTER 2

One Pip Up

University life was a dream come true after six weeks of military training under Sergeant Sessford. I am sure that none of us forgot him for the rest of our lives, but I often wonder if any of us met him again in later days as commissioned officers. However for the moment we were civilians again, treated with a respect that we had forgotten existed. We were assigned to student halls with our own rooms and a freedom of action that was unfamiliar to us. Six weeks of military training had usurped all our ideas of freedom of the individual. Suddenly we discovered that we had a series of lectures to attend that were not summoned by a bugle call and if we failed to attend that was our responsibility. No one would put us on defaulters for failure to be on parade.

I was assigned to Macklay Hall on the other side of Kelvin Park and looking out on the imposing Gothic university buildings. At first the other students regarded us as an odd lot of quasi-military intake, but we soon integrated into student life. The course was demanding for we had to try and cover a three year degree course for a BSc Engineering Degree in six months. But there were no sergeants or military instructors to jolly you along – it was up to you to make what you could of it. Some tried harder than others.

There was of course the usual student rag which at Glasgow went by the name of Daft Friday with the customary excesses in the name of charity. There was also one memorable day when Ex-President of Czechoslovakia, Dr. Benes, recently deposed by a Nazi putch, visited the University. A sad but dignified little figure. I helped tow his car around the University buildings which I gather was some part of University tradition for distinguished visitors.

After about six weeks at Glasgow I had an unexpected stroke of luck that altered my life completely. The sappers found that they had underestimated their requirements and those who had passed out high enough in the army exam were transferred to the sappers. To me it was manna from heaven; to others who had wanted to become a gunner it was very different – they felt cheated of their ambitions, but such is the wheel of fortune.

Once I knew I was destined to be a sapper I started to double my efforts at University. I ceased to play liar dice during complex chemistry lectures on the Benzine Ring and tried hard to understand the essence of the lectures that covered physics, advanced mechanics and dynamics etc. I tried hard but the pace was fast. Cramming a three year BSc course into six months was bound to make it so for the most brilliant of students and I was not of this class, also I had other distractions as did everyone on the course. For some it was the girl students studying social science or the arts, for me it was rugger. It was my passion and my ambition to play for the Varsity Team. An ambition that did not take me long to realise. In my first Varsity match I gathered the ball inside our own 25 and timed my kick just right, finding touch a few yards from the opposition goal line. It was a lucky kick that went just right, and luckier still the press had a photograph of me making the kick and the try that resulted from a forward rush from the line-out a few yards from the opposition goal line, where once again my height had enabled me to gather the ball and touch down. From then on my place in the Varsity Team was assured, but my knowledge of the complexes of the Benzine Ring were diminished as I was practising or playing at Murray Field or elsewhere when I should have been studying.

Glasgow was an exciting place full of life at night. Every nationality of seaman put ashore for a brief interlude in their constant waltz with death on the high seas. At sea they lived under the constant shadow of death from a U-boat attack. Always conscious that at any moment of day or night the silent track of a torpedo could be heading straight for them. Ashore they did not have time to adjust, life was just a moment in time, it was only the present that was real, no one thought of the future. When ashore in the pubs of Glasgow they seemed to shoot and knife each other with unfailing regularity. They drank too much and quarrelled; their quarrels were finally resolved in death. The human contents of the pub vomited out into the streets and were dispersed within seconds. The poor police when they arrived had nothing but the evidence of the dead man on the floor, the barmaid who had seen nothing and the knowledge that the suspects were a mixture of Poles, Latvians, Norwegians, Laskars and a dozen other unidentifiable European seamen who at that very moment could be weighing anchor and slipping out to sea for unknown destinations.

By the end of March 1942 our six months at University were all too quickly over, final exams of which we never saw the results before we were recalled to the colours, as army orders phrased it. I was posted to the 2nd Training Battalion Royal Engineers D Camp, Barton Stacey, near Winchester. I arrived at that bleak downland camp on the 1st April

1942, for a nine weeks pre OCTU training course.

I obviously enjoyed my time at Barton Stacey. The work was hard but it was all field engineering which was what I had always wanted to do. Knots and lashings, derricks and scissors, wiring, demolitions, bridging (small box girder and Ingles, no Bailey yet). We also had plenty of lectures and another exam set by 141 OCTU for which I was destined. It was mostly maths and engineer calculations and I got 95% which assured my entrance to OCTU and left me very elated. One other thing that the army was very keen on in those days was training for gas warfare, we had to smell and recognise chlorine, phosgene and mustard gas and we all had to experience DM which was tear gas. You were marched into the gas chamber with your gas mask on to demonstrate how effective it was, then on the command "masks off", you took them off just to prove how genuine their protection was. We emerged coughing, spluttering and eyes streaming. There was also a night exercise with gas masks carried but not worn until at some point gas was released and you had to use your own judgment as to when to put on your mask. Some who left it a little late learnt their lesson the hard way. What really sticks in my memory of that night was wandering about in thick clouds of tear gas whilst all around the nightingales were singing away completely unaffected, presumably they have no tear glands.

My pre-OCTU training finished, I moved on to 141 OCTU R.E. at Aldershot on 8th June 1942. The OCTU was situated behind the old Garrison Theatre just opposite the Officers' Club, a mere four miles from home. Being so close to home I could get back on my motorbike so easily that no letters exist as an aide memoire to my days there. One realises how these letters home, read thirty-five years later, help to trigger the memory to recall other incidents not mentioned in the letter, but without that record as a lead in, the memory is mostly blank. However, as it turned out we only spent three months at Aldershot after which the OCTU moved to Newark and letters home continued again.

My only other unprompted memory of 141 OCTU at Aldershot was church parade on Sundays. In those days church parade was still obligatory and a Garrison affair. We marched there with other units from the Aldershot Garrison with regimental bands playing all the way. After the service we marched back forming up in a rather limited space behind the church with a march past a saluting base just inside the churchyard. We were packed like sardines behind the church so tightly that there was no room for the bands; they fell in in front of the church, ready to lead in with their units as they came up to them. The effect could sometimes be disastrous because different regiments have different marching paces. I remember one occasion when we were directly behind a light infantry regiment who had a very quick marching pace, and the sappers have one of the slowest. It was all right starting behind the church where the respective CSM's bawled out the time. The light infantry snapped out their quick staccato pace and we followed with our measured left.... right.... left, but once we came round the church and in sight of the saluting base the light infantry band struck up their regimental march, a quick infectious tune that drowned out the voice of our CSM and in no time we were all changing step to keep pace with their band. The sapper band master, seeing with horror the chaos in our ranks as we strode to master and keep step with the light infantry pace, was quick to react, with the pride of the Corps at stake he ordered his bandsmen to play louder than they had ever played before. They swung into position between us and the light infantry, blasting out our regimental march, Wings, giving it everything they had got. The wind section going purple in the face, the drums crashing out the steady measured rhythm of the sappers marching pace by the crash of cymbals. They completely drowned out the light infantry band which was just passing the saluting base. Some of the light infantry tried to change their pace to the new rhythm that was swamping them while others tried desperately to maintain their accustomed pace in spite of the opposing rhythm of our band. The result was quite catastrophic, for not only had they all become out of step with each other but they were also in the position of 'Eyes Right' as they passed the general on the saluting base and could not see whether the man in front was in step or even marching at the same pace.

Men were treading on each others heels, tripping over each other and changing step every three or four paces to try and get in step with the man in front who was also changing step to keep pace with the changing step of the man in front of him. It was a complete shambles. The colour sergeant went puce. The NCOs' were hissing threats out of the side of their mouths. Fortunately the officers leading their troops were unaware of the chaos behind them, but the general on the saluting base had a distinctly old-fashioned look on his face. By the time we reached the saluting base we had more or less got under control and in step. We marched past to the steady crunch, crunch of feet at 120 steps to the minute held by the rhythm of our own regimental march. The light infantry were furious and convinced that they had been deliberately nobbled. The fact that they spent most of the following week marching up and down their barrack square confirmed that the inspecting general had not failed to remark on their church parade performance to their CO.

After three months at 141 OCTU Aldershot, the army decided to move the OCTU to Newark in Nottingham, where there was more space and facilities for training. They had sensibly set up the new OCTU with new staff and called it the R.E. Field OCTU. We moved to it as a going concern, so there was no break in our training.

After a time we became more aware that the countdown to commissioning day had started when we were instructed to start ordering our officers' uniforms from the military tailors. Here Messrs. Plumb and Son seemed to have cornered the market and were doing a roaring trade. I was fortunate that most of my father's uniform would fit me with little alteration and, though he was still serving, he had acquired quite a lot of spare in a lifetime of soldiering. I had to have one set of service dress made for the passing-out parade. The other one I got from my father. It was of far finer quality material, a beautiful smooth barathea, but it was not possible to hide the fact that when it was made officers wore their insignia of rank on the cuff of their sleeve and the colour was paler and greener than the regulation service dress khaki of the day. The other item I was forced to buy was the officers' regulation greatcoat. The hem had to be nine inches from the ground and the chest was very tightly fitted for the effect of smartness but unfortunately this sacrificed any effect of warmth which was supposed to be the object of the garment.

I remember little of the final passing-out parade. We were just another wartime run of the mill batch of young Emergency Commissioned Officers to feed the insatiable appetite of the military machine. Passing-out parades were more like glorified kit inspections. We already had our posting orders and mine was to 224 Field Coy R.E. in 48 Div. and I had to report to them on 29th November, 1942, at Wragby, a small market town in Lincolnshire. I was now nearly 19½ years old.

CHAPTER 3

From Halifax to Bangalore

No letters home survived to reflect on my time with them, so perhaps I was too busy to write. I remember that the officers' quarters were in a commandeered house on the edge of the market square where the whole company paraded every morning at about 7 a.m. I also remember that I had great difficulty in getting on parade in time. Suddenly every officer left the mess for the market square and I was left struggling into my place at the head of my platoon after all the other officers were on station, just before the OC appeared. I lived in fear of the day when I had to sneak onto parade after the OC had arrived. I saw the occasion as the contemporary cartoonist H.M. Bateman would have portrayed it – 'the junior subaltern who arrived late on parade' myself creeping into position with no tie and a gaiter missing.

My only other memories are of building a Bailey bridge across the village pond, the only handy training gap we could find. Also endless reconnaissance on a motor cycle over the frozen minor roads of Lincolnshire. They seemed to be paved in black ice and I parted with my mount on every bend. It just slid away from me leaving me standing on one leg with the other cocked as centrifugal force with no containing moment of friction allowed my bike to migrate to the nearest ditch. It was all done in slow motion, I rarely damaged myself but expended considerable effort in retrieving the Norton 500 from road side ditches.

This was my first month as an officer. Very keen to live up to the part and very conscious that everyone from the platoon sergeant up regarded me as the lowest form of officer life, a shining raw one-pipper with no experience of life or anything else.

Everyone looks down on a bright, newly commissioned 2nd Lieut. My stay at Wragby was pretty short, just a month, for on 21st December 1942 I was drafted overseas. This was in fact just what I wanted. I had an ambition to end up in the jungle which contained all the wild life that fascinated me. At the time one had no idea of one's ultimate destination other than Halifax on draft RWAW. I was to report there on 7th January, 1943, and await to discover where this magical draft coding would deliver me. It could be the deserts of N. Africa or the jungle of the Far East or a host of other hard pressed stations of the British Empire at that time. The unexpected bonus of this posting overseas was that I would now enjoy Christmas and New Year at home on embarkation leave.

I lost no time in packing, saying goodbye to my fellow officers and catching the train back home. I managed to get back to my family just before Xmas eve. It was perforce a quiet wartime Christmas but, in spite of rationing, my mother had been saving up all manner of little extras to ensure that the occasion was marked by the traditional culinary delights of Christmas. It was also to be my last Christmas at home for she knew not how many years.

By New Year's Eve I felt I had started the count down to my last days at home and the start of a new life style somewhere overseas but where I had no idea. One could not discount the possibility that it might be the last I would ever see of my family, such are the fortunes of war. However, one did not dwell on such thoughts.

I spent New Year's Eve quietly at home with my mother and father. Next day my Belgian relations, Grand Père, Aunt André and her daughter Annie, who had escaped Belgium just ahead of the German invasion called in to wish me luck. It is at times like these that one realises the true bond of the family.

Next day started at 5.30 a.m. with my last breakfast at home and I left our house, Norway Lodge, with my father who had insisted in seeing me off at King's Cross. I said my farewells to my mother as I left our home. I could she was much more cut up by my leave-taking than she was prepared to show but she could not hide it altogether.

When my father and I reached King's Cross, dawn was just breaking. Most of the carriages were full of RE officers. I said goodbye to my father with the deep understanding that exists between father and son coupled with the restraint that is observed when we were both serving officers in the King's uniform. I would not see him again for nearly five years.

We changed trains at St. Dunstan's where it was snowing hard. When we arrived at Halifax we were met by two officers who gave the impression that everything was in hand and well organised. However, four hours later we were still on the station awaiting the return of the transport for the second wave to the depot. The depot was not what I had expected. A large house with a barrier inside. By now we felt more like refugees. No home, no food and very cold.

A list of names is called out and the owners sift out of the mob and pass through the barrier. Fifteen minutes later they appear looking a bit worried, they are off tonight! This is a surprise to us all and more speculations fly around. Then there is a request for any four officers and we start passing through. We enter an office where we are given a slip of paper with details of our billet on it and we are promised supper; our speculation of immediate departure overseas is restrained by one of our company who claims to have had four lots of embarkation leave already and never got further than this depot at Halifax. We resign ourselves to awaiting our chances on the roulette wheel of the system.

Halifax in mid-winter. Black buildings and white snow. Here we stay in suspended animation for three weeks, attend vague training lectures, but really just mark time until the moment when RWAW was posted on the notice board.

First clue to the destination of Draft RWAW – we drew tropical kit. This narrowed the field somewhat but it must be remembered that in those days Britain had a vast Empire and even though a lot of it was now in enemy hands, the Japs in the Far East and the Germans in Africa, it still left the final choice wide open to anywhere from British Guiana in the South Americas to half the African Continent, or India or Ceylon in the Far East.

The tropical kit we drew had been a long time in the quartermaster's store. It consisted of sun helmets, reminiscent of the relief of Mafeking, and long shorts with turnups almost a foot long that were buttoned up and could be let down after sundown to give added protection against mosquitos. Many essentials were just not available. The mobilisation of hundreds of thousands of men to defend the Empire had drained the ordnance resources down to the last leftovers from the South African War. I was fortunate as I made up what they could not supply from my father who was able to let me have his valise, officer's folding canvas bath and wash basin etc. (also left-overs from the Boer War). He also sent me up 'Warrilow', a superb double damascus barrelled shot gun, made for him by a gunsmith in Chippenham at the turn of the century for 12 gns.! It turned out to be my most treasured possession during the next five years.

Life continued at Halifax depot with the dreary monotony of occasional lectures, hanging around, orders then counter orders, until on January 13th, 1943, we are told we will be parading in the Odeon car park tomorrow in battle order. A lot of argument ensues about what constitutes full battle order, everyone having different ideas.

We park our hand baggage and harness and go off to the Swan Hotel for a last good dinner. Prof. Joad is dining at the next table and we speculate on who had to listen to his familiar turn of speech tonight. After dinner we are invited to visit 'The Legion of Frontiersmen'. Have no idea who or what they are but it is very quiet in the Swan and we are prepared to try anything to relieve the ennui of our last night ashore in England. The title sounds appropriate. We make our way to another dark hall in the blackout. On the stairs a flashy redhead passes us, our expectations are raised but she has little bearing on the scene inside. A Mr. Horsefield greets us and introduces us to the President and his wife who are busy spilling beer over a Union Jack covered table. The President stands the drinks which are brought by a proud looking corporal in a white tunic with chains on his epaulettes.

I got caught by the President's wife who has a son in the R.E.M.E.; one of those for whom the Army never does anything right. He had failed to get his commission because he was too young being only 22 years. I did not tell her that I was only nineteen, but stuck the tale of woe out sympathetically. My friend Hugh seemed to have let himself in for a deep discussion on the parkin industry. At ten o'clock, The King, sung in many varied keys, we say goodnight and take the Legion Magazine and enrolment forms as souvenirs.

We walk back in the moonlight to our billet where our kind hosts have left supper for us. What magnificent people they were, all understanding and kindness. We feel sure that tomorrow really will be departure day. It had better be, we could not stand another anticlimax.

On the morrow, January 18th, we make the mess for breakfast in our own time. There seems no urgency. We dump our kit at the station and go off to the bank. When we get back to the station at the appointed hour the usual chaos is getting under way by the direction of the R.T.O. We get into one train and then get redirected to another, finally the train gets under way and we seem to be travelling due west, so Liverpool is the most likely destination. We pass through country new to me. The hills are on top of you and the industrial blight scars the valleys below.

We pass one factory. I have never seen such an immense place – miles of it. Every time the train stops more people start to get ready to disembark, but the right time is obvious when it does come as the train winds around in the docks and practically takes us to the quayside. Off we get and await action. Form 2606's are collected. Ten minutes later more action, they are handed back again. Some tea arrived in a dixie. Then we exchange our 2606's for a card giving us our cabin number. What luck. Hugh and I are next door to each other.

There are two troop ships docked, and we seem to be heading for the larger one, a fair sized vessel 27,000 tons. With disgust we see that the decks are already crowded with the RAF. As we found out later 3,000 of them. The RTO looks fogged so we leave him and go on board. On board at last and everywhere RAF wander, their hands in pockets slouching around getting in the way. God, what a slovenly collection. This is some ship. The *Dominion Monarch*, a 1938 luxury cruiser. Lovely fittings and very nice cabins for the officers. Spring bunks, wash basins, cupboards, chest of drawers all in walnut.

Our baggage comes up by crane. I see my case go into the hold and my trunk is deposited on deck and I soon have this in my cabin. Dinner time at last and a damn great queue for it. I suppose they are not used to catering for 400 officers. The dining room is the converted cocktail room, green leather arm chairs and a host of very busy stewards in their white coats; the lighting is modern, indirect and vertical yellow tubes against the pillars. And what food, this journey looks like being very healthy. Soup first, roast beef, leeks, baked spuds and sweet corn, apple pie with cream on top, then coffee. Everything perfectly cooked, plenty of lovely white rolls and butter. You could never get a meal like it in London for love or money.

The troop ship *Dominion Monarch* was to be my home for the next two months. She was at that time the largest diesel liner in the world and held the record of 11 days from Britain to the Cape. However, in convoy the pace was set by the slowest merchant man with its salt-caked smoke stack, and zig-zagging halfway across the Atlantic to avoid the German U-Boat packs was not going to achieve anything near its record capabilities. In fact it took over a month to reach the Cape on this occasion. But in spite of this we were luckier than we realised for she had not been fully converted for troop carrying. The other ranks' quarters had been converted and they were packed like sardines below decks, but there had been no time as yet to convert the officers' quarters and we enjoyed cabin accommodation practically unaltered from her normal cruising layout except for a few extra bunks in the luxury cabins.

I sent a letter off to Dad telling him what I could. I think my guess is right. I sent him my photograph and his sweet ration card. I hope we shall get some post while we are here. After dinner we sat in the lounge and had a few whiskies, 8d each and I got 50 Players for 1/8d.

On our seventh day at sea the air was noticeably warmer. Two ships appeared from the east to join the convoy to sail east whence they had come. We guessed that we must be off Gibraltar and the entrance to the Mediterranean.

On 1st February, the ninth day at sea we saw land off both bows, we were passing through the Canary Isles. At night it was a great thrill to see them all ablaze with light, a sharp contrast with the blacked out world we had left behind in Britain.

Four days later and we are noticeably in the tropics now. Heat and haze predominate. By 10.00 hrs. the convoy form single file and Freetown eventually appears out of the haze. We pick up a pilot and file through the gaps in the anti-submarine boom.

At first we only see thick bush and palm trees interspersed with small bays of yellow sand, lonely palms and white surf. Then Freetown passes on the starboard bow. A jumbled mass of odd shaped houses and big broad streets of red earth. A very British church with square Norman towers stands out amongst the tropical buildings. We drop anchor about ¼ of a mile away.

Night falls, the harbour, such as it is, lights up and the other ships, once but dark shadows on the ocean, become sparkling jewels. A real breach of peace time is felt and the band and singsong on the upper deck is like a shot out of a musical number in one of Hollywood's spectaculars on a tropical ocean. The sky is full of stars, the breeze is warm and a sort of unreal picture of peace is painted.

The heat of the tropics now makes itself felt by the liberal manner that one perspires here. The air, now still as the ship has no movement, is only kept in circulation by the air conditioning and the waft of humanity coming up the stairs from the bowels of the ship. I spent the morning with my field glasses (what a blessing they are). Some of the natives canoes are most picturesque. There are two definite species of canoe to be seen, one of the most amusing things about them is the writing on the sides. I saw one called 'God never Hurry' being paddled lazily along by an old nigger who evidently thought it was not for him to try to do better than God.

The next day I had a very interesting chat with an R.C. Padre who came on board. He has been in this part of the world for ten years. He told me the names of various birds and all about malaria. The first signs of which he says can be recognised by the taste of a cigarette becoming repulsive. I saw some of the currency and we talked about the problem of native labour and what it would lead to after the war. Naturally many men were getting paid for jobs they are not qualified to do and after the war they will not be satisfied to go back to their old jobs.

I hear we sail tomorrow.

We up anchor at 9.30 and slowly drift out of Freetown Harbour. *Dominion Monarch* hangs back then opens up her engines to full power just to show for a brief moment what she can do and why she holds the record to the Cape, very impressive with a giant creaming bow wave. All too soon we are back on station in convoy and our speed is once again that of the slowest merchantman.

I saw a flying fish in the morning. I also hear that nineteen subs have been sighted since we left Glasgow! Who would have thought it?

The convoy was always changing course as a routine to make it more difficult for any submarine that might be lurking round. Our escorting destroyers and corvettes would periodically go shooting off in one direction or another in a very businesslike fashion. Various planes from the aircraft carrier were constantly taking off and patrolling around the convoy so presumably any sub spotting was done by them, but I never saw any depth charges dropped, so suspect most of the sub spotting proved negative, unless the action took place too far away for us to feel the detonation. However, I noticed on occasions the destroyers had a black sphere hoisted on their yard arm which I later learnt was the signal that enemy submarines were suspected of being in the vicinity. I am glad I discovered this fact fairly late in the voyage. It is really better not to know.

A few days out from Freetown the sea changed colour to a muddy green. The steward says we must be passing the mouth of the Congo River which colours the sea for miles around. There is no land in sight so it must be 'some river' to affect the sea so far out.

On February 22nd the steward informs me that Table Mountain is visible on the port bow. We go aloft and South Africa is coming into view through the mist. Our convoy forms line and the majority of ships head in for Cape Town. We separate out in a convoy of nine ships on course for Durban. Table Mountain and the other hills look very impressive in the early morning light. I see my first albatross sitting on the waves quite unconcerned. A sitting shot even with a crossbow.

Two more days at sea before Durban hoves into view on 25th February. It looks a beautifully clean place with its large white buildings along the sea front. We stop in the bay for an hour then steam round the bar into the harbour.

On getting ashore we found that women of S.A. are stunners one and all, but that is where it ends. These stories we've heard about the towns' hospitality no longer holds good. The soldiers merely seem to be a commercial proposition and apart from putting all the prices up the inhabitants don't go out of their way to give the troops a good time.

Durban itself is certainly a very impressive town; it's very clean with big white hotels in various styles of architecture. They all have cool verandahs where people sit and drink. There is a surprising number of big American cars on the road (Pacard, Dodge, Chrysler etc.) There are also a large number of rickshaws pulled by Zulus. They are very amusing as they try and attract their passengers by odd whistles and hoots. They look just like a slow motion picture when they get moving, all their weight being counterbalanced by the passengers; they take long graceful strides.

On 1st March our ship left Durban. As we passed the quay point we heard a woman's voice singing 'Land of Hope and Glory'. She had a lovely powerful voice which came floating over the still water to us. It was a moving sight as she stood alone on the quay point like an opera star on an empty stage. I am sure she was an opera star for from the quality and strength of her voice, coupled with her poise and gestures, she could be nothing else. Everyone on board was deeply affected by this lone gesture of patriotism. An immense and assuring cheer broke out from the boat deck. The South Africans had not been very hospitable to the British on this wartime visit. I had heard of Afrikaans who had turned their back and refused to shake hands when introduced to British officers. This lone woman did more to restore relationships between Britain and her country than anyone else ashore at that time.

The next fortnight sailing up to the Indian Ocean was eventless save for some ships leaving us for what we guessed must be the Mombasa and later a larger contingent breaking away to the west for Aden or some other port serving the North Africa campaign.

By 16th March we dropped anchor off Bombay. The Taj Mahal Hotel and the famous gateway to India were clearly visible. At last we felt that we had arrived but rumour had it that we would be anchored off Bombay for a week. The rumour proved to be about right. We disembarked on 23rd March, 64 days after embarking at Liverpool.

There was one effect on me of this long voyage on the *Dominion Monarch*. For two months every meal was heralded over the ship's tannoy by the tune 'In an English Country Garden' played on a xylophone. After a few weeks I was so conditioned that my mouth started to water when I heard the tune and the effect remained with me for many years. Even back at home after the war was over I only had to hear that tune on the wireless and my gastric juices immediately turned on.

However, while we lay at anchor off Bombay it was not all inactivity. Certain formalities took place that had a profound influence on the future even though we did not appreciate their significance at the time. On 18th March I noted in my diary...... "The sappers seem the quickest off the mark around these parts. A sapper major came aboard today with our postings. I had the choice of Poona, Bangalore or Ceylon. The last one was very tempting, as it meant white troops and what I thought would be a pleasant climate. The old major had other views. He maintained that the climate was too moist to be pleasant, that I would be stuck there for at least a year and that I would only get English rates of pay".

So I chose Bangalore. The Garden City and pleasure resort of India with Indian pay – £31 per month (over double my British pay). "I will be attached to the Madras Sappers and Miners and have to learn Urdu. Oh well, roll on Bangalore. Let's have you. P.S. They have got a few Bailey Bridges."

A few days later we were allowed ashore. What a shambles! The smell is the first thing that strikes you, then you start to look around. Outside the dock gates are quite a few garries and taxis but before you get 100 yards the great assault starts, every five yards there is a beggar, more female than male, who all say 'Buckshees Sahib' like mechanical dolls. Every yard someone is trying to sell you something. You adopt the only course open, fix your eyes on a distant object fairly high up and walk straight ahead. To hesitate means at least three beggars clutching your arm.

"This is East all right and there is not much resemblance to the West. Went to the Taj Mahal Hotel, very smart inside as well as out, most impressive, so are the prices. I now understand why Indian pay is so high. Not only standards but cost of living as well is high. Went back to ship and dined on a few oranges. Have got the money complex. Long may it last."

We disembark at last. We leave Bombay and as our train pulls out into the night I watch the countryside by moonlight for a time and then go off to sleep.

Travel all next day through pretty desolate country. At every station we stop, and a crowd of little kids come asking for bakshish.

We reach Bangalore the following evening. Nothing laid on. With the help of Movement Control we get a lorry sent down which turns out to be a bus. We arrive at the Mess all ablaze with light.Col. St. John Forbes offers us a drink. We are provided with bearers and push off in lorries with our luggage to find our bungalows. How like Halifax, only it isn't snowing.

Bangalore, the HQ and the depot of Queen Victoria's Own Madras Sappers and Miners or Q.V.O.M.S.M., as we were understandably known. Here I was in for a slight shock. Having come from war weary Britain with everything rationed, restricted or unobtainable and the whole of the continent of Europe in enemy hands with Britain very conscious that it was the last bastion of freedom on the continent, with our backs to the wall, we were very serious about the war effort. It came as a bit of a shock to find life in India unmoved by the events of time. Admittedly the nearest Japs were some 600 miles away in Burma, but their advance across the countries of South East Asia had already been meteoric. Hong Kong, the Phillipines, French Indo- China, New Guinea, the Dutch East Indies, Siam, Malaya and Burma had been overrun by the Japs with the same rapidity that had marked the German advance across Europe. There was no English Channel separating Burma from India but the officers of the Bangalore mess regarded the situation with a remote equanimity as though it was just another native uprising or a mere frontier incident.

Life in the cantonment went on without the slightest concern for the war. Although there was no English Channel there was a vast mountainous region, an extension of the Himalayas that extended from

Nepal to the Arakan and Malaya, that was an equally imposing barrier to any invading army. The social order was the thing that mattered. The peck order that was the basic fundamental of social life. To be a subaltern arriving full of the spirit of making the last stand against the invading Japanese it was a difficult adjustment to make. To find that what really mattered was that you should leave your visiting card on the silver tray provided at the bungalows of all your superior officers seemed quite incongruous after one's training in the U.K.

Apart from this, life was very pleasant at Bangalore. The officers mess was spacious and its long verandah faced a row of tall shading trees. Here you could sit out in the evening with a cool drink and a smartly dressed mess servant always within call and ready to replenish your glass. Mess nights per force were very formal. The tables were decorated with immense pieces of mess silver, though the piece I liked the best was the least pretentious. It was a mule's hoof mounted on a silver stand. The inscription recorded that this mule had unexpectedly foaled during the Tibetan Expedition of 1902! A most unusual occurrence and well worth recording in silver.

We were allocated comfortable bungalows and a bearer to look after our needs. No doubt our Commandant, a Col. Jeakes, thought that we needed toughening up and smartening up after two months at sea. He was probably right. We did a lot of P.T. under the instruction of an Indian naik (corporal) which we felt was a bit undignified, even more so when the Commandant rode amongst us on his horse shouting exhortations. We felt as though we had gone back to being cadets again. We also spent quite a lot of time under riding instruction. This we felt was more worthwhile as it taught us how to handle horses over difficult terrain, such as sliding down the steep slopes of dry riverbeds or nullahs, as they are called in India. One particularly uncomfortable part of this obstacle course for me was cantering through a plantation of closely spaced trees. Weaving in and out of the trees my horse knew just how wide his flanks were but made no allowance for my knees which were very bruised and sore by the end of the day.

Apart from this he was a good responsive horse and enabled me to save a nasty situation when some piedogs rushed out of a small village we were passing. They appeared so suddenly, barking and snapping at the horses that several of the other horses reared up and one threw his mount and started to bolt dragging the rider, who could not get his foot out of the stirrup – a dangerous situation on that rough stoney ground. I spurred on my horse to try and head off the bolter before too much damage was done to the officer it was dragging. My horse went off like a rocket and I was quickly able to get in front of the other one and ride it into a convenient wall. As it threw its head up I was able to grab its bridle and the situation was soon restored. The instructor arrived and disentangled the rider who was bruised and scraped but not seriously injured, thank goodness. The instructor was suitably impressed and treated me with great respect from then on.

Apart from the riding we spent a lot of time being taught Urdu which was not a difficult language as it had no definite or indefinite articles, and no genders to worry about. It was the lingua franca of the Indian Army but not of the Madras Sappers I discovered. Their language was Tamil with some three other languages scattered amongst the men, none of which had any relation to Urdu. Your NCOs' spoke a little basic Urdu as it was a necessary qualification for promotion. Many knew more English than Urdu and one's VCO invariably spoke English.

I discovered later that in spite of this multiplicity of language, communication was no great problem for whatever language you gave your orders in they were quickly translated by someone into one language or another and on the whole your instructions seemed to get understood, though occasionally mistakes did happen.

After three weeks at the depot in Bangalore I began to feel both bored and frustrated. I had arrived all keyed up for active service and this seemed the most inactive service to me.

The day came when I found myself up before the brigade major or some such staff appointment. I was accused of behaviour unsympathetic to the social rules of the cantonment, whatever that might imply. I do not remember the exact offence. Either I had failed to attend some boring social function that was apparently obligatory for subalterns or I was incorrectly dressed for some occasion. I forget the detail. I was threatened with a posting to Burma if I did not mend my ways. When I told him that this was what I had travelled 6000 miles to achieve, the position was confirmed, though the establishment obviously could not understand my reasoning.

CHAPTER 4

On the road to Burma

So began my long journey to the war front in Burma. A fantastic journey of nearly 2000 miles by rail, river boat and road, through plains, marshes, jungle and mountains rising to over 6000 ft. I began to understand why the staff of our HQ depot in Bangalore felt so remote from the war. It was equivalent to being stationed at Chatham with the nearest enemy troops advancing on Moscow! Even Calcutta was over a thousand miles from Bangalore and Calcutta was a good three hundred miles from the Arakan front, and Tamu, the start of the other gateway to India, was 800 miles by road and rail from Calcutta. As it turned out Tamu was my destination.

The journey from Bangalore to Calcutta took 3-4 days, an incredible journey by any standards for Indian railways were rather unique. As an officer one travelled 1st class which meant that you had a compartment to yourself, or if conditions were very overcrowded you shared a compartment with another officer. You did not have a seat, you had a chaise longue on which you could lie and watch the world go by through a large window. This window had a series of screens that you could pull down in front of it. One was tinted glass if the glare was too bright, another was a form of wooden venetian blind; if it was oppressively hot you could leave the window open and have the maximum amount of air with both privacy and security from the world outside. The third was a mosquito grill that would let in a certain amount of air but exclude the mosquitoes. You lay on your leather couch and watched the panorama of the Indian countryside pass gently by outside. You travelled in stark contrast to the 3rd class carriages further down the train. These were just slatted wooden benches packed tight with humanity and its baggage. So crowded were these carriages that they overflowed and at times there were as many passengers clinging on to the outside of the carriage as there were within. They stood on the outside running board with an arm through the window or clutching the outer rail, put on the side of the carriage for their security. They travelled like this for miles shouting and gesticulating with their free arm. Not exactly a comfortable means of travel but at least they would be cooler than those with a seat in the hot interior of the over filled carriage. In the Sahibs 1st class carriage there was a loo at one end and a little annexe room at the other where you kept your bearer and the ice box, so that he could keep you supplied with iced drinks during the journey.

There were no restaurant cars but your requirements were telegraphed ahead to a suitable station where a meal was prepared. When you arrived there all the 1st class passengers got out and went along to the station buildings where in a room beside the station master's office a large table was already laid with the necessary number of places, and waiters in white coats and turbans were waiting to serve you with drinks and your dinner. Here the train waited patiently while you fed leisurely from the soup course to the final coffee, brandy and cigars. It was fantastic and a wonderful example of how the British Raj had organised the railways around the civilised necessities of life.

I well remember at one such station dinner which had been particularly good, but rather slow, and we had at last reached the coffee and brandy stage, when the worried guard of the train came in and apologetically appealed to the diners. "Sahibs, the train is more than an hour late. Would you be so kind as to get on board so that we may proceed with our journey".

There was a cold silence at the interruption, broken by an officer who had obviously spent many years in India.

"What, only one hour late? Boy, bring me another brandy".

We quietly stayed there savouring the last refinements of a good meal for another half an hour with the train waiting patiently outside and the guard and the station master getting more agitated, but without the slightest effect on the 1st class passengers who saw no reason to hurry the conclusion of their meal. When it was all over we rose from the table, bid each other good night, and sauntered off to our respective compartments where our bearers had our beds ready made and waiting for us. Not until the last compartment door was closed did the guard blow his whistle and the engine let out a cloud of steam and started puffing its way into the night, straining to make up the lost time.

In contrast to this very civilised aspect of our journey there was the other side of the coin. By day we stopped at many wayside stations where the 3rd class Indian passengers sorted themselves out, some leaving, others joining, but while this ensued, we were plagued by beggars of every shape, size and denomination. At the lower end of the scale were the small boys and girls out to make a little pocket money who came and chanted the beggars song of India, "Buckshees Sahib" in a monotonous unison outside your carriage window. If you good humouredly scattered a few pieces to them there was a scramble and a few fights like sparrows picking up crumbs. It was all over in a matter of seconds before both the successful and the unsuccessful were chanting again with renewed vigour, but your response would not have gone unnoticed by their accomplices trying their luck further down the train, and sensing that some one had struck a rich seam the numbers outside your window quickly doubled and you were conscious that your prestige amongst your fellow travellers was visibly halved by their presence. Just another young officer who had not got his knees brown and had not learnt that charity in India was something that only the foolish and uninitiated indulged in. After the children came the professional beggars. They relied on shocking your senses into parting with your money from pity or conscience. They aim to appear miserable, starving or, better still, crippled or mutilated. The real professionals are prepared to mutilate themselves or their children to enhance their begging potential. It is a pretty horrifying thing to say but it is true. Some have been mutilated by misfortune and seek to make the best of their misfortune as an asset for begging. Others are prepared to inflict self mutilation to enhance the potential of the only profession they know – begging.

It is shocking but true in a country where real poverty is endemic. Years later when I was in Bengal with a Bengali doctor, we were approached by a woman begging with a child that had its eyes bandaged and was screaming incessantly. By that time I was inured to brush all beggars aside, but the Bengali doctor said he would open my eyes to the problems of India. He snatched the child from its mother and quickly untied the bandages around its eyes saying he would give her no money, but, as a doctor, would give his services free for her child. Under the bandages were half walnut shells over each eye and the half walnut shells were full of ants destroying the child's eyes! This may seem quite horrific to a Westerner but to a professional beggar it was an expediency for survival. A screaming child attracted sympathy and compassion. It was a far greater asset even later to have a hideously blinded child to attract compassion and the chance of receiving buckshees would be infinitely more promising than touting around a perfectly healthy child, for even in the begging world life is highly competitive and you have nothing to sell but compassion. In this market it is, as in most other markets, the most ruthless who succeed.

After about four days and 1100 miles we pulled into Howrah Station, Calcutta. Stage one of this incredible journey came to an end in the unbelievable turmoil of Calcutta. Howrah Station must have been modelled on Victoria Station. Architecturally it was very similar, but this was where the similarity ended. Everywhere were sleeping bodies, the station was littered with them. As you picked your way through them some came to life and, like Lazarus rising from the dead, cried "Coolee Sahib" and subsided back to their somnolent posture.

Calcutta was the end and the beginning of the journey to Burma. It was the great transit camp of the Far East. Trains arrived from all quarters of the vast Continent of India and the occupants passed into transit camps to await the next stage or, if you were an officer, into the Grand Hotel, the Officers' Transit Hotel where you waited for movement control to sort you out and move you on to your final destination. Like every other officer en route for Burma, I ended up at this vast and fantastic hotel to await the final stage of my journey. It was the only Grand Hotel that lived up to its name space wise. The foyer was small and like the floor of the Stock Exchange where the business of your onward journey was transacted. The lounge was immense, a sea of cane armchairs and tables littered with groups of officers drinking gin and something or other. Some had settled in for the duration, others, like myself, had hopes of moving on, but it all took time.

Calcutta was very hot and very humid. I learnt one lesson very quickly. It is fatal to go to sleep, stripped under the cool airstream of a punka (ceiling fan). When you are hot and sweating it is a wonderful relief, but if you fall asleep you awake chilled and shivering and spend the next 24 hours with a chill on the stomach and racing for the loo clutching your stomach.

The second largest city of the British Empire I had been taught at school, but no one had mentioned if this distinction was based on area or population. I suspect the latter. It had a sedate European centre, an impressive park with the usual statue of Queen Victoria as its centre and impressive European style shops and offices on its perifery. It could have been the West End of London. Gun shops like Mantons with the euphoria of Purdeys; stationers that could have been lifted straight from Bond Street called Newmans. All the refinements of western civilisation were on sale, from grand pianos to the best of French wine, with obsequious European salesmen in attendance; but one street away from the select centre the change was dramatic. Poverty, squalor, sacred cows sleeping on the pavement, piedogs, excrement, ghee tins, beggars and that very special aroma that this kaleidoscope of mixed life and spice produced in the humid atmosphere that was so distinctive to Calcutta.

Calcutta was a great business centre exporting the tea, rice and jute of Assam and importing all that was so necessary for the development of these industries and the life of the great river complex of Northern India fed by the everlasting snows of the Himalayas. The best known of these waterways is the Ganges, but a whole series of rivers run parallel through Uttar Pradesh to join forces at Patna and assume the common title of Ganges, which ends in a great delta at the Bay of Bengal. The Hoogly is really a tapping off of the vast shallows of the Delta and is therefore navigable, which makes Calcutta, 75 miles from the sea, the only port for that vast area of Northern India watered by the Himalayas. Here life abounds. Hence the Hoogly is referred to by the more ribald soldiers as 'the Arsehole of India' and Calcutta was 70 miles up it.

The Europeans who generated the trade on which the teeming millions of Calcutta thrived were a fairly close knit society, whose temple of worship was the Calcutta Club. The Calcutta Club was very select. Its high priests in the trade of jute and tea were known as Box Wallahs. They regarded the military invasion of their territory with disdain. An unwarranted intrusion on the order of life as it had always been. That their world, well-ordered, secure and successful, was on the threshold of extinction should the Japanese invasion succeed never really came within consideration, so that they never regarded the military presence as a necessary inconvenience to the continued survival of their select existence, or so it seemed. Obviously some were more imaginative than others but in those days the British Empire was as indestructible as the solar system. It had weathered innumerable native risings and to them the Japanese threat was remote and of no immediate threat to their way of life. The real problem was whether club membership should be confined to brigadiers and above or whether the threshold should be lowered to allow colonels to enjoy temporary membership. After all you had to maintain standards, and there were some very odd people who had become colonels during the so-called emergency.

My stay in Calcutta was an education but unfortunately short lived. After a few days, movement control informed me that the next troop train to Dimapur via Gohati was due and I was back at the station. Nobody travelled light in those days. An officer bound for active service in Burma would travel with at least one tin trunk, possibly two. Labour was cheap and plentiful, there was never a shortage of coolies competing to carry your luggage, however heavy or awkward. It was expected that all Sahibs had at least one tin trunk of uniforms to cover all ceremonial occasions.

Calcutta station had a surprise in store for me. There, amongst the tumult of officers and coolies with their luggage struggling to claim a seat in the musical chairs of movement control, the atmosphere was very different from the journey from Bangalore to Calcutta. This was an entirely military train and the pressures of the time meant that there were always more officers than seats available. Here influence and rank ruled the day and no one hesitated in exploiting them to the full. I was new to the game and was making little progress in obtaining a carriage, for though many of them were not yet occupied they all seemed to be reserved and the Anglo-Indian RTO seemed to be doing a roaring trade. Then who should I see walking down the platform with a parrot on his shoulder and followed by a string of coolies bearing his trunks, valises and rows of other packing cases, but Rae Steele, my boyhood friend who had preceded me to India. The only close friend I had and here he was catching the same train as me and bound for the same destination – Dimapur. Even now I am fascinated by the mathematical odds on such an encounter.

Rae knew the ropes. In no time we were occupants of a reserved carriage. A short sharp exchange with the RTO soon settled the matter in basic English and the RTO retired with a shrug of the shoulders that said, "Oh well, you can't win every time". Undoubtedly he was making the best of his small sphere of authority but he knew better than to push his luck when confronted with someone who knew the game. We were joined by some more officers from the 4/5 Marathas, Rae's Regiment. We eventually pulled out a full train, with some carriages more overcrowded than others.

It was an incredible journey from Calcutta to Dimapur. One travelled by the broad gauge up through the Great Plains of the Bramah Putra to Duhbri. Here the broad gauge ended and one transferred to a Mississippi style river boat. The railway just ended at the riverbank. No station, just a platform packed with coolies competing to carry one's luggage on board the river steamboat. A transition of chaos, all up a plank from the muddy river bank onto the steamer. You stood beside your luggage while coolies fought amongst each other for the privilege of carrying it on board. They eyed it and quoted you a price which you promptly halved. If you did not, two or three would be fighting over it for the inflated fee, none of them looked capable of carrying a handbag let alone a tin trunk, but somehow these emaciated figures were able to carry anything once it was balanced on their head, and they padded up a thin bending gangplank onto the steamer. You beat them down to a mere pittance in annas to carry your pile of luggage on board. You sauntered aboard and found your coolie on the luggage deck standing guard over your pile of baggage that he had brought aboard. You checked it and if it was all there you paid him the few annas agreed and dismissed him with little thought that that was his living wage for the day.

These river boats were not unlike the Mississippi steam boats that one had seen in films, but in wartime the deck space was strewn with other ranks and their kit, together with the more impressive piles of officers' baggage. The main deck with awnings was reserved for officers and laid out with tables and white tablecloths, all ready for lunch. An army of waiters in immaculate white coats and turbans decorated with the colourful sash of the riverboat company plied drinks and later served lunch while we sailed up the Ganges, or Bramah Putrah whichever it was called at that point, to Gouhati. Here on the opposite bank the narrow gauge railhead for Assam started as abruptly as the broad gauge had ended on the other river bank further down stream. The journey from Duhbri to Gouhati by steamer was an experience itself; about 80 miles by these romantic old paddle steamers with the panorama of riverbank life, and the river traffic sweeping quietly by as you relaxed in a cane chair with a drink in one hand and watched it unfold.

Gouhati was an awakening. If you were lucky there was a train waiting on the narrow gauge siding. If you were not so lucky there was a trek with your luggage to rest camps – a strange misnomer for a collection of bamboo huts where you fought for space not knowing if you were settling in for days or hours before a train arrived in the desolate siding to take you on stage two of your journey to Dimapur road. Dimapur was the end of the line by rail and the beginning of the final journey by road to 'The Front' as it was loosely termed. On this occasion we were lucky: the narrow gauge train was awaiting us in the siding and we made a quick scrambled transfer from the river steamer to the train. However, this train was very different from the style we had previously enjoyed. We had crossed the 'Rubicon'. From now on it was war conditions; the contents of 20 carriages up to Duhbri had to fit into 10 very inferior carriages at Gouhati and what would not fit in ended up in open style cattle trucks. Nobody minded. They knew the form and scrambled for places. Most of them knew that from now on it could only get worse. It was only 100 miles to Dimapur Road – the railhead where the train load of humanity spewed out into the night and they all ended up in Penis Park.

Penis Park what an incredible place. This was where the true primary jungle started before the steep ascent up to Kohima 4000 ft. up in the hills. Its origin was lost in the mists of the past, a sort of Far Eastern Stonehenge in a clearing in the jungle and encircled by a crumbling wall of great antiquity. Within this wall were rows of huge phallic monuments carved out of stone. At one end were about three long rows of great stone erections symbolising the male penis; at the other end were equally vast stone monuments in the shape of a V that symbolised the female genitalia. Archaeologically the site was unique and one realises now the sacrilege of using the site as a staging camp for the re-conquest of Burma. However, possibly it was a stroke of genius, for being so remote and lost in the jungle it would never have been seen by anyone

Penis Park, Burma.

but the most enthusiastic archaeologists, as it was it was seen by thousands of troops on their way to and from the Burma campaign and I doubt if these splendid stone monuments suffered much as a result, though possibly there were a few initials scratched on to their surface. At that time in the war the staging camp only had male personnel to contend with. Some years later when the great advance into Burma gathered momentum and the administrative tail of the advancing army reached Dimapur a number of service women reached this strange outpost of the Empire. The army administration tactfully segregated them into huts built around the female phallic symbols (out of bounds to male personnel), but forced them to walk through an avenue of stone peni to the joint mess hut for meals and of course right through the centre of the male bivouac area. Running the gauntlet of ribald remarks that are too obvious to record here.

I digress, for the present I was allotted a charpoy in one of the bamboo huts, the floor of which was woven bamboo known as chathai, a loose weave of pieces of split bamboo. We were warned not to walk on it in bare feet for scorpions often took up residence beneath it and their tails could come up through the holes in the loose weave with disastrous effect! My first night in this staging camp introduced me to another unwelcome arthropod. I had barely settled into my bed when I felt something crawling over my thigh. I guessed that it was probably a cockroach but something made me resist the natural reaction of brushing it off and I threw back the bedclothes to check. Just as well, for it was a nasty looking six inches of centipede almost half an inch wide and I had been warned by Rae that if you brushed them off against their direction of travel they dug their legs in and the front ones were equipped with poison glands that could be very uncomfortable. I let it crawl over me until its course took it off me and back onto the bedclothes and at this juncture I drew my sheath knife and cut it in two, but to my horror this had little effect other than to produce two very active half centipedes trekking around in my bed. Not without a certain element of panic I finally speared both halves on the point of my knife and impaled them on the chathai floor. Here I felt they could remain as evidence of my ordeal until the morning. I had reckoned without the scavenging ant population. Next morning my knife stood impaled in the chathai, but not a morsel of centipede was left in evidence. The ants had eaten the lot!

The other unforgettable resident of that camp was the Tucktoo lizard, not so much seen as heard. Its amazing call punctuated the jungle at night with a staccato clucking culminating with 'Tuck-too Tucktoooo' from which it got its name and needless to say the British soldiers were quick to rechristen it as the 'Fuck you Lizard'.

My stay at Dimapur Road staging camp was not as long as it might have been if I had had to rely on the vagueness of movement control transport. Rae's battalion, the 4/5 Mahratahs, had sent transport back for him, and I was able to travel up with him. It was a spectacular journey, up the L of C of the forgotten army. The wide flat road through the primary jungle bordered by innumerable little parked groups of vehicles, stores, dumps, petrol depots, mule lines and all the other service units necessary to supply an army in the field, ended abruptly as the road narrowed to a rough earth track that entered the hill section and ascended nearly 4000 ft. in 46 miles to Kohima. The ascent was through bamboo vegetation, its delicate tracery arched over the small tortuous track, that wound its way up from one hillside to the other. In places cascades of water fell down the mountain side raising water vapour that sparkled in the sunlight, but for much of the way you drove through a green tunnel of bamboo but always conscious of the precipitous drop on one side and the hanging hillside above you on the other. If you knew your road you also knew where to stop. A small finger post by the roadside labelled A.R.C. or some vague equivalent and pointing up a little track to nowhere, led up a footpath with a bamboo handrail to an unexpected clearing and a few bamboo huts commanding a view of indescribable beauty. Here a RIASC major lived in forgotten oblivion. His job was to provide refreshment for those who were travelling up or down the road. It was 134 miles from Dimapur to Imphal and practically all on a road cut out of the mountainside. It was unsurfaced most of the way, full of ruts and potholes, very narrow on the more difficult sections where one-way systems operated on a time basis. Traffic moved one way on the odd hours the other way on the even hours.

The rules had to be strict, if you arrived after the tail of the convoy was out of sight you had to be a personal friend of Movement Control Officer or of impressively high rank to be allowed through, otherwise you had a two-hour wait until the tail of the return convoy came through. In the dry season you drove through deep choking red dust that invaded everything and dissolved into the sweat on your body so that you soon looked like an over made up Red Indian Nigger Minstrel. In the rainy season the dust was converted into a deep slurry of mud, but there were other hazards brought on by the torrential rain. Land slides occurred frequently, blocking the road, and in the more difficult sections these became major obstacles. The whole mountain side, saturated beyond capacity by the torrential rain, would become plastic and start to creep down the slope, road and all. In one place this happened on such a scale that the only solution was to bridge the gap with an aerial rope way. The road was cut and had disappeared hundreds of feet below in a slurry of moving mountain. The sappers constructed a vast form of funicular on steel cables bridging the gap, but it meant that no transport, only stores, could cross the gap. Every vehicle moving up the L of C had to be unloaded and its contents transported across the gap by the ropeway in this way. Food, ammunition, reinforcements, medical supplies and petrol, going up the L of C, but coming down, on the return journey to India, it was mostly casualties and the last of the refugees of the retreat from Burma.

This was the grand scale but the road was perpetually being cut on a smaller scale by landslides that spewed hundreds of tons of waterlogged shale down the mountainside onto the road. I remember at one point a large D12 dozer pushing this creeping slurry off the road and about a dozen vehicles could get through before the hillside slowly crept across the road, the gap narrowing until even a Jeep was risking being held in the liquid shale and forced over the side. At this moment the traffic was stopped and the dozer would carve out the roadway to its original profile again so that another dozen vehicles could squeeze through before the seemingly endless supply of mud creeping down the hillside had oozed across the road to danger limit and then the performance was repeated.

I have mentioned this now because it shows why the rest camps came into being. It was only a 134 mile journey from Dimapur to Imphal but it was a hazardous and very unpredictable journey. If you were lucky you might do it in a day, but in the monsoon it could take two or three days. Under these conditions the rest camps were a haven where you arrived tired, soaked to the skin and exhausted. Here you could get out of the pouring rain, get a hot meal and a relatively dry spot to put down your bedroll for a night's sleep. They were a real haven when times were difficult but you had to know where they were. They were not very well advertised, as I have already mentioned, possibly the officers in charge of them were not anxious to invite custom, it only meant work. They had built up a clientele amongst the old timers who had been on the road since the early days. They welcomed them as old friends dropping in for a chat and a meal. They in turn introduced others. This way it was like keeping open house for your friends at the army's expense.

I was fortunate to be travelling up the first time with Rae who had been up and down the road many times and was able to point out most of these rest camps and introduce me to the OC of the best ones where we stopped. Being May the road was mostly dry; the monsoon was still three weeks away.

I shall never forget that first journey up the road. It was another world of incredible beauty and contrasts. The giant bamboo that curtained the steep ascent up to Kohima gave way quite suddenly as you reached this hill station 4000 ft. above the plains. It gave way to neat white bungalows, grass and delphiniums that were in full bloom around the tennis court by the District Commissioner's bungalow. Tall spruce and very English looking deciduous trees lined some of the roads. Plum and pear trees could be seen in most of the gardens together with all the cultivated flowers from roses to hydrangeas that were so reminiscent of English country gardens. The contrast with what we had left only 46 miles away at Dimapur was very remarkable. The next 22 miles to Mao, the old one-way staging post, was even more remarkable for it became rolling downland reminiscent of Salisbury Plain in some ways except that the downland grass descended steeply into the valleys a thousand feet below where they gave way to a patchwork of paddy fields. Here white egrets were the most visible occupants both of the grasslands and the paddy far below. These little paddy strips were the characteristic of the view downwards. They followed the steep contours of hills and looked like an intricate assemblage of mirrors, a wonderful patchwork quilt of water reflecting the sky above. They were small paddy fields by any standards because of the steep slopes, but were fed by water conveyed along the hillside in a complex system of bamboo aquaducts made from giant bamboo split to form the equivalent of 6 inch guttering that conveyed clear spring water from wherever it emerged from the mountain side down to discharge into the paddy, hundreds of feet below.

The scene and the vegetation was directly linked to your height above sea level. At 4000 ft. it was almost temperate, but 2000 ft. down it quickly became tropical again. The road was the tenuous life line from Assam to Burma and all points along it were known and located by the mileage from Dimapur. Imphal was milestone 134, Kohima milestone 46, Palel M.S. 164 and Tamu, just into Burma, was MS 200.

Rae's battalion, the 4/5 Marathahs, were at Imphal so this was the end of the line for my free lift up the road. Imphal was the capital of Manipur State, in fact it was the only town in the State of Manipur so it had to be the capital. Manipur was a plateau in the middle of the chain of mountain ridges that separated Burma from Assam. It was one of those unique Principalities that characterised the Indian Continent. It had a Maharajah and a great reputation for polo. It also had some of the most colourful and beautiful women to be found in the Indian Continent, if in fact it was a part of the Indian Continent, for it was really in a no-man's land suspended between India and Burma. I shall never forget the market on the edge of Imphal. I have never seen such colour; the women dressed in saris of the most wonderful colours. Peach, apricot, pale green, subtle blue-green colours that any impressionist artist would have found intoxicating. Metro-Goldwyn-Mayer in all their extravagance could not have outdone the wonderful kaleidoscope of colour of the Manipuri women in the Imphal Bazaar. I have no idea to this day where they got their dyes from but I have never seen such beautiful pure colours before or since. It was so different from the Indian bazaars where most of the women wear dirty, plum coloured saris. I regret to this day that colour photography was almost unknown and strangely enough my brother officers were not equally impressed by the colour values, but were not however, entirely blind to the erotic values of the Manupuri women.

    I left Rae at Imphal, and eventually obtained transport to take me on to my new unit, 59 Ind. Fd. Co., on the road between Palel and Tamu. This section of the road had been nothing more than a bridle path but was now being rebuilt to ever increasing standards demanded by the military situation. It had to maintain supplies to the small force guarding the frontiers of Burma at Tamu. Eight months ago it had been the main evacuation route for the retreat from Burma. In May and June of 1942, thousands of exhausted and diseased refugees from Burma had struggled out along this route from Tamu to Imphal. It was an inhospitable route and hundreds died of cholera, dysentery and typhoid or sheer exhaustion. When cutting the new road out of the hillside we exhumed many of their corpses from the shallow graves where their fellow refugees had buried them, but as skeletons with no means of identification they were just moved from one side of the road as one cut into the hill and buried under the fill on the other side. The pressures of war left no time for respecting the unidentified dead.

    I reached my new unit after a last frightening drive along what was little more than an earth track carved out of the mountainside. I would have been much more frightened if it had been daylight and I could have seen the precipitous drop beyond the edge of the road. The driver negotiated all bends with a wild abandon and no thought that a vehicle could be coming the opposite way around the bends. Fortunately only the last few miles were driven in daylight when I could see just what we were negotiating in this manner. Later the driver confessed to me that he had done a crash course in conversion from bullock cart driver to M.T. driver. It was wonderfully simple: the accelerator was equivalent to your toe up the bullock's backside, the brake was the rope you had through its nose. Steering was the only thing you had to learn because at bullock pace the animal normally did this for you. I was glad that I had not known this when we set off from Imphal at a breakneck pace!

CHAPTER 5

The Forgotten Army

My final destination of 59 Ind. Fd. Co. in 23rd Ind. Div. was at some milestone that I forget, but we were encamped a few miles from Tamu just up in the hills and our main occupation was road construction, but with the onset of the monsoon this soon became just a desperate attempt to keep the road open.

A field company consisted of the O.C., a major, the 2nd I/C (second in command), a captain, who did most of the administration and paperwork, and three lieutenants, each commanding one of the three platoons. A platoon consisted of about a hundred men if you were lucky and up to strength. We also had two British N.C.O.'s (non-commissioned officers), one in charge of M.T. (motor transport) and one Q.M. (Quartermaster) in charge of stores and equipment. The next layer of command was the V.C.O.'s (Viceroy Commissioned Officers). They were the invaluable link with your men, one jemadar to each platoon and a subadar at company headquarters. As a platoon commander you soon learnt the value of your V.C.O. jemadar. He could speak English which few of your men could master. The lingua franca was Urdu, the common language of the Indian army, but the Madras sappers spoke Tamil, Malayalam, Telegu, Kanarese and Concanee, all of which bore no relation whatsoever to Urdu which was related to Hindi and the language of Northern India.

Our road construction was quite effective until the monsoon started, then slowly it became a desperate struggle to keep the road useable until finally all our forward units had to withdraw, defeated by the weather, not the Japs. As the road collapsed under the torrential rain it became impossible to supply them and once again they were pulling out to survive the monsoon on the Imphal Plain.

However, this was to come. For the moment I had at last obtained my goal of an active field company in Burma building what was to become, twelve months later, the great L of C for the reconquest of Burma. For the moment it was the great exit route from Burma being rebuilt to do no more than allow our forward troops to maintain contact with the Japanese. Life was hard and very basic. The task of rebuilding this road was the responsibility of a few engineer companies supported by the very minimum of excavating machinery plus a vast assortment of manual labour. The most effective of which was the Indian Tea Association (ITA) who had rallied their forces in the early days of the evacuation of Burma to make a road passable for the refugees retreating from the Japanese invasion. It was a superb action of humanity by the tea gardens of Assam to mobilise their labour forces to help extricate the thousands of exhausted refugees who were pouring out of Burma along this difficult and inadequate route. They had volunteered as an act of humanity being the only available source of manpower that could boast of command and administrative ability under their European overseers that was capable of being mobilised at the time of this emergency. They stayed on for a time to continue the road constructing function which they had performed for the benefit of civilian refugees, but as the sad exodus of civilian refugees came to an end it became a military problem of re-entry, and their humanitarian commitment being completed they started to pull out to return to their tea gardens in Assam. They were replaced by a hastily recruited military labour force, the Bengal Pioneer Battalions.

The idea was sound enough but the result was not quite what India command had anticipated. We were desperately short of earth moving machinery for road construction so the shortage could only be made good by manpower. The ITA had shown what could be done by thousands of tea garden workers to effect road construction. Bengal had vast resources of manpower and as most of its inhabitants were permanently on the edge of starvation it was not difficult to recruit them for military service with the promise of fóur square meals a day and pay as well. Officers to manage and control these hastily constructed units was more of a problem but the effect of war on many commercial business enterprises in Calcutta had no doubt made a large number of white civilians redundant. In a wartime emergency you cannot be too selective and if the Bengal Pioneer Battalion alloted to our Forward Company for road construction was anything to go by they had been far from selective in recruiting its officers. All its officers from the CO down to the platoon commanders had been in civilian employ a few months previously. They must have had some training to understand the military administration procedure, but little else. Basically their purpose was to be a pool of road construction labour under military control and discipline. The latter was necessary because purely civilian labour in the form of coolies had the habit of melting away at the first shot fired in anger.

The idea of these hastily formed pioneer battalions was sound but in practice it did not work out so well. Because of their size their commanding officer was a Lt. Colonel but the engineer companies building the road were only commanded by a major. The latter could only request manpower but was outranked when it came to insisting that the labour was forthcoming. Our allocated pioneer battalion was about a thousand strong but you were lucky if you could get 200 men out of them for road construction, the remainder seemed to be permanently employed on camp duties which appeared to consist of building the most incredible bamboo palaces I have ever seen. The Bengali was skilled at working with bamboo. Not only were the officers quarters and mess built out of the most intricately woven bamboo, but all the pathways interconnecting the various parts of the camp offices were bordered with beautiful and quite artistic bamboo fences as well. The CO's palace was a work of art all woven from split bamboo and lined with white cotton. His and his orderly's beds stood side by side, masterpieces of woven bamboo and white sheets. After I had been sent to try and get more labour out of this battalion I began to realise the root of the problem. He regarded his first priority was the construction and beautifying of his camp, anything surplus to this requirement could be released for work on this beastly road we were building. He went to great pains to explain to me how he had been associated with the Bishop of Calcutta in a campaign to save certain small boys from corruption (he even had his wallet full of their photographs) and though he had a charming young orderly he could not wait to get back to his responsibilities in Calcutta.

It was so incongruous that in my innocence I took some time to realise that he was a monumental queer. He spent his day in a little ornate bamboo palisade built on the highest point in the camp gazing through his field glasses because, as he explained to me, he was sure that he was being spied on. His nights were no doubt spent with his orderly. However, he just was not interested in supplying more labour for our beastly road when there was so much to be done in his own battalion lines!

His second in command was, to my surprise, a German with no great enthusiasm for anything beyond the pure administration of the battalion. What it was used for was no concern of his. As long as their transport was up to strength and all the necessary returns were filled in and sent off in time that was the end of his responsibility. It was up to the CO to allocate labour, not him. It seemed incredible that I should be appealing to a German in British uniform, very German, gutteral accent and all, yet still being refused the release of labour so vitally needed in the war interest.

The whole situation was like Alice in Wonderland and became more so when I met the quartermaster. He was an Armenian sporting the rank of captain and quite a character. He invited me to his temporary home as he put it. Not that he could do anything regarding the release of labour for road construction, but we were all in this war together and camaraderie was what mattered.

His temporary home was even more like a Lewis Carroll creation. It was in fact an amazing construction that looked just like a house built with solid bonded walls, but the bonding was not of brick but of packing cases, packing cases of tinned fruit, bonded like bricks to make a very substantial house. These cases of tinned fruit were the accumulation of rations issued to the battalion over the previous months, but, as he explained, Bengalies did not need tinned fruit, all they needed was rice and a little fresh goat to make a curry, so he had used the cases of tinned fruit for more practical purposes – building himself a house.

He extolled the wonderful fruits of Armenia and offered me peaches, figs, pears, the lot. When I accepted his offer of peaches he attacked the packing case wall with a wrecker bar until a cascade of tins fell onto the floor. Alas they were pears. Undaunted he started attacking another section of the wall and this time a cascade of tinned peaches fell to the ground. He picked up one of the tins and opened it tipping the contents into an enamel bowl which he offered me apologetically. "Ah! In Armenia the peaches are twice the size." Meanwhile his orderly had appeared and was busying himself stacking the other fallen tins of fruit back into their cases and taking up the boards.

I devoured the whole tin of peaches while he rambled on about the wonders of Armenia. When I had finished he said "how about some figs" and started to search the walls for the right packing case. I had had more than enough and fought a rear guard action out of this fantastic 'Gingerbread House', constantly plied with the promise of all the fruits of Armenia regretfully in an inferior tinned form.

As I made my way down to the road below I was fascinated by the labyrinth of paths throughout the camp, all of them bordered by a wonderful tracery of split bamboo fencing. It had the intricate artistry of Victorian ironwork and must have taken hundreds of man-hours to construct. Man-hours that should have been expended on the construction of the road into Burma.

Back at our company camp, life went on as usual. We had one Bengali company camped beside us commanded by a Lt. Edwards and here at least we could get a few pioneers to help with the task of road building. It was however a far from normal military set up. Lt. Edwards was large, rubicund, and very like the Jimmy Edwards of the theatrical world, even including the moustache. He was also in the advanced stages of D.T. In those days we had rum galore. It was part of the rations, a sort of waterproofing agent issued liberally to help us survive the monsoon. It was issued on a per capita basis without regard to the fact that in the Indian Army many of the capita were forbidden to drink alcohol by their religion. This meant that in some units with a majority of Mohammedans there was a large amount of rum available for those few members of the unit whose religion bore no such constraints.

    Lt. Edwards found himself in a predominantly Mohammedan unit with the responsibility of consuming the rum ration for the entire unit. A responsibility he took very seriously. He also had an addiction for roasted peanuts. As he was the only European in his unit he came over to our mess tent every night for social reasons. He was always accompanied by his orderly who carried a gallon jar of rum and a vast supply of peanuts together with a device for roasting them. He was always welcome. We played cards, drank his rum and ate roasted peanuts until far into the night, when finally Edwards was gently steered back to his lines by his faithful orderly and we had the promise of his men for road works next day. Unfortunately, the strain proved too much for Edwards. Eventually he shot his bolt in a haze of rum; he held a special parade and tore the badges of rank from his VCO for some imaginery indiscretion, which was sad for the VCO was the one man who kept the company going under these difficult circumstances. The inevitable Court Martial ensued and Edwards disappeared.

    By this time the monsoon was well under way and our road was becoming a river of mud. Though we struggled to keep it useable by building miles of corduroy it soon became a losing battle and the forward units were ordered to withdraw before it became totally impossible to keep them supplied. They sent their transport out first, winding and grinding through the deepening mud on the road. We soon could do little to keep the road open other than extricate vehicles which had sunk to their axles in mud. We cut down trees and laid stretches of corduroy in the worst places. Corduroy is a log road made of thousands of trunks laid in close order across the road and held together by longitudinal trunks along the edge, spiked to the cross members. It is slow work felling, trimming and moving the trunks down to the road and requires the felling of some 7000 trees for a mile of road. As conditions became critical the road was closed during the day when we struggled to reinforce the worst stretches with corduroy and reopen it for traffic at night. The situation was becoming desperate and if a vehicle stuck or broke down it often brought the whole exodus of transport to a halt and the only solution was to push it over the hillside to keep the traffic moving for the track was now so deeply rutted that it was not possible to get past broken down vehicles. Many vehicles did not have to be pushed over the edge, they slipped and slid over it of their own accord. If they went over the edge they had a 600 ft. drop down the precipitous hillside. As they cartwheeled down through the rocks and trees their headlights swept the night sky in great arcs of light until they were suddenly extinguished as they shattered against some obstacle in the course of their descent.

It is strange how callous men can become under these conditions when life and death is balanced on the razor's edge. There was a medical unit, a M.D.S., situated on a spur not far from us. It had a wonderful view of the road winding up from Burma. In the evening the doctors would sit outside drinking and taking bets with each other on how many times the headlights of the next vehicle to go over the edge would arc across the night sky before they were extinguished either by being smashed on the descent or on arriving at the bottom. They sat outside their field dressing station, drink in hand, counting aloud. "One, two, three, ooogh, that could not be half way down. Yours again Pete". Or, 'I demand a recount".

Hours later the mangled remains of the surviving occupants would arrive on stretchers borne carefully through the glutinous mud right up to the M.D.S. where their bones would be set and their lacerations stitched up with loving care by the same doctors.

In a strange way it made sense. The headlights of a vehicle tumbling down the hillside were too remote. For all you knew the driver could have jumped clear before it went over. While you were remote from the disasters that were commonplace every night you kept sane by remaining remote and indifferent. It was no good getting worked up about the situation over which you had no control, so you made light of it to preserve your own sanity for the moment when you had to act. This strangely enough was the philosophy of survival under wartime conditions.

The seasonal withdrawal from Burma at the onset of the monsoon started with the transport and ended with the infantry slogging it on foot through the deep mud created by the churning wheels of the vehicles. The last of the vehicles were generally the gunners with their heavy, ammunition laden quads towing guns. Their weight created special problems for the recovery units as they sank deeper and got into more inextricable situations, as they were not, in the last resort, as expendable as a worn out three ton lorry that could be pushed over the edge to keep the rest of the convoy moving. I remember one such problem when the weight of a heavily laden quad was left balanced on its belly on the edge of oblivion. There were four gunners perched on the front seat but as they started to get out from the nearside door the last two realised that their weight was the only counterbalance that was preventing the quad from toppling over the edge. As they stepped down the nearside rose up almost to the point of no return. They quickly got back in and the balance was redressed but there they were, stuck. If they got out the quad would certainly topple over the edge of a 600 ft. drop and be lost; if they sat tight it would remain balanced on the edge but at any moment more of the road edge could collapse under the weight and they would have little chance of getting out before it fell down the ravine. Full marks to the gunners; they sat it out for an hour, balanced on the edge of life until we got steel wire ropes attached and anchored the vehicle so that it could be safely winched back onto the road and live to fight again. If they had panicked and got out it would have undoubtedly rolled over the edge, so finely was it balanced. It took a lot of courage to sit it out under those conditions.

The withdrawal of the infantry was less dramatic but had its moments. I have never heard the bagpipes playing to more stirring effect than those of a battalion of the 1st Seaforth Highlanders marching out along this tortuous mountain road. At first just a faint note on the evening breeze, the distant sound of pipes rose and fell as they negotiated the endless bends along the mountainside, but slowly it became more and more audible as the long columns emerged from the mist until finally the full skirl of the pipes filled the air as they passed beneath us. The effect was quite eerie. It made the hair stir up the back of my neck. This was the true setting for the bagpipes. I had never heard them like this before. I realised just what it must be doing for the morale of that weary column of 1st Seaforths slogging through the mist, rain and mud from Burma. They were thousands of miles from their Highlands but you could see the effect they had on all who watched them pass through. British and Indian troops were spellbound by the magic of those pipes. Tradition and pride transformed a weary mud bespattered column of soldiers into heroes of the moment. It not only sustained their morale, it boosted ours. Long after the column had passed and the sound of the pipes faded into the mist, one wondered if it had all been a dream, but the effect it left on us was real. Full marks to those pipers who marched out through those conditions, and still had breath to spare for their pipes.

Eventually even the engineering units could do no more under those conditions and we finally pulled out to our monsoon quarters near Palel. This camp was not far from the famous Longtak Lakes, a huge shallow area of water and reedbeds that was the focal point of the great migration of wild fowl from Siberia. Vast numbers of duck and geese made this their winter quarters. When they flighted in the evening their numbers would darken the sky like an eclipse of the sun. Unfortunately, the winter months were our dry season and we were forward working on the road. By the time the monsoon forced us back it was summer in Siberia and the wild fowl had flown there to their summer nesting grounds. However I did occasionally get sent back from the line in the dry season and saw the amazing population of wild fowl that migrated to these lakes. Driving past in my Jeep the clear sky was suddenly overcast with black clouds of flighting duck. How I longed to be there with my gun at this time of the year, but fortunately for the duck this was not to be.

The monsoon brought more than rain and mud to contend with. Green mould grew on everything overnight, even my wallet turned green. Worst of all was a complaint known as Burma foot, a fungus that attacked your feet when permanently encased in soggy wet boots. It reduced you to a hobbling wreck, and in the end I discovered that it was better to walk barefooted through the mud with your boots slung around your neck. Worst of all was the various forms of dysentery that became endemic under these conditions. This really knocked the stuffing out of you and sapped your will to live. I recall falling out from a march in the pouring rain and curling up under a bush for an hour or so until I had the strength and the will to continue and catch up with the column. A foolish act for had it been a leech infested area it could have been fatal but I was beyond caring at the time.

Leeches were something very special to the jungle in the monsoon. They were creatures that I had always associated with pond life in England but here under the constant humidity of the jungle they had evolved a terrestrial species. Fortunately they were localised and not all jungle was infested with them, but when you came across an infestated area it was an experience that you did not easily forget. Suddenly you realised that every leaf had a leech on it. As you passed they seemed to sense you and reached out towards you, extending themselves into long thin threads always pointing towards you until you were close enough to make contact, when in a flash of momentary contact they released their hold on the leaf and were on you. Forcing your way through the jungle it was easy not even to notice them or to be aware of their lightning transfer until later, when you stripped off your clothes, you found you were festooned with their blood gorged bodies and in the most awkward places. Their invasion was barely noticeable; you felt nothing but there they were embedded in your skin and full of your blood. The drill for their removal was a military instruction, but like so many military instructions it failed to envisage the conditions under which it had to be carried out. It recommended putting salt on them, but in pouring rain this had little effect. The alternative was to touch them with a lighted cigarette. This too had its problems in torrential rain. You could get through a week's cigarette ration and be left with a pile of sodden cigarettes for a poor return of dislodged leeches. You were warned that pulling them off was liable to leave their jaws embedded in your skin to go septic. I eventually discovered that safety fuse, a part of our demolition equipment, was the ideal solution for their dislodgement. It was the slow burning fuse that was used to ignite demolition and it burnt at 2ft. per minute even under water, but it needed skill and care in the more inaccessible parts of one's body or you could end up with burns that were worse than leech bites.

While we were back at Palel waiting for the monsoon to abate we also did a bit of re-equipping. At that time our transport was mostly ex-desert campaign cast-offs. Fifteen and thirty hundred weight trucks still in their sand coloured desert camouflage and generally still fitted with sand tyres! Nothing could be less suitable for the conditions in which we had to operate. I was given the job of taking these vehicles back to Assam where a sort of M.T. remount depot was established at Sylhet. There, I was to hand over these clapped out veterans and be issued with American Dodge four-wheel-drive equivalents. I set off back down the road full of hope and expectation. It took several days to reach our destination under monsoon conditions. Needless to say when we got to Sylhet no one had any instructions to issue replacement vehicles, only to take in our old ones. So there we sat refusing to hand in our vehicles until assured of replacements.

Sylhet was about as hot and humid as you can get. We were soon suffering from prickly heat, an inflammation of the sweat pores. We tried to cool off by bathing in a local tank (artificial pond) until we discovered that it contained elephant leeches. They were anything up to five inches long and rumour had it that if one end attached to one knee and the other end to the other knee you were hobbled for good. We did not wait to find out and burnt these disgusting monsters off before they could get embedded in the more inaccessible parts of one's body. After that we kept cool by driving up and down the road with the windscreen down. It was heaven while you kept moving but as soon as you stopped the hot humid reality was worse than ever.

At last the order came through to issue replacement vehicles and we set off to Dimapur in wonderful Dodge four-wheel-drive troop carriers. Not new but an exciting advance on the old clapped out desert campaign vehicles we had handed in. We reached Dimapur by nightfall and entered Penis Park rest camp in the dark. As I picked my way towards the guardroom I trod on something soft that hissed. My shouts brought out the Sikh guard with hurricane lamp to reveal a banded kriat. One of the most venomous snakes of the jungle. The dim light revealed a snake banded with black and lemon yellow segments still very much alive and very angry. However, within seconds the Sikh guard had beaten it into a pulp with their bamboo poles.

Next day we set off in pouring rain up the climb to Kohima and beyond, but various delays made it a late start. Halfway up the mountain ascent a tiger stepped out into the road in front of me. A wild tiger is a beautiful creature, full of poise and disdain for interlopers on its territory; it stood in the middle of the road regarding us with complete disinterest, then quietly disappeared over the edge of the road into the jungle below.

Within a few more bends of this tortuous road another of nature's giants, a huge moth, homed in on my headlights and as it struck them I instinctively braked and leapt out to find it stuck in the mud in front of my wheels. I had never seen such an enormous moth. Its wing span was 11½ inches across and I guessed that it must be an Atlas moth.

We reached Kohima after sunset. I stopped to ensure that the other vehicles were still with us. The evening was still luminous and magical at 4000 ft., yet more magical still was the faint sound that came drifting on the breeze. It sounded like a mass choir singing, and there was no mistaking what they were singing – 'Abide With Me'. The effect was dramatic in the extreme. Thousands of miles from Britain in the remote Naga Hills to hear a mass of voices singing 'Abide With Me' was both unforgettable and inexplicable. Slowly it grew louder until around the bend of the road the choir appeared. Not a contingent of Welsh miners but several hundred Naga tribesmen who had been working on the road. They passed us in full throat and wound their way down the road until the hymn hung on the air like a fading dream. It seemed quite incredulous that such a moving hymn should have come from the throats of a bunch of Naga tribesmen known to practice head hunting. Dressed in their colourful shawls, a beaded loin cloth, a necklace and a spear they looked impressive. Fortunately, they were also pro-British. This particular group had been helping with road building and were returning to their village on the hilltop. I later discovered that there had been an active Welsh Methodist Mission in this remote area. I do not think they made many conversions to Christianity but it certainly explained this unexpected and very moving rendering of 'Abide With Me'.

Back with my company, life was improving as the monsoon diminished and once again we moved forward to re-open and occupy the route into Burma. Back in England the press had discovered our existence and someone had coined 'the forgotten army' phrase which was a good press standby when news from the other fronts was slack.

Just as it began to seem as though we would spend the rest of our lives building and rebuilding the road into Burma, news came that our company was to be sent back to India to form part of a special jungle warfare training division. Our destination was Chindwara in the central provinces, nearest town of any size being Nagpur. The great day arrived and I was off with my platoon to form the advance party. We had the long drive back to Dimapur Road, hand in our transport and then an even longer rail journey ahead. I made the mistake of deciding to ride one of our motorcycles back. I thought it would give me greater flexibility of command, easy to turn round and dash back along the convoy to make sure there were no dropouts due to breakdowns. The monsoon was over, it was the end of September and getting hot, so I reckoned that I would have better air cooling on a motorcycle, but I had not reckoned with the state of the road post-monsoon wear and tear. By the time we had covered the hundred miles back to Dimapur I was a shaken wreck. The jolting of handlebars over endless potholes had overflexed my arm muscles to such an extent that next day I could barely straighten or bend my arms. I swore I would never do that again and I do not remember ever riding a motorcycle since.

CHAPTER 6

Training for Jungle Warfare

I remember little of the long train journey to Chindwara except that it was long and very uncomfortable. I do however remember one small station somewhere in Assam where we waited for our train to arrive in the dark. I walked down the single track that skirted the edge of the jungle; on the other side was a large thorn hedge and it extended into the distance illuminated by the light of millions of fireflies. Their pulsating white light lit up the hedge like an endless neon tube. I had never seen such a display. I must have walked about half a mile admiring it when, from the edge of the jungle on the other side, the most blood curdling cries started, rising higher and higher in pitch and intensity every moment. I was frozen with fear, the hairs on the back of my neck I could feel rising like those on a cat's back. It was so close that I felt that at any moment whoever they were must burst from cover and attack me. Then the weird banshee chorus reached a peak and started to lose intensity and diminished down the scale that it had ascended until suddenly it was deathly still again. It would have been undignified for an officer to run, but I got back to the station at a walking pace that would have been near to disqualification in a walking race. My men to my surprise were quite unmoved. They squatted in little groups chatting away just as I had left them, yet they must have heard these blood curdling yells. I found my jemadar standing quietly talking under the hissing pressure lamp that lit the station. I asked him as casually as I could whether he had heard that strange disturbance in the jungle. "No, Sahib, I heard nothing, what sort of disturbance?" I tried to imitate the blood curdling yells I had heard so close to me in the dark. "Oh yes, Sahib, I heard those jackals" he said smiling. "Noisy brutes those jackals, we hear them every night in my village. Good thing we did not have them in Burma or the Japs would start imitating them to infiltrate our positions unnoticed".

I then realised that they were so familiar to my men that they had barely noticed them, whereas I, who had never heard the jackals before and at such close quarters, had been scared stiff. Just as well that my introduction to them had not happened in Burma where I should have assumed that it was the war cry of a Japanese regiment about to attack and reacted accordingly. If I had opened fire on a pack of jackals my men would have had a good laugh at my expense.

The rest of our journey was long, hot and tedious but eventually we arrived at Nagpur and completed the last stage to Chindwara on a very slow, narrow gauge, single track railway. The next week was the usual round of collecting stores and equipment from ordnance quartermasters who behaved as though they were parting with their own personal possessions. However, by the time the rest of the company arrived we had our new camp site layed out in a large clearing in the jungle. In India any wooded area is called jungle. This was pretty sparse jungle, small trees and large clearings with a small river at one end. On the other side of the river was an area of tall grass and reeds which we later discovered was a favourite haunt of wild peacock. It was a tented camp and unlike our tents in Burma, which were so rotten that we had to thatch them to keep the rain from pouring through, these tents were near new and quite a luxury.

Our training programme when it got going was receiving new recruits who had done a short period of training at their depot. We had to toughen them up for the experience of jungle warfare. This meant long patrols into the thick jungle a few miles away, sometimes marching all night and bivouacing by day making our own shelters out of jungle materials.

The monsoon was not fully over and our shelters were frequently tested with torrential rain, though often our night marches were helped by brilliant moonlight. By day the jungle was different from the jungle on the route into Burma but equally fascinating for me. There was more colour and more game for a start. The colour came in the form of flowering trees, the most beautiful of which was the 'Flame of the Forest', as the name implies its upper branches were a mass of flame coloured flowers. Then there was the jacaranda which had mauvey blue flowers cascading all over it, and another tree growing on the higher, more barren, ground that at that time of year had no leaves but great yellow flowers on its bare branches.

The animal life was equally varied. Different species of monkeys abounded, the most noticeable being the langour that frequented the more open country. They were large and had long tails and seemed to prefer the ground to the tree and went bounding across the clearings in a loping canter. There were various species of deer from samba which were not unlike red deer, to barking deer that were small and shy and kept to the thicker undergrowth but could always be heard with their dog-like bark at night.

There was wild pig and smaller game like the chickor, a maddening partridge that kept calling with a sound like its name. I spent hours hunting these in the cultivated land near villages. The bird went on calling until you were a few yards away and then stopped. I was sure I had pinpointed the spot he was calling from to a few square yards and walked the ground up and down practically trampling it flat but no bird would get up. I would hear another bird calling and off I went after that one where the whole infuriating process was repeated. Very occasionally I managed to put the bird up and got a shot but walked miles in this process for a brace of these elusive birds. Oh what I would have given for a good dog! To this day I do not know if they sat tight or sneaked off when they stopped calling. From my letters home I see that I also came across some frogs as large as partridges. In my letter I said I was going to try cooking them as I had heard that frogs legs were like spring chicken. I do not remember eating them, so perhaps I had second thoughts on this.

My great ambition was to shoot a tiger or a leopard. This may seem strange now but in those days there was no environmental lobby or conscience regarding the future of the large cats and the threat of their extinction. They were plentiful in many parts of India. They were regarded as a menace to the remote villages where they took a steady toll of their livestock and frequently of the villagers themselves. They were still regarded as the ultimate trophy in the sporting world. To bag a tiger was the highest accolade for the big game hunter involving both know-how and an element of risk. It was like being awarded your colours in the First XV. A leopard was equally rewarding but psychologically was only equivalent to Second XV colours. I was determined to get both. The local villagers assured me that there were plenty of both in the nearby jungle.

All villagers tend to exaggerate and when you try and pin them down they become rather vague. 'Plenty tiger here Sahib' because my brother saw one here three weeks ago and my uncle had his best bullock killed by a tiger last year. However, I was determined to have a go. I found a large climbable tree on the edge of a clearing, its branches went out horizontally from the crown to form a natural foundation for a machan (a platform for shooting tiger). I borrowed one of the goats from the company ration compound (in those days your meat ration was delivered alive, there being no refrigeration and you killed it when you needed it). I selected a large white goat which I felt no hungry tiger could fail to see. My driver helped me bundle it into the back of the Jeep together with a camouflage net from which I intended to construct my hide, a ·303 service rifle with which to shoot the tiger plus a powerful torch to spotlight it at the last moment before the kill, and we were off. I had read how these things were done. We stopped the Jeep about a hundred yards from the selected site. The plan was that I should shin up the tree and make my hide with the camouflage net and get settled in. When I was ready I would signal my driver who would come and tether the goat below me and then turn round and go back to the company camp. The goat would believe that it was abandoned and on its own in the jungle and start bleating, the noise would attract the tiger and when he attacked the goat I would have him in my sights just below me and Wham – I would bag my tiger.

The first part of this operation went according to the plan. The big horizontal branches of the tree made me an ideal platform. I soon had the camouflage net arranged suspended above me falling down like a curtain on all sides. My driver brought the goat and tethered it below and as instructed walked away without so much as looking up at me. The goat felt abandoned and gazing at my retreating driver started bleating away. All was set for action. I heard the Jeep start up and saw its lights disappear back to our camp. As the light began to fade so the mosquitoes began to appear. Just the whine of the odd scout at first, but before long I was besieged by clouds of the brutes. Most of me was well covered but my face and hands were not and they homed in on these targets with deadly accuracy. When they bit me I had to resist the temptation to slap the site of the attack for fear of giving my presence away to the goat below, instead I had to be content with aerial passes with my hands that only momentarily dislodged them before they settled in for a second feed elsewhere.

As it got darker shadows appeared. The longer I looked at them the more they looked like tigers waiting to pounce. I distinctly saw one such shadow moving closer to the kill. This was it. I decided to get the barrel of my rifle through the wall of the camouflage net and pointing in the direction of the goat ready for the moment of action. As I manoeuvred the Lee Enfield through the netting the foresight somehow became entangled. The mesh of the net was, I realised, rather too small to allow sufficient room to manoeuvre. The mosquitoes took their opportunity to deliver a mass attack, the net became inextricably entangled in my foresight, and I could move my rifle neither forward nor backward without pulling on the net. The shadow moved closer to the goat. I became desperate and pushed the rifle forward in the hope that it would clear itself should the tiger spring. Unfortunately, it did not, but the pull on the netting dislodged its attachment above me and the whole net fell down enveloping me. I felt like a vanquished Roman gladiator ready to accept the thrust of the trident as a just reward for my incompetence.

I vented my anger on the mosquitoes and the camouflage net with little effect on either but my expletives dissipated the tiger shadows and reassured the goat that it was in good company. It stopped bleating, looked up at me, made a low chuckling noise and lay down and went to sleep. Half an hour later I had at last extricated the camouflage net from the tree and was walking back to camp with the bundle of net on my back, the rifle on my shoulder and the goat by my side. It was not the triumphant return that I had envisaged, and I was glad to find that everyone was in bed and asleep. The duty sentry challenged me and demanded the password for the night, but a good English swear word and the sight of his officer leading a white goat and burdened with a bundle of camouflage net seemed sufficient evidence of my authenticity for him to entone, 'Pass friend, all is well'. The expression on his face confirmed that he was well aware that this was not the case.

My first attempt to 'bag a tiger' had been a miserable failure but not long after this event we started losing goats from within the camp itself. On two nights running, goats were taken from the ration compound. My men were convinced that it could only be a tiger or leopard that could be doing this. At the sight of their meat ration disappearing so fast, they turned to me with faith and encouragement. "Sahib you are a great shikar (hunter). Only you can destroy this villain for us". And, "Sahib, only you have the courage to face this tiger and kill him. We are afraid that when he has eaten all our goats he will be hungry and start on us".

What worried me was that our camp site was in a large clearing and the trees were all too small to support a machan. In fact, there was nothing with a trunk much thicker than a man's arm, so if I was to confront this tiger it would have to be on foot, and if I did not make a clean kill I would be very vulnerable to a wounded and enraged tiger. However, my reputation was at stake. You cannot go off into the jungle to shoot tiger and chicken out when one is threatening your own camp just because there are no big trees to make a hide in. I did not want to lose the faith of my men and I wanted to bag a tiger, but I was also aware that this was a situation of considerable risk and one in which more experienced men would have made special preparation in the form of a man-made platform near the goat pen. In the end I just remained in the mess tent after everyone had turned in for the night, drinking my way through the whisky ration with my shotgun across my knees. It was loaded with two contractile cartridges and a powerful torch strapped underneath the barrels. I was doubtful if the animal would really return. It was starting to get quite cold and I was considering the merits of retiring to my bed as it was nearly 2 a.m. and the whisky ration was looking a bit depleted. I picked up my gun, extinguished the hurricane lamp and paused outside to survey the peaceful scene. There was no moon but a soft luminosity which just enabled me to see my way to my tent without bumping into anything in my path. Then suddenly a large pale shape was moving around not far away. It seemed to be quartering the ground. I stood frozen. It was coming towards me. It was in range. It was a long pale form moving silently across my front. I raised my gun and switched on the torch. All I could see was two irridescent eyes and a bit of striped flank. My heart was pounding within my chest, it was now or never. The sudden shaft of light had momentarily frozen the animal and I knew it would not last. A thousand thoughts shot through my mind. There was no retreat, not a rock or tree to afford shelter if I failed to shoot it dead. I aimed for the striped flank to the right of those glowing eyes and pressed the trigger. This time I had the range right, thank God. The tiger fell as though pole-axed. The ball must have gone straight through its heart. All I heard was a long, low fart!

I had read a lot about shooting tigers. Always approach with caution, it could be momentarily stunned and a second shot at close quarters makes the difference between life and death. I approached with every caution, my finger on the trigger of the second barrel. At last I had won my First XV Colours. Later generations may find it hard to understand just what this meant to me. No doubt its origins are tribal and the initiation into manhood by proving oneself in self imposed danger are all part of the age-old ritual. However, my elation was to be short-lived. As I advanced on my tiger ready to deliver a second shot should it show signs of life I became aware that it was not a tiger. It was too pale and too small. It was a hyena. A very large one and beautifully striped, but not a tiger. I had gone through all the anxiety and fear of shooting a tiger under those very risky conditions only to discover that the trophy was just a hyena. I sauntered off to bed like a pricked balloon.

No more goats were taken from our compound, so no doubt he was the culprit, but his demise did not have the glamour that would have been accorded had he been a tiger. However, my men were appreciative that their meat ration had been saved by my efforts. They had the hyena skinned and cured and presented to me as a rug to go by my bed.

My reputation as a shikar was now established and not long after this incident a group of highly excited men came to my tent to announce that there were peacock in a nearby jungle clearing and they would drive them for Sahib to shoot. They were as good as their word and positioned me in the river bed while they drove through an adjacent piece of elephant grass with much shouting and noise. They flushed them successfully and as they shot overhead with all the velocity of a good game bird I downed one of them and it fell with a thud in the grass behind me. With whoops of excitement my whole platoon converged on it and brought it triumphantly back to me. They were as excited as children by the whole incident. I was their hero for the moment. I mention all this because of the contrasting sequel to the event which shows how men's minds can be influenced by circumstance.

One of the aspects of our jungle training was the battle course. A very popular feature with the directing staff of training establishments. No good training unit should be without a battle course and we were duly ordered to build and operate one. The idea was a form of obstacle course with simulated battle effects to make it seem like the real thing. You crawled under wire while live bullets were fired over your heads. You scaled a series of obstacles with NCO's screaming at you and letting off thunder flashes. You crawled up ditches filled with smoke and as a finale, if it was possible, crossed a river by a rope bridge with demolition charges exploding in the water beneath. It was probably more valuable for impressing visiting staff officers than it was for training men. The men knew they were not going to be shot or blown up so their behaviour was very different from what it would be in battle. They just pressed on regardless to complete the course like extras in an M.G.M. film. We had our battle course and it ended with a river crossing over a rope bridge (one rope to walk on and two to hold on to). In the river were placed slabs of guncotton wired up for electrical detonation by an NCO instructor on the opposite bank. He could see the river and the bridge and judge the right moment to set off the charges. The effect was quite realistic as shell fire for it sent up a great spout of water with a muffled explosion, but was relatively safe, even at fairly close quarters, as the water absorbed most of the detonation wave.

Unfortunately, the unforeseen can always happen. A few days after the peacock hunt a class was due for the battle course. All went well until one of the class fell off the rope bridge into the water below. The bridge was not very high nor the water very deep, so he quickly got to his feet and waded ashore. The NCO in charge of the underwater demolitions held his hand until the man was well clear of the water and on the shore beneath him. Unfortunately, because the bank was steep and he was lying down he could no longer see the man or he might have noticed that he had got his foot entangled with one of the electric cables leading to the charges, and had dragged the charge out with him. All the NCO saw was that the water was clear and proceeded to fire the next charge. He knew something was very wrong when instead of it exploding in the water it went off at the foot of the bank beneath him. When he stood up and looked down he saw a man lying shattered beneath him.

When I was called to the scene a few moments later I sent a runner for the doctor for the man was still alive, but only just, and there was little hope for him. The charge must have gone off pretty close to him for it had blown half his clothes off and I could see that his stomach was split right open as though cut with a sharp knife. His intestines were lying beside him though apparently undamaged. I was pretty shocked by the scene, but I remember picking them up and placing them carefully back inside him having first removed a few bits of gravel that were adhering to them. There was practically no blood. Explosive force does strange things. I noticed that both his boots had been removed and lay on the ground a few yards away – the laces were still done up tightly, his socks were still on his feet. He was still breathing and groaning slightly when the MO arrived with a stretcher. He was a good Indian MO. He looked at the body carefully and said "I will do what I can, but I am afraid he will die from the shock anyway". He was right. The man died in the night.

There followed the official enquiry and the unofficial military inquest by the latter. I mean amongst the men themselves. They were mostly new recruits and without experience of violent death. The battle course had proved more realistic than they expected. Misfortune had fallen on them and simple people look for simple causes – amongst the first was the displeasure of their Gods. In some parts of India the peacock is sacred though not in the C.P., but my men came from the Hindu south and someone amongst them had said this trouble has befallen us because the Sahib shot a sacred peacock – he has offended the Gods and we are all to be punished.

The beaming faces that summoned me to the peacock hunt were now black and sullen. No one would look me in the eye and say why, but it was all too obvious that their regard for me had changed dramatically. In the Indian Army in such circumstances it is your VCO who bridges the cultural gap between the British Sahib and your Indian soldiers. I turned to my VCO and as ever with a foot in both camps he was able to explain and advise. "One man has been telling the other men that this has happened because you shot a sacred peacock, Sahib. I know who he is and he has told them that you will break out in boils for doing this. It is better to do nothing at the moment and as long as you do not break out in boils, I will make sure he gives no more trouble for the future".

A subtle philosophy and thank goodness I did not break out in boils. Within a week we were back to normal again. Thank heavens we had eaten the peacock before this happened. Very good it was, too, like a gamey turkey, but it might have stuck in my gullet if we had yet to eat it after this incident.

In the middle of all this training others, I was sent on a jungle warfare course in the South of India. It took a day and a half by train to get there but well worth the journey to me. This was real primary jungle again. An exciting fauna of snakes, crocodiles and, above all, the painted jungle fowl whose amazing cape of feathers were prized for salmon flies due to a natural blotch of white enamel on each feather.

The course was partly on how to survive in the jungle and how to improvise everything out of bamboo, from cooking pots to defences of sharpened and fire hardened spikes on which the enemy were supposed to impale themselves. There was a very mixed bunch of officers taking the course with me, a few old hardened ones who had lived half their lives in India and knew it all, a few young staff officers who had never been in the jungle before, and had no intention of ever doing so again, and a few like myself anxious to learn everything that might help us survive our next stint in the jungles of Burma.

One part of the improvisation was booby traps. These form part of every sapper officer's training, not just setting them but clearing and making safe enemy booby traps. So this part of the course I found doubly interesting though some of the other officers had got to the stage where they found the whole course a bit of a laugh, as they had no intention of ever going outside Bombay or Calcutta in their administrative capacity. The chief instructor had set up a very good booby trap alley where we were shown every conceivable form of improvised booby trap. One very simple and effective one was made with a small tin such as a cocoa tin fixed on one side of the path and a hand grenade just fitted into the tin, the sides of the tin preventing its handle flying up and releasing the plunger. A fine black wire was attached to the grenade and stretched across the path about a foot from the ground and was fixed to a tree on the other side. The enemy walking down the path would knock into the trip wire which would pull the grenade out of its tin, the lever would fly up and three seconds later it would explode.

The chief instructor sensing his audience were none too attentive called over his havildar instructor, a burly great Sikh who looked as though he knew everything about jungle warfare. He was bristling with knives and guns and had several hand grenades clipped into his belt. "Now Havildar Jador Singh will show you how this is done for real because if you don't set the trap correctly you may get surprised and not the Jap". The instructor looked at his watch. "Ah, nearly tiffin time, come on Havildar Jador". The havildar leapt forward with a nervous grin. "There's no time to get a dummy, use one of those grenades on your belt and show the officer Sahibs how to attach the trip wire to the grenade and place it in the tin". "Achah Sahib". This was obviously the havildar's great moment for which he had been waiting a chance to demonstrate his skill to the Sahibs. However, he seemed a bit nervous and clumsy as he attached the trip wire to the grenade. "Right now, watch carefully everyone. This is the important part. You must remove the safety pin before you place the grenade in the tin because it's no good if you leave it in for you can't get it out once it is in the tin – Right?

– Carry on havildar".

Jador Singh seemed to be having trouble getting the safety pin out. The more he struggled the more nervous he became, then suddenly the pin came out and with a cry of "Whoops" the lever flew up in the air. Even the bored young staff officers knew what this meant. We had three seconds to take cover or be killed by the exploding grenade. One's sense of self-preservation took over. In a flash I had noted where the stupid havildar had let the grenade fall and the position of a large tree a few yards away. There was precious little cover around so I dived towards the tree, put my arm out like a rugger tackle and swung around the tree until I was on the opposite side from the grenade. Though it skinned my arm I felt I had gained a position of survival. I judged three seconds had elapsed but as some grenades have seven second fuses, I clung tightly to the ground waiting for the inevitable explosion. As time passed I realised that not only was more than seven seconds up, but there was a sound of suppressed laughter emanating from the instructor and his havildar. I raised my face from the dirt and saw them sitting on the ground beside the booby trap, holding their sides in convulsed laughter. All around there were officers lying prone with their faces pressed into the earth awaiting the expected explosion. I must have been the first to realise that we had all been the victims of a carefully planned hoax. At least I had the benefit of seeing the other members of the course, some previously so bored and disinterested, now lying face down on the ground and pressing themselves into it in a desperate bid for survival. Some I reckoned were too close to the grenade to have achieved survival had it been live. They were mostly the bored staff officers, others who knew the possible effects had the grenades been live had achieved better positions, but all were equally furious at being tricked in this manner. I do not know if every class was subjected to this hoax. If they were the instructors must have had a lot to laugh about for it was well staged and demonstrated that we all had the same will for survival come the crunch.

The course was soon over, I saw but never shot my painted jungle fowl. Others saw but failed to shoot a mugger, and in no time we were all back with our various units just that little bit wiser about jungle warfare.

By now it was December, and the weather was the endless sun of the dry season, but this did not deter the British element from thoughts of Christmas and the celebrations that went with it. Even the traditional turkey appeared on the ration indent. Half a pound per British personnel on the strength. With five officers and two British warrant officers the promise of a 3½ lb. turkey did not seem very exciting. Various ingredients for a Christmas pudding were also available but no one had the faintest idea about what went into the traditional Xmas pudding. Least of all our Bengali cook. Nevertheless we indented for our share of the magical ingredients allowed, such as suet, dried fruit etc. I made a special trip to the local hospital and chatted up the matron who supplied me with complicated instructions on what went into a Christmas pud. I remember it even included grated carrot. Determined to succeed, I wrote it all down and one way or another all the ingredients were obtained and correctly mixed according to the magic formula. I carefully supervised the mixing which I remembered was part of the essential ritual. The resultant dough was wrapped in a cloth like a sacred football and handed to the Bengali cook with instructions that it had to be boiled for four hours. Unfortunately, I did not mention that the process had to be continuous. Life in an Indian cookhouse was punctuated by demands for tea which necessitated boiling water. Every time someone came in and shouted "Cha orderly" a fresh brew was made which caused the Xmas pudding to be placed on one side whilst fresh water was boiled and the Xmas pud cooled down awaiting its return to the fire. The numerous interruptions in its four hours of boiling had an amazing effect on its consistency, which was not fully appreciated until it was finally reheated on Xmas day and ceremonially piped into the mess flaming with cheap Indian brandy substitute. The effect was the real thing and as Officer in Charge of Christmas Pud I was warmly congratulated, but when it came to serving it up problems arose. No knife, let alone a spoon, could make any impression on it. In spite of all the meticulous adherence to the magic formula supplied by the hospital matron the result was just like synthetic rubber. It just could not be cut with a knife. Someone drew his kukri and eventually succeeded in hacking off a small piece but when he tried to eat it, it was only to confirm that it was the nearest thing to synthetic rubber we had come across and that the formula would be worth a fortune to the war effort. In the end we worked off the Christmas spirit playing football with it. Even this seemed to inflict more injury on the player than the ball.

    Christmas over there was New Year to be celebrated and the CRE had decided that an impressive mess night for the other officers of the division would be a suitable way of marking the occasion. To accommodate this splendid dinner a large marquee was produced and duly erected.

    To ensure the success of the occasion many more senior officers than would normally concern themselves with catering arrangements, began issuing instructions and counter instructions which reduced the poor officer who was Mess Secretary at the time to a nervous wreck. As is the way in the Army, he was elected Mess Secretary not because he knew anything about catering, but because he could not think up any reason fast enough why he should not be Mess Secretary when proposed at the last mess meeting. This is generally how Mess Secretaries are elected.

The whole idea of a pucka mess night in a jungle camp seemed a bit of an absurdity, but no doubt the CRE thought it good for morale in some strange sort of way. As we were entirely dependent on army rations, apart from eating two days' rations at one sitting, the dinner itself could not be that exciting. However, the mess waiters would be in their starched white coats with colourful turbans on their heads and a corps sash around their shoulders to give the right effect. Rumour had it that the CRE had managed to secure some extra booze including port to toast the King's health. All the officers were expected to appear in well starched khaki drill. There was a guest list of senior officers from other regiments in the Division. In fact from a junior officer's viewpoint, all was set for a thoroughly boring evening. However, no one had reckoned on Cocoa, a pet monkey recently acquired by one of these junior officers. Cocoa was a bit of an unknown quantity as he was always chained up outside his master's tent and apart from some rather rude habits, and a passion for eating anything, he had given little trouble to date.

Unfortunately, shortly before the appointed hour for the mess night his owner was seen wandering about with a very worried look on his face. Cocoa had managed to release himself from his chain and had disappeared. Only his owner seemed worried, but everyone else thought he had probably legged it back to the jungle where he belonged.

On a mess night it is incumbent on the junior officers to be there on time, in fact to be correct you arrive in reverse of seniority. Juniors being present to welcome their immediate seniors and so on up the scale. When I arrived there was a handful of lieutenants and a very worried Mess Secretary. Something had already gone wrong. There had been a large silver cigarette box on the table full of cigarettes and now it was practically empty, except for two broken ones in the box, and a few others strewn along the table. The Mess Secretary wanted to accuse someone, but did not know where to begin. It was unbelievable that one of the mess waiters would have behaved in this way. To prevent the Mess Secretary having an apopleptic fit we all rallied round and collected up cigarettes from our own cases to make the contents of the box look reasonable if not full again. We had hardly done this when a small figure appeared from nowhere, bounded onto the table and took a large fist full of cigarettes from the box and disappeared under the wall of the tent. It was obvious that Cocoa had not legged it back to the jungle. Time was short as the next echelon of officers was due at any moment, but you cannot catch a monkey in a hurry. To our horror we discovered that Cocoa had sought refuge between the inner and outer flys of the marquee. His evil little face appeared in one of the air vents in the roof from whence he showered bits of broken cigarette at us. Various attempts by his owner to coax him down with everything from bananas to more cigarettes were to no effect whatsoever. As more officers started arriving we decided it was better to ignore Cocoa but left instructions with the mess bearers that if they got the opportunity they were to catch him and tie him up.

The senior guests arrived and all went well until we were seated and the soup was served. Then I saw Cocoa peering down through the air vent directly above the head of the table where the CRE sat with the divisional commander on his right. They were engrossed in a very personal conversation for the CRE was leaning right over to the general and appeared to be telling him a very funny and probably very dirty story. At the same moment I saw a thin trickle of liquid falling from above straight into the CRE's soup. To my horror as I looked up I could see the source. Cocoa was standing in the air vent and peeing into space. The mess havildar had also seen what had happened and leapt forward to remove the CRE's soup. However, the CRE got the wrong impression. It is normal to wait until the senior officer had finished before the course is cleared, and the CRE thought that he was being hurried with lack of respect for his rank and told the mess havildar to stand back and wait until he had finished, in no uncertain terms. The mess havildar did not dare explain that a monkey had just urinated in the CRE Sahib's soup so just stood there frozen in indecision while the CRE finished his soup with relish and then waved for the havildar to remove his plate, which he did with obvious relief. I was not alone by any means in observing what had happened. According to their rank the various observers thought it extremely funny or extremely serious, but at this late stage no one dared do anything but contain their mirth or their anxiety.

Fortunately, the rest of the dinner went without incident. I saw Cocoa's face gazing down from his secure observation post in the roof vent. Eventually the port was passed around and we reached the ritual of drinking the King's health. The CRE banged the table and called out, "Mr. Vice", whereupon I, as junior subaltern present, had to rise, a symbol for all to rise, after which I proposed the King's health. "Gentlemen, the King". The words had hardly left my mouth and been repeated by all present, "The King", when a grey shadow leapt onto the table, deftly gathered up all the cigarettes in the silver box and was gone before the heads, tilted back to drain their port glasses, had returned with the odd strain of "God Bless Him".

Then the CRE called out, "Gentlemen, you may smoke", as per tradition, for you must not smoke before the King's health has been drunk. Somehow those of us who had a few cigarettes left palmed them into the box as it was passed to the top of the table where they quickly disappeared whilst we sat dying for a cigarette to relieve the tensions, but had to pretend to be non-smokers while a steady confetti of chewed up tobacco descended from the roof of the tent.

After the top table guests had departed we set about sorting out Cocoa, but this time we were all a little the worse for drink and he had no difficulty in eluding us, though, as more and more officers joined in the chase, the mess marquee was practically demolished in the process, but Cocoa remained free.

Towards the end of the recruits' training we were doing jungle patrols of ten days to a fortnight's duration, and as this was the culmination of their training I decided to make it more purposeful and designed the assault on Pachmari. Pachmari was a sort of quasi hill station that was situated on top of a towering block of cliffs that rose from the jungle in which we trained. It was about 50 miles to the north of us and was the Army Education Corps Centre, a sort of retreat for school masters and professors caught up in the net of conscription and formed into a corps to further education in the Army, combined with a little mild propaganda called current affairs. Their stronghold seemed to offer just the target we required as a final test. Though it was easily reached by road on the north side, the south side was the scarp slope of the feature and consisted of rugged cliffs that towered above the jungle plains below. The cliffs were steep but not unclimbable for they were good hard rock with deep ravines cut into them that would allow their six or seven hundred feet to be scaled. I made up the usual military background to our training objective – a 50-mile jungle trek to our target where we had to scale the cliffs up to Pachmari and demolish a secret enemy military installation. The position was well defended on the approach roads from the north but they regarded their southern flank as unassailable because of the cliffs and relatively secure.

We set off in full battle order and, moving by night by compass bearing, arrived at the foot of the Pachmari escarpment on the evening of the third day. The cliffs towering above us really did look unassailable and I began to have my doubts, but we camped for the night and set off at first light for the final assault. This proved as difficult as it had looked the previous evening. Time and time again we climbed half way up only to find that the last few hundred feet were too sheer for anyone but expert mountaineers which we were not. So down we clambered and started up another route. Finally we found a route that was possible and by nightfall we were within 100 ft. of the top and the way ahead, though steep, seemed possible so we camped there for the night, sleeping on a ledge with just enough room to lie but not to turn over without dropping several hundred feet. I must admit I was a little nervous, not for myself but for the men I had been training. Perhaps I had set my sights a little too high. If the exercise was a success the army would say "Well done, Henslow", but if there was an accident and one of them fell to their death the army would want to know with whose authority I was conducting such a hazardous operation and I would have to admit that the scheme was mine alone and no approval had been obtained for the exercise. With such thoughts I fell asleep.

At 5 a.m. next morning we were all awake and no one was missing. We struck camp and scaled the last hundred feet in no time at all. At 5 a.m. Pachmari was asleep. We wandered around at will. If they had guards or sentries they were not to be seen on this side of the station. The symbolic charge of 1lb. of gun cotton had to be sited, but where? I did not want to risk shattering windows so in the end settled for an open spot on the edge of their parade ground. In the still silence of early morning the explosion was quite deafening. Fortunately it was the hot season and most windows were open and probably survived the force of the blast. Not so the occupants. It was like stirring an ants' nest. Soon men started to appear from every doorway, some scantily dressed in assorted gowns, questioning, ordering, counter orders, confusion. Possibly their current affairs lectures on the downfall of Burma and Malaya triggered their imagination that their safe and secure outpost in Central India was the next to be over-run by the audacious Japanese Army.

Young as I was I had enough sense to realise that this was not the moment to rush forward, explain and apologise. It is one thing to frighten people and apologise, but if you make them look foolish as well it is better to say nothing and withdraw. We withdrew quietly over the edge of the cliff whence we had come and left them in disorderly confusion; calling out their guard and preparing themselves for a heroic defence against the, as yet, unlocated enemy.

The assault on Pachmari was a very good training exercise for my sappers and I like to think that it also was of some military benefit to the Army Education Corps who, as non-cambatants, might now give a little more thought to some basic military precautions which might in turn serve them in good stead in the future. My men were also delighted with the success of the operation, but it was still a long march back to camp in full marching order.

Before we got back to camp I had agreed with my jemadar that it was best if the OC did not hear of our explosive exploits at Pachmari. He assured me that he could ensure that the VCO's would not talk of it to their British officers and they in turn would make sure that no NCO spoke out of turn. As none of the British officers were fluent enough in Tamil they were unlikely to overhear anything from the men themselves. When we arrived back at camp two days later we were all too tired to talk about anything.

My time with the training division was nearly over and I was more than due for a fortnight's leave. This I planned to spend at Outicumund, a hill station in the South of India. It boasted of everything from strawberries to trout fishing and big game hunting, not to mention tennis and even a pack of hounds and above all female company. I fixed the date with my OC and started ticking off the days on my calendar.

CHAPTER 7

Back to War

On 15th April, 1944, I set off on 28 days leave to Outicumund. I took all my baggage with me as my time was up with the training division and after my leave I was to report back to the depot at Bangalore to await my new posting.

I made friends amongst the new arrivals, and had an eye on the future prospects for a female companion, but little did I know that fate had other plans in store for me. Within a week of my arrival I received a telegram headed 'Immediate' Report to 421 Ind. Fd. Coy, Cox's Bazaar, Arakan.

Censorship is a two-edged weapon. News had filtered through to the press in India that the Japs had launched an offensive in the Arakan and that our troops had it contained. Like all bad news from the front it was watered down by official censorship to appear as no more than a major skirmish so as not to cause alarm or panic within the civil population of India. In fact, it was no skirmish but the major Japanese offensive for the invasion of India and had very nearly succeeded. An extract from the history of the 7th Indian Division written after the war when all the facts were known is worth quoting here as it sets the stage on to which I was about to appear as a member of the cast. 421 Ind. Fd. Coy. was part of the 114 Brigade in 7th Ind. Div.

'The offensive launched by the Japanese on 4th February, 1944, was to be the opening phase of the march on Delhi. Its objective was to destroy the 7th Indian Division, then the 5th Indian Division, as a preliminary to a limited advance towards Chittagong. This might not unreasonably be expected to draw all available reserves to Arakan, thus opening the way for and securing the flank of an advance through Manipur state into the Assam and Surma valleys.

The strength of the force operating under General Hanaya was about 30,000. Japanese accounts state that by 1st February, 55 Division had been brought up to a strength of 24,000 but this excluded attached units. The advance into Assam would isolate the Chino-American forces in North Burma by cutting the Assam valley railway and the Assam trunk road, would overrun the Fourteenth Army advance bases and the great airfields from which supplies were being flown into China, and provide an admirable base for a full-scale invasion of India – a base, moreover, rich in vital commodities: rice from Manipur state, coal from the Ledo coalfields to keep the railway going, and perhaps even oil from the Digboi oilfield.

It was confidently expected that the arrival of Japanese forces accompanied by Bhose's so-called Indian National Army in Assam and East Bengal would be the signal for open revolt in Bengal and Bihar which would paralyse the supply lines to the Fourteenth Army.'

When I read the telegram I thought 'this is it'. The real thing at last. Enough had been filtering through on the news for me to realise that there was a serious Japanese offensive in the Arakan and that 7 Ind. Div. was in the thick of it. Though I felt somewhat cheated of my hard earned leave, being recalled after only eight days, it also made me feel that I was of some value to the war effort. That I was chosen to report immediately to the battle front and all those other officers on leave were not required and could carry on enjoying themselves gave me cause for some satisfaction. Such is the conceit of youth.

I packed and departed and made every effort to join my new unit with the least delay. I found them at Bawli Bazaar licking their wounds and enjoying a momentary rest from the battle. They had survived this major Japanese offensive but not without losses. The Division had been overrun by the Japanese and, whether by accident or design, they had not retreated but formed a box and stuck it out until they could turn the tide and the Japs were forced to withdraw beaten for the first time.

Casualties amongst Engineer officers had been high. The CRE, Lt. Col. Cator, had been killed on a reconnaissance and his successor, Lt. Col. Bishop, had been wounded three days later. Major Cooper was killed at the same time as Lt. Col. Cator and Captains Street and Higgins were both killed in the first few days of the fighting in the Admin. area. 421 Coy. Commander, Major Bewoar, was also killed at this time. By the time I caught up with the company they had a new OC, Major Tony Dixon. His greeting words to me were, "We were not expecting you for ages. What on earth made you get here so quickly?". I felt a little deflated and wondered if I had not been a little too enthusiastic to terminate my leave and join my new company.

They were a very pleasant bunch of officers but they had been through a tough time together and I was a new arrival who had not shared their recent experiences, so felt a bit of an outsider to start with. There were also certain undercurrents that I could sense in relationships but it took time for me to realise their significance. Firstly there was our OC Tony Dixon, a young very fair-haired major who I gathered had been posted in as a replacement for the previous OC, Major Bewoar, who had been killed in action. Major Bewoar was an Indian officer, trained at Sandhurst and held with great love and respect by all ranks in the company. Not an easy position to succeed to. Everyone had expected the 2nd I/C, a Capt. Selby Pride, to take over, but Tony Dixon had been posted in over his head while he was on secondment to Div. HQ. A delightful Scot, Jock Meldrum, had taken over 2nd in command and no doubt Selby Pride felt cheated of his inheritance. An inheritance for which he had to wait until Tony Dixon was repatriated more than a year later from the banks of the Irrawaddy at Prome.

I thought that I must be a replacement for another battle casualty but this did not appear to be the case. In those days an Engineer Fd. Coy. consisted of a major in command, and a captain as second in command, and three subalterns commanding the three platoons. 421 Fd. Coy. had lost no subalterns killed but one of them seemed very relieved at my arrival and quickly disappeared. It was years later that I learnt the true story. He could not face the realities of war and pretended to be sick every time he was given the job of a forward reconnaissance and our amiable 2nd I/C, Capt. Jock Meldrum, had to do the job for him. Jock was a wonderful character, a broad-shouldered, well-built Scot from Banff. He had a quiet dry sense of humour, there was always a twinkle in his eyes and he was completely unflappable. The other great character in our company was Tigger Royale. Somehow his initials had formed his nickname of Tigger. He had started life in the Bengal Sappers and Miners and had been transferred to the Madras Sappers and stayed with us to the end of the war. He had a quite unique sense of humour that would cut the most pompous staff officer down to size. He could turn the most serious situation into an amusing exploit; he was the safety valve of all tension. I am sure that faced with imminent death Tigger would still be able to see the funny side of the situation. His unique sense of humour was infectious and did much to preserve the sanity of his brother officers under difficult and dangerous conditions. However, it was not always appreciated by those in authority. Even our own OC, Tony Dixon, would get up-tight towards Tigger, suspecting he was undermining his authority at times.

The other platoon commander was David de Souza, an Eurasian, probably originating from the Portuguese state of Goa on the West Coast of India. 'Little David', as he was often referred to, was young and a little uncertain of himself, but managed very well to conceal the inferiority complex that must lie beneath the dark skin of an Eurasian in a British officers' mess in those times. It was not that anyone would dream of saying anything to offend him but in a very close community the difference in background was bound to make him feel excluded from the conversation at times, particularly when one was reminiscing about England. I made up the third Platoon Commander to complete the strength of five officers in a field company.

There were two other Engineer Field Companies in the Division. 62 Q.V.O. Madras Coy. and 77 Bengal Fd. Coy. together with 331 Q.V.O. Madras Field Park Coy. In overall command of these companies was the CRE and his staff at Divisional H.Q. The CRE was Lt. Col. Tom Wright O.B.E., a very taciturn officer and reputed to be singularly lacking in a sense of humour. He was in fact a very shy and reserved man. It was nearly six months before he even spoke to me and almost as long before I even knew what he looked like.

By the time I joined 421 Fd. Coy. the Japanese offensive in the Arakan was almost spent. Having failed to break through in the Arakan the Japanese launched a second offensive with fresh troops along the central route through the hills into India, through Manipur to Kohima on the threshold to the Plains of Assam. The incredible fact is that had they launched both offensives simultaneously, we would not have hoped to have held them. However, through this strategical blunder we were able to switch the battle weary 7th Ind. Division and 5th Indian Division from the Arakan to reinforce the hard pressed troops on the Manipur Road and hold their advance until the monsoon broke and eroded their 200 mile L of C through the mountainous country of the Naga Hills that lay between Burma and India.

They so nearly made it. When they reached Kohima it was downhill all the way, a mere 46 miles of twisting road descending 4000 ft. to the rich plains of Assam in India below. Some of their patrols may have reached Indian soil but Kohima was astride the only road and it was still held by the local garrison but only just. They had been forced to withdraw to the small promontory on which stood the District Commissioner's bungalow but which completely covered the road into Kohima from both Imphal and Dimapur. Here they held on heroically, lobbing grenades across the D.C.'s tennis court at the Japs dug in on the other side until 161 Brigade of the 5th Division broke the encircling ring and relieved part of the hard-pressed garrison with fresh troops, to be later reinforced by the 2nd British Division with 33rd Brigade of 7th Ind. Div. under command and later to be reinforced by 114 Brigade whilst our other Brigade 89 was flown to Imphal to reinforce the surrounded and cut off garrison there.

This, however, was yet to come. When I joined my Division my Brigade was resting at Bawli Bazaar, that is all except the sappers who were busy building huts for the other troops to rest in and reorganise after their battles in the Arakan. The huts were never completed. News of the second Japanese offensive to the north got worse and soon we had our orders to move by road up to Dimapur and the other two Brigades were to go by air. One to Imphal and the other to Dimapur. Thus we set off on a fascinating road journey of about 500 miles right up through Assam, through Chittagong, and Comilla to Shillong where there was a staging camp and thence on to Dimapur and Kohima. Like all large convoys the pace was slow and the road surface varied a lot. All-weather tarmac to start with but after Comilla they were very much dry season roads, often just country earth roads that would become an impassable sea of mud in the monsoon and this was about to break at any moment. Then there were long stretches of brick roads. I have never seen such roads before or since. Mile after mile of beautifully bonded brick like a garden path. They must have been built a long time ago by an army of bricklayers. Unfortunately once a brick was displaced the bond was broken and a vicious pothole quickly formed.

At first the countryside we passed through was typical of low lying Bengal in the great Delta of the Ganges. Very lush, very green and water never far away. One was always running alongside a watercourse or crossing it. Generally one crossed on wooden bridges of doubtful strength. The watercourses were solid from bank to bank with water hyacinth, a floating water plant, with pale mauve flowers.

Occasionally we stopped to brew up tea and have a short respite from driving or sitting cramped up in lorries. Sometimes we stopped because of a breakdown or obstacle further up the convoy. On one such occasion I found a number of my men standing around in a circle of locals. There appeared to be some form of entertainment going on. Looking over their shoulders I saw a man squatting in the middle of the circle. He was writhing about in a strange way rolling his eyes and making a noise not unlike the howling of a dog. I guessed he must be a fakir going into a trance. Whatever it was everybody's attention seemed riveted on him. At that moment the convoy restarted and my men dispersed to their vehicles leaving the ring of locals still watching. As I walked back to my Jeep I asked my jemadar whether the central figure of the entertainment was a Holyman and what he was doing. "Oh no, Sahib", came the casual reply. "That was not a Holyman, he was from the local village. He was dying from the bite of a mad dog. They have to watch over him until he dies, then he will be burnt on that spot and they must stay there to see that nobody touches him". He said it so casually that I was rather shocked but I suppose that if you have just spent several months fighting in the jungle of Arakan, death is pretty commonplace and I gathered that rabies was endemic in this part of India so that the ritual of taking a rabid man out of the village and watching him die was no more than a simple health precaution to safeguard the lives of others in the village.

They knew that as long as you did not touch him you were safe; they knew that there was nothing that could be done to save him so they drove him out of the village with sticks while he could still walk, then stood around chatting while he went through the final dreadful paroxysm of the disease to make sure that no passing child or stranger could be scratched by the mad man and inherit this frightful disease before he finally expired. Then they would pile firewood around him and burn him to a cinder so that no passing jackal or piedog could take a meal from him and perpetuate the disease. It left a deep impression on me regarding rabies that was to influence my behaviour a few days later in Shillong.

For the moment we were continually on the move in the low lying water dominated landscape of Southern Bengal. It was a land of kingfishers. We were held up for some time when a bridge collapsed and had to be rebridged with the ubiquitous Bailey bridge. I began to sense the wonderful camaraderie amongst the British officers, this little élite race commanding the Indian Army, who knew how to respect and command. It was a wonderful relationship seldom recognised by those reporting from the world outside. Each knew the others' merits and capabilities. Each was dependent on the other and openly recognised it.

Before the landscape changed I made one worthwhile discovery. We were halted temporarily near some dark green bushes. They looked rather like bay trees but were festooned with what resembled strawberries. My men quickly stripped them and brought them to me. "Lychees, Sahib", they announced as they handed me what looked like case-hardened strawberries. When one peeled off the hard strawberry coloured skin the luscious clear colour fruit within was a new gastronomic experience. Nowadays when one buys them tinned or occasionally so-called fresh they are already dried up to a dirty brown colour, though still quite good inside. One forgets how beautiful they look on the tree and how wonderful and succulent and reviving they were to a parched throat beside that dusty drive up through Assam.

As we went north we started to enter a landscape of bamboo, until we seemed to be driving through an endless green tunnel. Occasionally jungle fowl flew across the road and I was allowed to take my Jeep to the front of the column where, with my windscreen folded down and my shotgun across my knees, I was able to down the odd fowl that crossed over the road in front of us. Finally as the road rose higher we came out into the famous tea gardens of Assam. Here for the first time I saw the tea estates with their acres and acres of neatly trimmed tea bushes. Occasionally there was a long line of women in brightly coloured saris and tall cane baskets on their backs plucking the tea bushes and tossing the tea leaves over their shoulders into the basket.

Occasionally we passed a tea factory where they force-dried the tea and the aroma of tea was quite overpowering. Once on a temporary halt near some estate bungalows I chatted for a few moments with one of the European planters. He told me that the countryside was full of rumours that the Japanese had already reached the Plains of India and that they were already losing coolies deserting to safer areas.

The road rose higher still and the air became pleasantly cooler. We emerged from the trees to see a great plain before us with a sugar loaf mountain rising almost vertically out of it. This was the Khasi Hills and the town of Shillong was on top of it. The road wound up the steep hillside around innumerable hairpin bends slowly gaining ground towards the top. It started to rain. At first it felt wonderfully refreshing after the hot plains below, but soon we began to feel chilled in our wet clothes and we stopped to put up our hoods and windscreens. While we were stopped two very attractive girls suddenly appeared over the edge of the roadside from the steep slopes below. They were relatively fair skinned and seemed to be made up with rouge on their cheeks and lipstick. They wore black skirts with a white embroidered blouse and dark shawls. Their clothes were more reminiscent of Austria than India. Their heads had been lowered coming up the steep ascent, but as they reached the road they looked up and saw the long line of military vehicles filling the road as far as the eye could see. The expression on their faces was anxious surprise. Someone let out a low whistle; next moment they were over the road edge from whence they had come and were bounding down the hillside like two frightened deer. It had started to rain really hard so we got back into our vehicles and ground our way on up the steep hill road to Shillong. Later when we reached there, we were told two things about Shillong. One was that it was inhabited by the very attractive fair-skinned Khasi Hill tribes. We were also warned that V.D. was very prevalent amongst them and that the women believed that if they slept with a white man it would cure them. We were due to stay in Shillong for the next few days awaiting final orders to move forward. I was never sure whether the Camp Commandant's information about the Khasi girls was true or a very clever ruse to dissuade anyone from thoughts of promiscuous behaviour during their short stay in Shillong.

We stayed two or three days in Shillong, refitting, servicing vehicles and just resting before moving back into the battle. One day I was strolling through the colourful bazaar which was in a long broad street lined with trees. I was in the company of another officer from one of the other units in the division. Suddenly we noticed the crowded street parting in front of us as though an unseen wedge was being driven through towards us. The crowd was thinner at our end of the street and the next moment the people in front parted with understandable speed to reveal a dog snarling and snapping at everything in its path. With fresh memories of the dying man by the roadside in Southern Bengal I made for a nearby tree to dodge behind, but my companion just stood his ground and as the dog came for him he drew his revolver and shot it almost at his feet. It was a very cool and courageous action, but an awful risk as he discovered later, though at the time he pointed out that the dog was not coming that fast as it appeared to be slightly paralysed in the hind legs and kept collapsing. He explained that he had to let it get close before firing for fear of his bullet ricocheting off the road into the crowd. The news of his prompt action travelled fast. That evening the senior medical officer sent for him and explained that he would have to have the full course of anti-rabies injections. The dog had been close enough for a fleck of the spittle from its foaming mouth to have fallen on him. He had a small scratch on his hand that could have been infected when he took off his boots. It might seem a very remote risk but however remote the risk of rabies was too awful to be ignored. The reward for his prompt action was a course of 16 injections with a long needle into the stomach. I only just escaped the same treatment myself by insisting that I had not been within spitting distance of the dog while it was alive.

It was now early May 1944, and the Japanese offensive along the road to Kohima was at its height. Rumour was rife and as we set off on the last leg of our journey to the advance base at Dimapur we half expected to find the Japs had reached there before us. As we arrived at the great canopy of jungle that shelters the base of Dimapur from the sky above, I quickly recognised all the old familiar landmarks from my previous visits. Even old 'Penis Park' looked just the same though a little more crowded, but everywhere else things were different. Every clearing under the jungle canopy was crammed with guns, tanks, vehicles, mules, stores, dumps and soldiers. The atmosphere of the quiet, forgotten frontier of 1943 was completely changed. It was now seething with men and equipment. Everyone moved with a businesslike sense of urgency and all the time more troops and equipment were pouring in. We found our allotted space amongst all this humanity and settled in to await for orders. The Division was now somewhat dispersed, one brigade flown into Imphal, another, 33, had flown up ahead of us and was already in action at Kohima and my brigade was now waiting in reserve at Dimapur. Things can happen very quickly in wartime. Those at the top see the overall picture. Those at the bottom of the command structure only see their piece of the jigsaw puzzle and rarely get a glimpse of the whole scene into which they are eventually fitted.

CHAPTER 8

The Battle of Kohima

My next move into the jigsaw puzzle was when my platoon was sent on detachment to reinforce 33 Fd. Coy. at Kohima where the demand on the engineers was exceeding the resources of one company. On 11th May, 1944, I set off with my platoon for Kohima. The road up looked much the same as I led our little convoy, seated in my Jeep. The same bamboo arching over the road and brief glimpses of cascading water, but as we approached Kohima one sensed that one was getting near the battle area. At first it seemed as though there was no one about, no one could be seen standing about talking. Instead one realised that they were there but were dug in and watching you from their fox holes and slit trenches, then around the next corner there was a temporary barrier of petrol drums and poles. An M.P. sergeant and an officer stepped out from the jungle. Who were we, what were our orders? It was not safe to drive beyond this point, from now on it was on foot. Our vehicles and drivers were shown where to park and get camouflaged. The platoon would continue on foot to the next check point where they would be directed to their destination on Jail Hill. There we would find 77 Field Company in the area held by the 1st Queens. At the next check point we were on the outskirts of Kohima, but it was unrecognisable as the Kohima I had known some months earlier. I was confident that my prior knowledge of that lovely hill station would have made it easy for me to lead my platoon to Jail Hill that I remembered well, but I was not prepared for the transformation that confronted me — the Kohima I had known so recently with delphiniums growing around the D.C.'s bungalow and great trees shading the roads to the various parts of the town, which, being a hill station, were known by the various promontories they occupied such as Treasury Ridge, Congress Knoll, Hospital Knoll and Jail Hill. These were no more. What confronted me was something that reminded me of pictures of the battle of the Somme, a landscape of shell holes and truncated trees. Only the shattered stumps remained of those magnificent trees that shaded the roads when I last strolled down to them to visit my friend in hospital. There was, however, no time nor was this the moment to stand and stare at man's destructive achievements. Shells or mortars from one side or the other were sporadically exploding.

We picked our way past the turning to the hospital-that-was and up to Jail Hill, only recaptured from the Japs a couple of days before. There everyone was dug in and watchful. On the first bend in the road up to Jail Hill tanks were moving, mostly manoeuvring into little cramped parking spaces. We halted, uncertain where to go. In front of us a great camouflage net was suspended from the remains of two trees that still had most of their trunk left standing. The others were shattered almost to ground level. An officer of the Queen's Regiment came forward and said "I would not stand around here old man, you are in direct line of sniper fire. The camouflage net spoils their aim, but that's all". We moved on. A Major Mansel had been killed by a sniper earlier in the day while standing just where we were now standing. I soon found the OC of 77 Coy. under whose command we had been placed. He allocated a small area of ground and told us to get dug in as soon as quickly as possible and report to him as soon as this had been done.

"Make sure your men stay in their slit trenches until they have to come out to do a job of work. They shell and mortar this hill every now and then and we can't afford to lose men caught standing around unnecessarily. When they start shelling make it a strict order: all heads below ground level until they are called out. Then they will be perfectly safe unless they are unlucky enough to get a direct hit". I passed this useful bit of information on to my men and sited their slit trenches and left them digging enthusiastically. As soon as we were all dug in I made my way back to the company command post a little lower down the hill. It was difficult to know what was happening. There were sporadic bursts of machine gun fire all around and shells frequently whined overhead and exploded with a crump not far away. It was not very easy to determine whose shells they were until they landed, though the more experienced professed to be able to identify them by the characteristics of their whines. "Ah, that's a Jap 88mm", or "You can't mistake that, it's our own 25 pounder". In the moment of anxiety wondering just how close it was going to fall they all sounded much the same to me, only the shells from our tiny mountain artillery could not be mistaken. They sounded as though they were turning end over end in the air and many gunners swore that was just what they were doing.

When I arrived at the company command post the OC was out but his 2nd I/C was there and did his best to fill me in with the situation at the moment. He explained that the Queen's in whose area I was dug in had finally taken Jail Hill two days ago but had difficulty in getting the Japs out of the bunkers on the reverse slope. The 4/15 Punjab had also taken the adjoining D.I.S. ridge, but both were having difficulty with

Sketch Map of
THE BATTLE OF KOHIMA MAY 1944

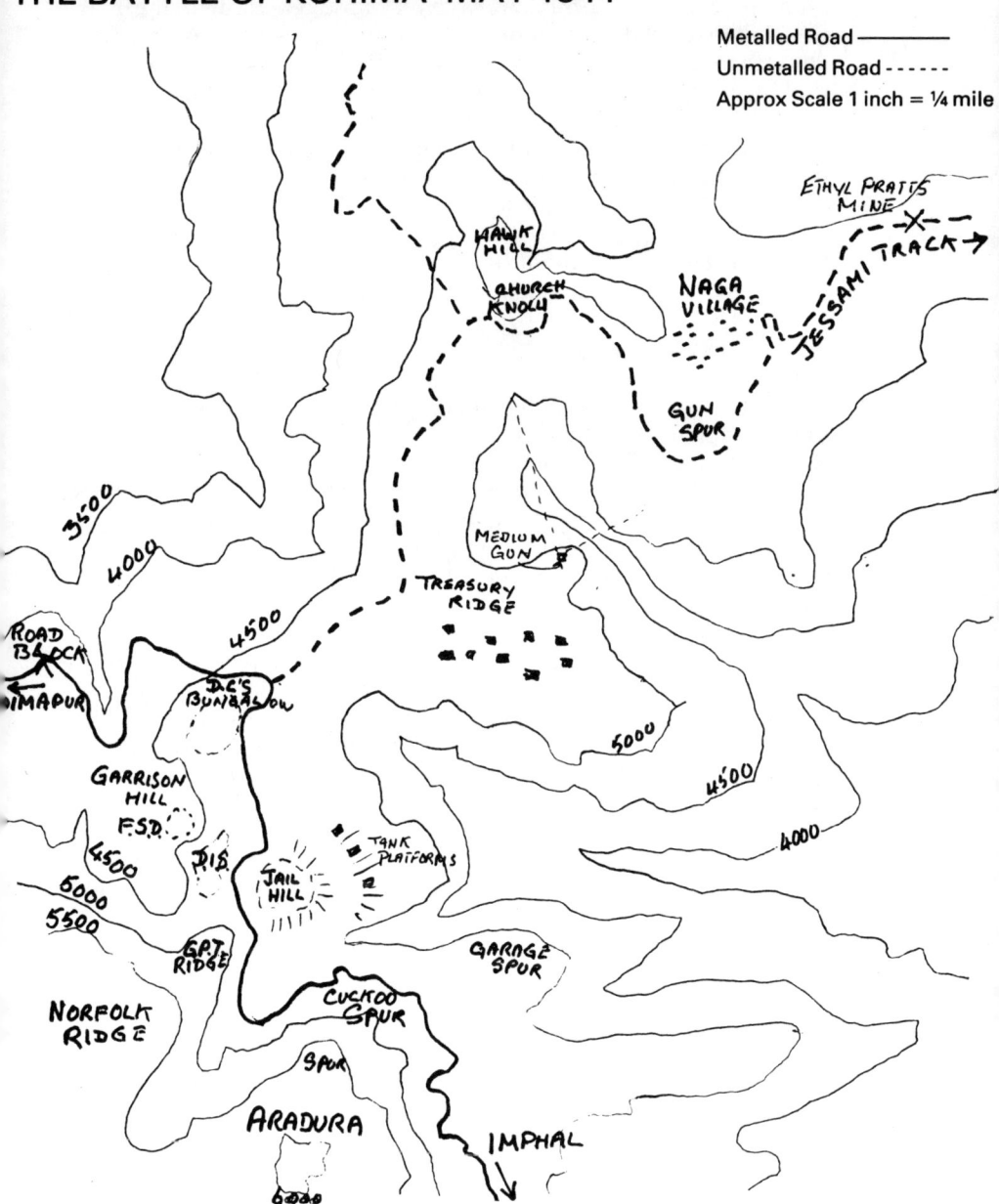

crossfire from other positions that were not easy to locate, particularly from the opposite slopes across the deep ravines that separated all these promontories. The Jap bunkers were very close as the crow or the bullet flies, but to reach them on foot you had to descend several hundred feet down the steep slope on your side of the hill and then climb up again the steep slope on their side and you were liable to be under fire the whole way. He also explained that 77 Fd. Coy. had been fully committed clearing minefields and providing bunker busting parties for the infantry attacks. These parties went in with the infantry assault, armed with pole charges – an explosive charge on the end of a bamboo pole. When you located a bunker the sappers had to get up close enough to thrust the charge into the firing slits in the bunker and pull the cord which detonated the charge inside the bunker, knocking out the Japs within. A very hazardous operation but it had proved a very successful way of knocking out these bunkers that were built to withstand direct hits by artillery on top of them. Needless to say the sappers had had fairly high casualties recently and had asked for my platoon to be put under command to help with the increasing demands on their services. At that moment the OC arrived and greeted me with the words "Ah, John. I've got a job for you tonight". It appeared that the Queen's were to make a fresh attack at first light on the Jap position on the other side of the valley. They wanted the support of the tanks as mobile pill boxes but unfortunately the slope on their side of the hill was so steep that when the tanks moved onto it they could not elevate their guns sufficiently to fire at the slopes on the other side. So they wanted the engineers to construct platforms forward of our positions during the night so that when the tanks came over the top of the hill they could drive down on to these horizontal platforms and fire straight across the valley at any Jap bunker located on the opposite slope. While this was being discussed another officer came into the post with the news that some officer that they all knew well had just been killed. Though his name meant nothing to me I sensed that it did to the others present, and that this was the reality of war. In my imagination I wondered whether tomorrow someone might wander in and say "I hear old John Henslow copped it last night". Fortunately there was no time to dwell on such thoughts; I had to get back to my platoon and organise the night's work.

Our plan was to pass through the Queen's forward positions as soon as it was dark. Every man would be carrying a pick and shovel plus two steel ammunition boxes. Each section would dig out two platforms on the hillside below their positions and reinforce the base of the platform with earthfilled steel ammunition boxes that would support the weight of the tank. The job had to be done under cover of darkness as we would be working in 'no man's land' between the Japs and our own troops' in full view of both. Fortunately it was a dark night and just starting to rain. This would soon produce mist which would help deaden the sound of our excavations.

We passed through an arranged point in the Queen's defences. I asked the sergeant in charge of that section if there was any password for the night as we did not want to be mistaken for Japs on our return. He looked up at my 6ft. 4ins. and said "Nobody is going to mistake you for a Jap sir, but if you whistle God Save the King in tune we'll not open fire on you". So out we went into the darkness and found problem number one was that it was so dark it was difficult to keep in touch and keep silent. I knew the rough distance in front of our positions where the platforms had to be constructed but by the time I had paced out this distance and halted the men, I had fallen in and out of so many shell holes that I was not sure which way to align the platforms. The OC had just said align them down the slope and you will be about right, but in this sea of shell holes it was not that easy to define 'down the slope'. Fortunately at that moment one side or the other fired a star shell and suddenly we would see everything and no doubt be seen by everybody, but it was a great help to get re-orientated. After that it was not difficult to mark out and site the platforms and allot each section to its task. While they dug away I just had to move from one site to the next to make sure they were being dug to the right size and pointing the right way and that there were no problems. Number two section had a problem. They had nearly finished digging out their platform when they unearthed an unexploded shell in the middle of it. "What should we do Sahib?" Sahib was always expected to know the answers. I examined it by the light of a pocket torch shaded by my hand. It was at least a British shell but my stay in the gunners was too short to remember to colour coding on the fuse. But it looked like an ordinary HE impact fuse that had failed to go off. It was obviously not the best thing to have sticking out of the tank platform. The simplest solution seemed to be to pick it up and carry it further down the hill, which I did. I had thought of throwing it but it was too heavy to throw very far and should the impact be just enough to set it off I would be too close to survive. I carried it cradled in my arms about 50 yards down the slope and laid it gently down in a shell hole. As I was returning up the slope someone opened up with a machine gun only a few yards from me on the right.

My first thought was that the Japs had spotted us when the star shell had gone up and had sent out a patrol to attack us. I did not know what to do for a moment. I had no grenades with me only my ·38 revolver and five rounds. I did not feel very confident in taking on a Jap M.G. with five rounds of ·38 so I sat tight, but not for long. Other L.M.G.'s opened up from the vicinity of the first one, then answering fire came back from the Queen's position then various lights shot up in the air, followed by the wham of 2" mortars. I began to feel rather frightened for it was obvious that the Japs were putting in a night attack on the Queen's and we were caught in the middle. I worked my way up the hill to get back to my platoon and hoped that no nervous sapper with his finger on the trigger would mistake me for a Jap. When I was what I judged to be about 20 yards from their position I called my jemadar by name "Jemadar Suri". To my relief the answer came from a few yards away in the dark; he had obviously been making his way down to find me. I crawled towards him and we made physical contact. A wonderful feeling in the isolation of darkness in this pig-in-the-middle position that we were now in. Every now and then the battle flared up and bullets were everywhere cracking overhead or kicking up dust around us. There was little we could do in this position except to lie low in the deepest shell hole we could find and wait for developments. Someone joined us for a moment in our shell hole but before we could do anything he had left again moving down the hill. It must have been a Jap. The firing became more spasmodic and then ceased altogether. There was not a sound. Suddenly it was so still you could have heard a leaf drop. My jemadar moved cautiously up the hill calling softly to the platoon. "Haveldar". An answer came softly back. "Inge Sahib" (Here Sir). Slowly he re-established contact with the rest of the platoon. They had all laid low in the shell holes and there were no casualties. We got back to work to finish the job. While they were doing this I was worrying about the next problem – getting back through our own defences, who might well be a bit jittery by now, without getting mistaken for Japs in the darkness. We closed up together and called a silent roll to make sure we were all together, then I led them back up the hill towards the Queen's positions, but it was not easy to find the same place we had come out by after all that disturbance.

If we arrived at another point in their defence they might have no knowledge that sappers were working in front of them and mistake us for another Jap assault. It was now terribly quiet. The forward defence posts could not be far away but there was not a sound. I imagined that those battle weary Queen's had everything pointing at the muffled sounds of our approach up the hillside. I decided this was the moment to start whistling 'God Save the King' but my lips were so dry I found I could not whistle a note, just suspicious hissing noises came out. This was worse than silence. In desperation I called out "Queen's, it's the sappers returning through your lines. Hold your fire", and kept going. There was not a sound in reply. It was well-known that the Japs used similar deploys to infiltrate our defences, calling out names of units they had identified as opposing them. I was very nervous at this point when a British voice whispered in my ear, "Well done, Sir. I'm glad you spoke when you did. I was just about to give the order to open fire". As I had feared, we had returned at a very different point from that of our exit through the Queen's defences.

At first light next morning the Queen's attacked the opposite slope and the tanks moved onto our platform to give supporting fire across the steep valley. Real progress was at least being made in winkling the Japs from the commanding position in Kohima. We now had a firm foothold on Jail Hill and D.I.S. Ridge but the enemy still held Treasury Ridge, Naga Village and Church Knoll, together with the commanding point of Gunspur. The 4/1st Gurkhas were sent in at night to try and secure the next feature which was Treasury Hill. Though this had been heavily manned by the Japs they found it deserted. The Japs had withdrawn for now we were firmly established on Jail Hill and D.I.S. Ridge we overlooked them at close range and they had considered it untenable. However the Gurkhas in turn found themselves overlooked by Naga Village and had to endure continual fire and night attacks from that commanding feature.

At this juncture in the battle the rest of my brigade arrived to help take up our expanding territory, together with our Divisional H.Q. and a Brigade of 5th Ind. Div. under command. This meant that our Division was now in a position to take on the task of capturing Naga Village and all other Jap strong points on the north side of the road. The 2nd British Division were having a hard time south of the road trying to dislodge the Japs from Aradura Spur which commanded most of the immediate approaches along the road to Imphal.

My company joined my position on Jail Hill and quickly dug in. It was good to see one's company again and we soon had a small dug-out built in the middle of our area covered with corrugated iron sheets with earth piled on top to make it reasonably proof from shell splinters. There we met to discuss our various allotment of tasks and we also fed there when the opportunity arose. There was one occasion I remember when we had just left our little bunker after the O.C. had given his instructions for the day. We were standing around discussing various aspects of the day's work when without warning shells or mortars, I forget which, started falling on our positions. It does not take you long to learn to dive for cover on these occasions and as one fell very close to where we were standing, I was into our bunker as the nearest point I could see to get below ground level. I literally dived into it. The bombardment stopped as suddenly as it had started. Before long we were all emerging above ground again. Then someone said, "Poor old John has been hit, get a stretcher". I looked around but I was the only John in the present company. Someone came up to me and said "You must have caught some shrapnel in your back, how do you feel?" He placed his hand on my back and showed it to me, his hand was covered with blood. I had felt nothing but presumed this was how it happened, in the heat of the moment one felt nothing. I was nearly convinced that I had been wounded by a shell splinter. I peeled off my shirt but the wound being in my back I could see nothing. I had to go by the reports of others. When the copious blood was staunched with a towel it became apparent that it was not a deep shrapnel wound but a long shallow cut right across my back. Being tall I had not bent down enough when diving for cover when the shelling started. Our central bunker had an edge of corrugated iron protruding over the entrance that supported the earth cover, and it became equally obvious that this had cut me across my back as I had gone to ground in a hurry. I had felt nothing but the wound, such as it was, was self-inflicted, superficial and a bit of a joke all round. Tony Dixon our OC said he was not sure whether he should recommend me for 'the purple heart' or charge me with self-inflicted injury.

My next assignment was another night job. On the north side of Treasury Ridge was an open grass spur with a large shed of some sorts on it. The shed commanded a splendid view across the valley to Naga Village and Church Knoll where the Japs were firmly entrenched. Like all Jap positions its main defence hinged on deep bunkers, well sited and exceedingly difficult to knock out. Many had such a deep covering of earth that they would withstand a direct hit from a 25 pounder shell. Someone at Div. HQ had had the novel idea that if they could get a gun from the medium artillery into that hut under cover of darkness it could fire over open sights at any Jap bunker that was proving troublesome in the attack. I was given the task of making the hut ready for this large gun to move into position that night. The spur was overlooked by the Jap position so one could do nothing in daylight except a casual reconnaissance. I was told that the spur and the hut were within mortar range of the Jap positions and if I went out there I would be watched by the Japs, so I must not give the impression that the hut was of any significance to us. I sauntered out onto the spur trying to look as casual as possible, with my ear cocked should they consider me worth mortaring. It was sunny for once and silent. I walked to the end of the spur past the hut taking a good look at it from the corner of my eye. There was a good track down to it so there was no problem there. It would need reinforcing with sandbags and the entrance would need considerable modifications if we were to get a medium gun inside. The only thing I could not see was what opening could be made on the other side to give the gun a reasonable field of fire. This meant I must go into the hut and study its construction to see how it could be modified over night. As I walked back towards it I made it very obvious that I was undoing my fly buttons in the hopes that any watching Jap would consider I was going into the hut for purely natural reasons. Once inside, out came my notebook and I started making notes and measurements to be able to plan the necessary alterations to make it fit for its role as a grand surprise for the Japs next morning. I finally emerged pulling up my trousers to make the deception complete. In my notebook were all the measurements to be able to plan the night's work.

That night I went out with my platoon and hundreds of sandbags. We strengthened the roof and covered it with sandbags and built sandbag walls around the front of the shed, knocking out the original front so that this large artillery piece had plenty of room to traverse its barrel to cover all the slopes up to Naga Village. We also widened the entrance to get the gun in. By the time we had finished there was little of the original hut left but basically we hoped it looked much the same. In the early hours of the morning the big gun arrived, together with its gun crew. Being medium artillery they were used to engaging their targets from well behind the front line. You never saw your target. You just laid your gun and fixed into the distance as directed. They did not seem overjoyed at this opportunity to get into the front line of battle. I heard the master gunner sergeant grumbling, "Next time they will be asking us to fix bayonets on the bloody barrel and charge". Never in his long service with the medium artillery had he been ordered to fire over open sights at a target and, as he pointed out, this target was so bloody close that the gun and crew were within their own shell burst area and liable to be hit by splinters from their own shells.

We had to have the gun in place before daybreak and the hut looking just as it had looked the previous day, for if the Japs observed anything unusual going on in its vicinity they might become suspicious and range their own artillery and mortars on to it. However, when we came to run the gun into the hut we came across a snag. The 55mm medium gun has two 'horns' sticking up, one on either side of the barrel. They are in fact part of the recoil mechanism. These had been overlooked when we were given the dimensions of the gun and now it was obvious that they would not fit under the lintel of the rear opening of the hut through which the gun had to pass. There was nothing for it but to dig down to gain the necessary clearance above. There was no possibility of raising the lintel as it was supporting the strengthened roof which was now covered with sandbags and time was running out. Already there was a perceptible glimmer in the night sky to the East and in those latitudes the sun comes up fast. We dug furiously until we hit rock and my tape measure told me that we had another three inches to go before the horns would pass under the lintel. The glimmer to the east was becoming a glow. There was nothing for it but to let the tyres down to lose those vital three inches. A medium gun is a very heavy piece of artillery to manhandle and with deflated tyres it would be even more difficult to move. I could see that once we had pushed it into the depression we had dug to get it under the lintel we would never be able to move it forward into the firing position, so once again, while the tyres were being deflated, we had to dig channels forward from the depression for the wheels to move further in without going up a slope. What made it all the more difficult was that everything had to be done without making any noise for we were well within earshot of the enemy. Even voices had to be kept down to a whisper. At last the gun was low enough to pass into the building but the tyres looked very flat. The gun team fixed their trail ropes and we all got round to push and pull as best we could in the confined space. The gunners felt it was now their job to get the gun laid in position, but on the command, "Run up" the gun only moved a few inches in a sluggish crawl and stopped. The night air was laden with grunts and muffled curses but it would not budge. Dawn was breaking but unless we could get the gun right into the building it could not open its split trail, without which it would be unable to fire as there would be no room to load.

Also until the trail was opened and the thrust spades dug in it would be unsafe to fire for the recoil from the first round would shoot the gun backwards out of the building again. The attack, relying on the gun for support, was due to go in at first light. Various worried liaison officers arrived with their wireless operators. "Was the gun ready to fire?" "Why not?" "What the hell had we been doing all night?" There was no time to explain the problem. I suggested they save their breath for helping to push to gun forward. This time I took command of the operation. I put men with chocks and levers behind the wheels and explained that everyone had to keep scrupulously in time pulling in short pulsations to get the gun rocking. I would give the timing.

Every time I said 'Heave' they were to lay back and give it every ounce of strength in their body. On the command 'Back' they would let the gun run back ready for the next heave. Every time the gun moved forward a few inches the chock men were to slide their chocks forward so that the gun could not run back.

It worked a treat, with a pulsating Heave... back... heave... back... heave... back, the gun rocked forward six inches at a time and as it rocked back the tyre mounted the chocks and with the right rhythm this gave added impetus to the next heave forward. In no time the gun was in place with its barrel trained on the opposing slopes, the trail was split and the spades dug in. The gun was ready to start firing over open sights, the wireless operators were bent over their crackling sets, it was first light and the attack had started. My platoon had finished their task and the last problem was how to get them back over the grassy spur without the cover of darkness. As orders for targets for the medium gun were already coming over on the wireless and I knew that the spur was within the shell burst area of the gun, speed seemed more important than concealment for our withdrawal. We formed up at the back of the hut, wished the gunners 'good shooting' and on the command 'Go' every man was to run as fast as his legs would carry him back to our company positions. I ordered 'Go' and we were off leaping and bounding over the open ground. If the Japs observed us they had little time to do anything about it. Long before we reached our objective there was an almighty grump as the first shell from the medium gun homed in on its target across the narrow valley. We listened all morning to the crump of that big gun. Unfortunately from our position we could not see the effect it was having on the Japs bunkers on the other side. By the evening news filtered through that the feature was in our hands and the Jap resistance was fading fast on our side of the road. I also heard that the medium gun had proved quite devastating to the Jap bunkers. They had used fractional delay fuses on the shells so that they had penetrated right into the bunkers before exploding, thus blowing them out of the side of the hill. There were reports of the occupants literally seen flying through the air.

 Not long after this we realised that the Japs were retreating. A few suicide squads were left to cover this withdrawal and they were winkled out by the 4/1st Gurkhas and the 4/15 Punjabis. Suddenly the battle of Kohima was over on our side of the Manipur Road but on the other side the 2nd British Division was still held up on Aradura Spur.

 I walked up onto the positions that had been held by the Japs the day before. They were littered with Jap corpses and equipment of every sort – guns, mortars, medical stores, and I even found a beautifully made set of dentist's equipment, all fitted into a stainless steel case no more than six inches square. The contents were horrifyingly practical. A real field emergency set comprised of weird shaped gouges and chisels and the usual extraction forceps. I later presented them to our own field dental unit on the condition that they would never be used on me.

CHAPTER 9

The Jap Retreat and Follow-up

The monsoon had now broken in earnest and we were informed that our higher command had conceived the brilliant idea that we would fight through the monsoon. It was undoubtedly the right decision for the Japs had to maintain 200 miles of jungle tracks for their L of C and we were sitting almost on top of our main supply base at Dimapur. They were at the end of their tether and if we could keep up the pressure on them throughout the monsoon the weather conditions would inflict more casualties on them than we could ever hope to achieve with bullets and guns. It would be hell for us but it would be death for them. Death from starvation and disease.

The immediate plan was to follow up their withdrawal down the Jessami track, a rough earth (now mud) road that wound its way parallel to the Manipur Road to Chakabama where it split. To the south it rejoined the Manipur Road at Mao Song Sang, the fork to the north filtered through to the Ukrul track which was one of the main Jap supply routes from Burma, used to bypass Imphal and attack Kohima. The plan was for my brigade (114) to advance down the Jessami track and take the right fork at Chakabama to Mao Song Sang where they would be on the Manipur Road behind the Japs that were opposing the advance of the 2nd British Division.

We had hardly started when news came down the convoy that the advance troops, the 4/5th Gurkhas, had spotted that the track was mined and they needed the sappers to clear the minefield. The track was very narrow so I decided to leave my Jeep and go forward on foot as there was no room to drive forward past the vehicles in front. I took my platoon havildar with me in case there were more mines and booby traps than we could deal with and he could be sent back to bring up more sappers if it proved to be a major obstacle. We plodded forward in deep mud and past all the halted Jeeps in front of us. At the head of the column was a Gurkha sentry and a Lt. Col. gazing ominously at an object in the centre of the track. There was the usual friendly greeting of "What took you so long to get here?", to which I did not bother to respond other than to say, "Now that I am here, Sir, where are the suspected mines?". I had expected to find the leading vehicle blown up on a mine, which is the usual first indication of a minefield. The Lt. Col. said something to the Gurkha sentry who took a smart pace backwards and stamped to attention. I hoped he realised that if they had spotted one mine there could be others and stamping to attention was not the best minefield etiquette. The Lt. Col. pointed at the mud in front of him and said, "It's a good job some of us have sharp eyes in our head". I sensed a feeling of resentment that the sappers had not done something about it before they got there and that this was something that we had overlooked even though we had no instructions to reconnoitre the track for mines. Mines were something that sappers were meant to find and deal with and the whole advance was held up because we had failed to spot them and clear them.

The Lt. Col.'s pointing finger indicated an area of mud in the middle of the track with two brass lugs protruding from it. They did look like what one might expect a mine fuse to look like but bore no resemblance to any Japanese mine that I knew. However, there is always a first and I crouched to inspect it more carefully. The officer and the sentry immediately retired to a safe distance. I started clearing the mud away with my fingers. As I wiped the mud away between the two brass lugs the body of the fuse was exposed and it had some letters on it, they were in English and they spelt out 'Ethyl Pratts', a familiar name to pre-war motorists as a proprietary brand of leaded petrol with anti-knock additives. I immediately recognised it as the top of a two gallon petrol can from the days when petrol cans had solid brass caps. I picked it out of the mud and wiped it clean then walked back to where the Lt. Col. was standing impatiently with a group of other officers. I handed him the petrol cap and said, "This is what has held up your advance, Sir. It is all clear now". I saluted and walked away back down the line of stationary Jeeps. It was neither tactful nor very kind of me but I felt his attitude had deserved it. My loyalty to the sappers had been strained by his insinuation that we were responsible for the delay in the advance.

There were no more hold-ups for suspected mines after that and the Jeep column ploughed its way along the Jessami track churning the mud deeper and deeper with four wheel drive all the way to the Chakabama Ridge. Here there was a very temporary hold-up by the so-called Indian National Army or the INA as it was termed for brevity. They were Indians recruited by the Japanese from the countries they had overrun, Burma, Malaya and the Dutch East Indies. Many of them were ex-Indian Army and had joined the INA under brainwashing by the Japanese who told them that they would be the spearhead for the conquest of India and its take over by the Congress Party under Subhas Chandra Bhosc. But the majority joined as the best hope of defecting

The Ethyl Pratts Mine on the Jessami Track. Kohima. May 1944.

back to their own troops rather than rot in a POW camp. They quickly surrendered at Chakabama but the Japs held the mountain top village of Kidima a short way beyond and here we were stuck until they could be dislodged from their commanding position. The Chakabama Ridge was high grassland and scrub in contrast to the surrounding tree-clad mountainous country. It was also the main junction on the Jessami track. The right fork went back to join the main Imphal-Kohima road at Mao Song Sang.

For a time we were held up on the Chakabama Ridge. We were dug in and our small living quarters where we fed and met to discuss the day's work was a hole in the ground about 8 feet by 6 feet by 5 feet deep. It was covered over with tree trunks and earth on top and the ceiling was lined with the fly sheet of a 140 lb. tent to stop the thin trickle of dust from the earth covering falling into our food at meal times. The situation was momentarily static again. Occasionally Japanese shells or mortars homed in on our position and our own 25th Mountain Artillery seemed to be continually lobbing shells over our heads at the Japanese positions that lay ahead. The chief casualties on the Ridge were mules for they could not be dug in below ground and these invaluable beasts of burden were all too frequently the victims of shrapnel from enemy shells. What is more, nobody had time to bury these victims so that they lay where they fell and quickly putrefied in the tropical climate. The smell of their putrefying flesh became overpowering, but far worse were the flies that went with it. One gets used to a high level of flies in a tropical climate, but we were caught in an amazing population explosion of blue bottles such as I have never seem before, or want to again.

The ceiling of our mess bunker was so thickly coated with them, that you could not place the end of a pencil between them. At first we tried spraying them with flit with the result that apart from nearly asphyxiating ourselves in the confined space, it also rained dead and dying flies into our food, into our hair and down our necks. A flitted fly takes time in dying and where they fell they wriggled and buzzed for several minutes. By the time we had removed them all from inside our shirts and out of our food, reinforcements were already pouring in and our stew tasted strongly of flit.

Sappers are known for their resourcefulness and ability to improvise. A quick conference decided that a flame gun was the answer. Burn them up, then quickly lay the table and eat our meal before their numbers built up again. The only snag was we did not have a flame gun. I volunteered to improvise and in a matter of minutes produced the MK I Anti Blue Bottle Flame-Gun. It consisted of a large brass fly spray filled with kerosene, an igniter mechanism consisting of a piece of stiff copper wire extending for a few inches below the nozzle, the end of the wire being twisted round a piece of cotton waste soaked in kerosene. One lit the cotton waste and sprayed the kerosene through the flame. The fine spray of kerosene ignited and produced a sheet of flame several feet long like a giant blow torch. With relish I set to on the hated blue bottles. As I swept the flame across the ceiling the flies frazzled and dropped by the thousand, and in no time the ceiling and wall that had been black with them were white again. I sounded the all-clear and we all rushed in to enjoy a meal without these filthy flies. My triumph however was short-lived. Halfway through the soup, the thanks and praises of the inventor of the MK I Anti Blue Bottle Flame-Gun died. Everyone seemed to have developed St. Vitus' Dance. Then I, too, felt things crawling up my legs. In another moment everyone was jumping up and down, slapping their trouser legs. A glance at the floor was enough to realise why. It was a seething mass of creeping blue bottles. The MK I Flame-Gun had only burnt off their wings. It had not frazzled them, just scorched them.

Fortunately, before the MK II Flame-Gun could be produced the 4/14 Punjabs and the South Lancs dislodged the Japs from their hilltop positions at Kidima and we moved forward again towards Mao Song Sang leaving Chakabama and its plague of flies behind us. It became evident that the Japs were now convinced that their positions forward on the Aradura Spur were untenable once we reached the main road behind them at Mao, so they withdrew their forces from the area where they were holding up the advance of the 2nd British Division with the result that the advance guards of our own brigade and those of 2nd Division reached Mao at the same time on the 19th June and the relief of Kohima was complete.

The 2nd Division then pressed on towards Imphal where they finally met the advanced element of the 5th Indian Division at Kanglatongbi, thus raising the siege of Imphal on the 23rd June.

My own brigade had now been in close contact with the enemy, except for the brief interlude of their move from the Arakan to Assam, since August 1943. The tremendous physical exertions of the recent fighting in the Naga Hills during the monsoon were producing serious signs of malnutrition.

The Brigade was ordered back to Kohima to rest and refit, and the 33rd Brigade who had been resting there for three weeks came up to take up the pursuit of the retreating Japs along the Ukhral track.

I had one more job to do before joining my company at Kohima. I was sent on a reconnaissance to Maram about 15 miles further along the road to Imphal. At Maram a small track led east through mountainous country to join the Jessami – Ukhral track along which the main Japanese forces were retreating. Maram was at Milestone 65 and that milestone was about all I could find of Maram. No doubt the village, like so many Naga villages, was perched on one of the many nearby wooded hilltops and not visible. However, the track was there and my job was to go down it and reconnoitre the crossings of the Sangu Lok River. The track was little more than a narrow worn footpath that descended steeply amongst the grass and scrub that covered the hillside. After a while I could see the Sangu Lok River about a mile below. It did not look very wide but it was a reddish brown and was obviously swollen with the monsoon rain and no longer fordable. The bridge was clearly visible. By the time I got down to it I was feeling distinctly off colour. My head was swimming and I had difficulty in focusing my eyes. My tongue and throat felt so dry I found it difficult to swallow. My water bottle was nearly empty. I was not looking forward to the climb back up the hill to Maram.

The bridge had seen better days. It was a narrow, simple timber construction of three or four roughly shaped tree trunks spanning the river with rough and partly rotten planks across them as decking. The swollen water had eroded the bank at one place so that one side of the bridge had sunk and the decking sloped dangerously into the water on the downstream side. I gathered that some advance units had already crossed and had great trouble in getting their mules across. Several had slipped on the sloping deck and gone over the side. They had retrieved the mules further downstream, but their precious loads had been lost in the deep brown torrent. It was obvious that there was little one could do to shore up the existing bridge as the water was already lapping the underside. If it rose any more the whole lot would be carried away and its bank seats were already collapsing. It needed a longer bridge to get its bank seats back onto firm ground. I made a rough sketch of the existing bridge with its measurements and notes on the length of bridging required to get it seated on firm ground. A dozen bailey panels with transoms and decking would do the job in no time. They would not require launching as they could be carried across and be assembled over the existing bridge, but how to get them down there was another matter. By now I was feeling distinctly ill. I felt I could do no more. I gazed up the slope and wished I had brought someone with me as I did not feel I was going to make it alone. That day there was a lull in the monsoon and the sun was beating down, my body felt as though it was on fire with the heat. For once I wished it was raining.

I started the ascent, my head pounding with the effort. I set myself a target of one hundred paces between rests, but the rests got longer each time before I could summon up the strength to start again. My water bottle was empty and my throat was parched beyond belief. If I had been down by the river now I would have gladly drunk the brown muddy water. Typhoid, cholera, dysentry, the lot, what did it matter. I felt I had them all anyway, but I knew that if I went back I would never get back to where I was, let alone the mile and half on up to the road. I struggled on slipping, sliding and falling about where normally I would have walked straight up without any difficuty. My vision was blurred, my head felt twice its normal size and seemed to be pulsating. I could not think very clearly but the instinct of self-preservation made me determined to keep going up. I knew I had to get back before nightfall. Then after only fifty paces of the next hundred I had started, there was a log, a long sunbleached trunk in a sea of grass and scrub, as inviting as a park bench. I weakened and sat down on it and as I did so I knew I was not going to have the will-power to get up again. I cupped my head in my hands and closed my eyes. I was past thinking or caring about anything. Then I started to shake. It welled up through my body in uncontrollable muscular pulsations until even my teeth were chattering. I recognised the familiar rigor of malaria but it had never been as bad as this before. I felt miserable and alone. I would have sold my soul for a mouthful of water. Then I felt a hand caress my cheek, gently but quite distinctly. I was far too gone to be startled.

At first I could not believe it, then I felt it again. With difficulty I opened my eyes and raised my head. An old woman was crouching beside me with her head on one side gazing inquiringly at me. She stretched out her hand and brushed the back of it gently across my cheek and smiled. The scene was coming into focus and I realised she was not alone for there was a small group standing back a bit. They all seemed to be smiling. Then the old woman said something and a man stepped forward, practically naked except for the striped cloak hanging neatly folded over his shoulder, a characteristic of the Naga Hill tribes. He was proffering a large gourd which turned out to be full of *zoe*, a slightly sharp tasting rice beer. To my parched throat it was nectar, and as far as I was concerned he could have been the Angel Gabriel.

I made signs to show how grateful I was to them and they made signs that it was a pleasure to help a stranded traveller. I indicated that I was going up the hill and stood up, for I knew that it was now or never if I was going to make it to the top. That was the last thing that I remembered until two days later when I regained consciousness lying on a camp bed in a small tent beside the main road. I discovered that I was in the A.D.S. (Advance Dressing Station). The MO informed me that a party of Nagas had carried me up the hill on an improvised stretcher made of spears and Naga cloaks. A very romantic Livingstonian arrival was how he described it. He also informed me that my temperature had been 105 on arrival and that I had been out for the last two days. Strictly speaking I should have been sent back to a base hospital, but they had arrived there almost as I had arrived up the hillside. They were on detachment to 33 Brigade and about to disappear with them down the track I had come up. "What about the bridge?" I said. "Oh, I gather the river had dropped sufficiently for mules to ford it; anyway most of the brigade got over somehow or other. We are off tomorrow so it's just as well you have come round as we shall have to leave you with 25 Mountain Artillery Regiment who will look after you until you are fit to move in a day or two".

I was lucky that my unit was resting back at Kohima or I would have been evacuated to a base hospital and might never have got back to them. For the next two days I enjoyed the company of the Mountain Gunners, or Goat Gunners as they were often referred to, but never within their presence. They were a bit touchy over their nickname. They introduced me to a card game called seven and a half. It was very like pontoon only all the 8 and 9's were removed from the pack and all tens and court cards were valued at a half. A pontoon instead of being 21 was 7½. It seemed an easy conversion but it was more tempting and more deadly than pontoon. They were very good at it, and in the two days that I stayed with them I lost most of the money I had saved up for my leave which was due at any moment. Then with a lighthearted wave they loaded their mountain guns onto their beautiful Mark One mules and set off down the track to the Sangu Lok River bridge and the incredibly arduous track to Ukhral. I waved them goodbye and secretly hoped that all those carrying my cheques for their winnings at cards would fall into the Sangu Lok and my cheques would be lost in the brown swirling waters. As it turned out they survived far worse trails than the Sangu Lok, but by the time they were presented months later I had had my leave and the money was spent and accumulating again.

The next day I set off back to Kohima where my unit was resting but I had hardly started when rounding a bend in the road I met a strange party of Nagas triumphantly bringing in a Jap prisoner, quite a rarity even then. What fascinated me was the method of securing their prisoner. About six Nagas surrounded the Jap and each had a rope tied to his waist so that he was the hub of their wheel and the radiating ropes acted as spokes but were in tension so that the wretched prisoner was held at a distance from everyone. He staggered down the road in their midst being pulled this way and that. He looked pretty well done in. I think they intended to hand him in but were not sure how to set about it. I found a Jeep load of MP's around the next corner and sent them off to control the situation. Thirty years later I can feel sorry for the Jap, but at the time I had no such feelings. A Jap prisoner was a rare curiosity and we were well indoctrinated in the belief that the only good Jap was a dead Jap. Within a few weeks we were to see hundreds of good Japs but they were nearly all skeletons.

Almost as an afterthought I realise that I had my 21st birthday somewhere between Chakabama and Maram. From my letters home I gather that I celebrated it with some officers from the mule company and my own brother officers who were not otherwise engaged that night. Frankly, I do not really remember it, just that it was the best one could do under the circumstances and a feeling that it was one more milestone missed out because of the war.

By July 1944 we were all back in Kohima resting and refitting. A lovely spot outside the battle torn town, high up on the grassy slopes with incredible views over the Naga Hills and on a clear day you could see the snow-capped Himalayas two hundred miles away. It was from here that I was sent to Calcutta to report to the W.O.S.B. (War Office Selection Board), to undergo selection for a regular commission. As I have described, I had taken the army exam and passed fairly well up the list, but 'the shop' had closed down in front of me and though I went for a potted Engineering degree course at Glasgow University, gazetting into the regular army had been stopped. It was eventually replaced by the WOSB when they realised that there was going to be a big age gap in the regular army if they did not do something to replace Sandhurst and the R.M.C. Woolwich which had both been closed down for the duration.

CHAPTER 10

A Battle Trophy

The WOSB was situated somewhere in a camp near Calcutta where I reported on 14th August, 1944. Most of the other officers were infantry and well-experienced in war. It consisted of endless interviews, I.Q. tests and one had also to give a talk on any subject of one's own choice (I chose to talk on the life history of the salmon). We also had a number of practical problems set. We had to get across a ravine, supplied with two planks of different length, some rope and a wheel barrow that had to be pushed across. There was also a high wire fence, electrified, and we had to get over it with a barrel and a few other stage props. As a sapper most of these problems were no problem at all. It was the sort of situation one was trained to take in one's stride, but I realised that the infantry officers found it more difficult. When faced with such problems they were trained to send for the sappers.

The result was that I passed fairly easily with a B Grade. Of the 25 officers taking it with me there were no A's, 3 B's, one C and the remaining 21 were failed. I felt that the whole course favoured the sappers, though I do not think it was intentional. The General in Charge told us at the beginning that due to the many applicants and few vacancies the standard would be higher than in peace-time. But I think they forgot that in peace-time the standards for the engineers and the gunners are very different from those required of the infantry. By taking them all together they lost a lot of very good infantry officers who did not require the technical standards they were setting. These were early days; maybe they got wiser later. Anyway, the result was not final. One was told that one would not be gazetted until the war was over and that when the day came one would be contacted and have a last chance to accept or reject one's regular commission in the light of the changed circumstances.

Somehow I felt it was not what it should have been. Rae took it sometime later by which time he was a major with great wartime battle experience, and had an M.C. and bar. He too, was rejected. Yet I, a miserable lieutenant with limited battle experience, was passed out a B candidate. Very nice for me, but no way to select regular officers. After my four or five days at the WOSB I went on to Bombay to take the leave that had been curtailed at the Outicumund earlier in the year. I pretended that I enjoyed it but really I was a lost soul and glad when it was over. Leave in a big city seems wonderful when you are in the jungle, but you need friends and by the time you have adjusted and settled into the new life in the city it is time to report back to your unit. This I did with an inward sense of relief not fully admitted at the time.

However, apart from taking the opportunity to send presents of tea and other luxuries back to my family, I also took the opportunity to equip myself with such things as films for my camera and above all a personal weapon that could be relied on. Shortly before I left to go on leave the army had allowed all officers another five rounds of ·38 revolver ammunition with instructions that the five rounds we had had up to now, but only to be used as a last resort, could now be fired in practice. We had duly celebrated the occasion by placing a 44 gallon drum in a sandpit and having a little practice with the revolver which we had been carrying as our personal weapon against the Japs. It came as a bit of a shock when the five rounds I fired at the oil drum never left a mark on the drum, even more so when I later found that all five bullets had failed to leave the end of the barrel and were jammed one behind the other inside it.

The truth was that the ·38 ammunition was so old that it had deteriorated. A bit of a laugh, but had one been confronted with a Jap it would not have been so funny. What was the good of an officer's personal weapon if there was virtually no ammunition available for it?

At that time the sten gun was the utility automatic weapon designed for the resistance in Europe. It fired 9mm. ammunition so that it could be used by the resistance with captured German ammunition. However, it proved so cheap and effective as an automatic weapon that it soon became standard in the British Army and 9mm. ammunition was always available, but no one gave a thought to the availability of ·38 ammunition on which the officer's personal weapon depended. While I was in Calcutta I took the opportunity to buy myself a new personal weapon of my choice. From the gunsmiths, Mantons of Calcutta, I purchased a Luger pistol, ex Dutch Army. It cost me 600 rupees but I felt it was a worthwhile investment on my own life. However, it seemed wrong that the army could not provide its officers with a reliable weapon so that they were forced to arm themselves at their own expense. I was by no means the only officer who had done this. Some bought their own, others bought them off the Yanks who had a very good light repeating rifle. Some even carried captured Jap pistols. A very poor reflection on British ordnance.

The Luger turned out to be a wonderful pistol. It sat in your hand as if it was part of you and when you aimed at something you hit it. It was more complicated than the revolver, with a unique knee action bolt. I soon learnt to strip, clean and reassemble it in a matter of seconds. It appeared to kick up when you fired but this must happen after the bullet had left the barrel because it did not affect its accuracy and with sten gun ammunition ad lib I soon found I could knock down five out of six tin cans at twenty paces which gave me a little confidence for the future.

Our rest period eventually came to an end and we were off to take up the advance into Burma. In a few months the pendulum of war had swung from desperate fighting to hold the Japanese invasion of India at its frontiers, to a counter-attack that had the Japanese in full retreat for the first time in the history of the war against Japan. It did wonders for our morale. In May 1944 we were fighting for every inch of ground at Kohima. By the end of June the Japs were in a desperate retreat. They had relied on capturing our bases in Assam before the monsoon destroyed their own tenuous L of C through the 150 miles of mountain passes separating India from Burma. Almost within sight of these bases they had been held and repulsed. They were now short of food, short of ammunition and all other essential supplies. Their L of C was turning into a morass of mud and fast becoming incapable of keeping them supplied with the basic essentials to survive. With the only all-weather road from India to Burma now firmly in our hands they were forced to retreat down earth tracks, which the monsoon had transformed into riverways of mud.

The decision of the 14th Army Commander, Gen. William Slim, to carry on fighting through the monsoon was hard for the battle-weary troops that had to carry it out. But their morale was high, they had their tails up and they knew it was the right decision. Having got the Japs in this position it would be fatal to let them get back to Burma and regroup to become fit and ready to fight again in a few months' time.

So our troops followed up down the main all-weather road and sent brigade groups off across country to intercept their line of retreat, cut them off and destroy them. It was a formidable task and only the fit survived, but the effect it had on the Japanese troops was devastating. They died in their thousands of starvation, exhaustion and disease. Those who managed to survive were allowed the privilege of being killed by our intercepting troops.

My return from leave along the old familiar route seems to have left me with strong feelings against the attitude of the white civilians in India. Certainly travel to the front across India had changed and the treatment of troops had become very under-privileged.

The reasons for this change were probably a combination of two things. Firstly we were now winning and with the threat of invasion past, the civilian population saw us in a different light. We were no longer the shield between them and the advancing Japs. Subconsciously their attitude changed when they were no longer threatened. The other significant factor is that there were now many more troops in transit to the front and pressure on limited transport facilities were proportionately more strained. Be that as it may, the effect was that the civil population no longer felt inclined to make the personal sacrifices in comfort once the threat of invasion was past. They demanded and got the best conditions of railway travel and were not prepared to share it with the military, so that the army had to make do with any clapped out rolling stock that was left over. The result was a heightened contrast between their respective travelling conditions and ours. The contrast was too great and, as always under such conditions, it bred a deep resentment of those civilians whom we had recently admired when they were working with us on the Burma Road to help the evacuation of refugees from Burma.

Back with one's own unit just inside Burma at Tamu this was soon forgotten. The spirit of the turning tide took over. This time we were in pursuit. The pace had to be kept up for we knew only too well that failure to exploit success only allowed the enemy to recover and mount a counter-attack.

It was not long before we received our marching orders. We were to move north (a bit unexpected) and develop the Thonan Thonhe track through to the Chindwin River so that the 19th Ind. Div. could come through and spearhead the attack on Mandalay from the north. We understood at the time that we would be following them through on this route.

We set off north from Tamu through sombre teak forest for Thonan. This village was in fact on the retreat route of the Japanese Army from Kohima through Ukhral and via Thonhe on the banks of the great Chindwin River. By now what had been mud was soft dry earth that broke down into deep dust under the wheels of our transport. When we camped for the night we were warned that the area was still patrolled by the Japanese. We harboured at night on the bare ground beneath the massive teak trees, posted our sentries and slept with one ear cocked for the slightest sound that might herald the Jap night attack to which we had become only too familiar.

The teak tree has leaves as large as soup plates. The dust from our vehicles rose in thick clouds into this foliage during the day and settled in thick layers on the leaves. At night the natural fall of the odd leaf was heightened by the strange sound of the falling dust as the descending leaf brushed past the lower leaves. In the deathly still silence of night in a teak forest the sound seemed magnified. It needed little imagination to turn this 'Tup, tup, Shhhh' of falling dead leaves and dust into the stealthy shuffle of a Japanese patrol. At the time we all heard this strange sound but few knew the cause of it so we all remained awake ready to react; only later did we discover its origin and wish we had not sacrificed our sleep so unnecessarily.

When we reached Thonan we realised for the first time just how great a defeat had been inflicted on the enemy. Not just by our direct action but by the monsoon, disease and the RAF pursuit planes. The jungle was full of predators of flesh. Everywhere was the evidence of their efficiency. The Japanese dead were everywhere. Not as the bloated, putrefying bodies we were used to seeing, but as clean dry skeletons, gleaming white bones picked clean of any flesh or sinews. They lay by the side of the track, they sat in lorries, they even sat on their latrines. Skeletons all, no clothes, no flesh, the myriad jungle ants had had the lot in a few weeks, only the indestructible remained. I shall never forget the sight of clean, white skeletons still with their steel helmets on their heads, a pile of bullets and buckles in their lap and their rifle and grenades by their sides. Maggots had consumed their flesh, and white ants, those voracious consumers of cellulose, had eaten their clothes, their leather and webbing equipment, so only the skeletons remained grotesquely sitting or lying in the very positions where death had finally overtaken them.

The Thonan Thonhe track was not easy to locate. In many places it was indistinguishable from the surrounding jungle save for the litter of Japanese trucks. On some of the steep slopes there was no track that vehicles could possibly negotiate, yet half way up the slope one would find a Japanese workshop lorry loaded with spare parts, perched on a ledge with no track up to it or down to it, nor was there any way around this feature that rose nearly a thousand feet in a few miles. There was only one possible solution to this riddle. They must have dragged their vehicles over it with elephants! There was no trace of a road over which even a Jeep could have driven. Of this I am certain, because I spent days cutting a trace for a road that could be developed into a track that 15 cwt. trucks could negotiate. It took us two weeks with bulldozers and tons of explosives to cut a road up this feature. It was a challenge that we sappers enjoyed tackling. Later some of the more challenging features that were negotiated were labelled with name plates such as David's Ditch and Banana Ridge. However, there were complications, for having been told to make a road for 15 cwt. trucks it was not long before we were ordered to up-grade it for artillery quads with guns and three ton trucks; the latter started to use it before it was finished to 15 cwt. standards. In the end the Div. HQ demanded that it be improved to a standard for tanks on transporters. This was the kind of absurdity that the sappers so often had to contend with. If you start with a road trace for 15 cwt. trucks you cannot just up-grade it for transporters by widening it, particularly on hill sections where turning circles are the limiting factor. Where you could get round a feature with a 15 cwt. truck the requirements for a tank transporter would demand a different route to avoid sharp bends which it could not negotiate, but these were problems that our superiors did not seem to appreciate. Why should they, for such was the pride of the sappers that they were prepared to move mountains rather than say it cannot be done. So in the end we moved mountains. Quite unnecessarily as it turned out for by the time we had moved them and made the road fit for the tanks on transporters the whole of the 19th Ind. Div. had slipped through without transporters and our final motorway was no longer required. Plans had changed and we were not to follow on but to move south again.

However, our task in building this road had its unexpected compensations. In the early days when we first arrived on the track things were fairly peaceful. We were there on our own except for a few forward patrols trying to locate their opposite numbers on the Jap side. Most of my time was spent surveying the route and leaving my men to cut the trace (clearing trees and scrub on the line of the road to be). Sometimes in the evening I would wander off on my own into the jungle with my shotgun in search of jungle fowl or any other edible game. When I went off alone I always took the precaution of being loaded with No. 6 shot in one barrel and contractile in the other. Contractile was a form of solid ball shot that was developed for shooting anything from large deer to tiger. I did not expect to find either but I felt it was a wise precaution in case I bumped into a Japanese patrol!

It was on one of these evening shooting forays, moving quietly along a wide track through the jungle, that I spotted a large thicket of dark green bushes all overgrown with creepers about a hundred yards into the jungle from the track. The cover in this part of the jungle was rather sparse so it struck me as just the sort of place that might hold some jungle fowl. I crept quietly up to it along a very faint track that seemed to lead directly to it. The thicket was surprisingly dense and dark. I wished I had a dog but without one all I could do was to walk around it beating it with a stick and hope that if there were any birds in it they might flush close enough for me to get a shot at them. I had nearly circumnavigated the thicket in this fashion when I came across what looked like a small tunnel-like path leading to the centre of it, and I could see sunlight at the end of the tunnel which suggested that the thicket might have an open centre. More out of curiosity than expectation of finding any game in there, I bent down and crept along the tunnel. As I reached the other end I realised that there was something large, black and shiny in the centre of it. For a moment I froze in my tracks and I could feel the hairs on the back of my neck rising in fear of what I might have walked into. The object was to one side of the end of the tunnel so I could only see a few bits of it through the thick screen of leaves, but what I could see looked vaguely familiar and certainly not like a piece of Japanese military equipment. I crept forward with my finger on the trigger of my gun, the trigger for the barrel which held the contractile cartridge. It was so silent, I felt sure I could hear if a man was breathing, if it was not for the pounding of my own heart. I reached the end of the tunnel and stuck my head around the corner cautiously. There within a few yards of me, dappled in the sunlight, was a shining black and chrome limousine. It was a Ford V8 De Luxe and it looked spotless. Just as though its chauffeur had parked it and then given it a final polish to leave it immaculate for the next day. It was so incongruous that I began to feel very suspicious. You just do not find shining limousines in the middle of the jungle miles from anywhere. Not in wartime, at any rate.

I walked around it cautiously, my finger on the trigger of my gun, and my nerves taut and ready to respond to the slightest movement or sound. I began to sense that I really was alone, one's animal senses become more acutely developed living in the jungle under wartime conditions. Always aware that you are hunting or being hunted. Those sixth senses so necessary for survival in our dim ancestral past, and dulled by civilised life still remain dormant within one's frontal lobes, capable of partial reactivation in a crisis, but one had to be able to recognise the signals and interpret them however faint the transmission.

I realised that I was alone but my military upbringing made me suspicious of the situation. If it was not an ambush then it had to be a booby trap of some sort. How had it got into the centre of this thicket without an apparent way in? This was not difficult to discover. At one end, the end that I first approached along the faint track, an entrance had been cut through the bushes and the bushes had been carefully placed back to conceal the entrance. What worried me most was that though they had been cut off and replaced they showed only slight signs of wilting which meant this must have been done very recently. The other thing that caught my eye was the bonnet of the car. It was slightly raised, exposing a gap of about an inch all round. This I was sure was where it might be booby trapped. Why else would the bonnet be ajar, so to speak? I worked carefully around the open gap feeling carefully inside it for a tripwire – there was nothing. I gave the same treatment to the driver's door but with no result. Unfortunately I was unfamiliar with the modern development in car bonnets. Having started off so carefully examining every possible location for a booby trap I ended up lifting the bonnet with all my strength until the front started to lift off the ground in my desperation. Only later did I discover the miracle of a bonnet catch where a slight pull released a catch allowing the bonnet to rise. It disclosed an engine devoid of carburettor, distributor and generator. It did not, however, take me long to find a piece of freshly disturbed ground from which I exhumed all these except for the rotor arm.

The inside of the car was as immaculate as the outside. Not a speck of dust or a piece of paper in the glove compartment to give a clue to its recent owner. The boot too appeared empty and swept clean, then I spotted a little black cloth case about nine inches long nestling almost invisibly at the back of the boot. I reached in and examined its contents – a small silk Japanese flag about six inches by four inches and mounted on a chrome standard that I soon discovered screwed into a hole on the front of the bonnet. It was obvious that this was the staff car of a very high ranking Japanese officer. The fact that it was not camouflage painted suggested that it had belonged to some general who never expected to get very near to the front and had been overtaken by the front falling back on him. It also looked from the way it had been so carefully cleaned and hidden that he had every intention of recovering it when the temporary setback in the Japanese advance into India was overcome.

With such an unusual find to report I forgot about the jungle fowl and set off back to my company positions. When I got back only the 2nd I/C Jock Meldrum was there. He made a quick appreciation of the situation. "Well, John, one thing is certain we must get out there and tow it in before some other bugger finds it and claims it". Within a few minutes he had a 15 cwt. truck and a tow rope and I was guiding him back up the track to where I had discovered this find. It did not take long to clear the branches concealing the entrance to the thicket. On my suggestion we had brought a very long tow rope as I still thought it could be booby trapped and might go up when it was first moved. When Jock saw my find he let out a low whistle. "That would come in very handy when we get to Rangoon, but it's a long way off and there will be a lot of envious staff officers working overtime to get their hands on it long before then. Still, not to worry, it may blow up when we start to tow it anyway". We fixed 25 yards of tow rope to it and eased forward. It followed us obediently out of the thicket and there was no explosion.

With rising excitement at our treasure trove, we shortened the tow rope and I got into the driving seat of this luxurious vehicle and shouted out of the window, "Back to camp, my good man". And we set off. As we reached the jungle track the 15 cwt. truck slowed to make the right-angle turn onto it and I discovered that at least my brakes worked, but as I tried to turn to follow the truck down the track nothing happened. The steering wheel was solid and would not turn at all. In the confusion I shot straight across the track and into the jungle on the other side, where fortunately the tow rope checked me before I hit anything more solid than a few bushes. Jock had seen my performance and had stopped before the situation was compounded. "What's up, John, you are meant to follow me not go off on your own. The camp is back this way." "The bloody steering's jammed," I cried. Then I noticed that the ignition switch was right against the steering column and not on the dashboard. I guessed that it must incorporate a steering lock as well. This was the last straw. It was getting dark and our plans to have our prize safely back in our company lines were so near and now were suddenly thwarted by this unexpected revelation in modern car technology. Neither of us had ever heard of a steering lock before but it was obvious that was what it was. We considered that the chances of picking the lock in failing light were out. If we left it where it was some chance infantry patrol could come along in the night and claim it as theirs. As far as we knew a Jap patrol could find it and destroy it to thwart our capture of this splendid bit of booty. There was only one option left – brute force.

We sat either side of the steering wheel, took a firm grip and put all our strength into forcing it around. There was a slight grating but if held fast. We tried it in the other direction, it grated and gave a little, then held fast. We continued to try forcing it one way then the other, and each time we seemed to gain a little more play. Then in a final desperate heave it broke, or something broke and the wheel spun. It was not without relief we discovered that the front wheels also turned when the wheel spun. We had broken the lock and not the steering! The last of our troubles were over and within no time we were back on the track and heading for home. As we entered the camp all eyes turned at the sight of this luxury in black and chrome being towed into our camp area. To understand its impact you must also understand that we existed in a land that was totally military and was at least 200 miles from any form of civilised life in its most basic form. A vehicle that was not camouflage painted stood out like a nude at a Methodist Convention. It was so alien to the life that we lived that it was eyed with the same mixture of horror and delight. Everyone's head turned to admire and ogle this brazen hussy in our midst. The sappers converged on it and it took the full whiplash of military discipline to disperse them back to their duties.

In the officers' mess the first euphoria of our new possession was soon displaced by the practicalities of reality. Reality was that it could be classified as a C.E.V. (captured enemy vehicle) and as such would have to be handed over to the Divisional Transport Pool.

However, it was agreed that it would have to be reported next day at Divisional Prayers, the nickname given to the daily conference of unit commanders at Div. HQ presided over by our Divisional Commander, General Frank Messervy. It was also decided that this would be a tactful moment to present him with the Japanese commander's pennant found in the boot of the car.

The result was a pleasant surprise. The vehicle was classified as a battle trophy and not a C.E.V., a distinction that we did not fully appreciate at the time but was quite invaluable later, for as Jock had so well predicted it became the envy of many staff officers, not only in Burma but later in Bangkok and Malaya when the war was won. They ordered its immediate surrender as a C.E.V. but were stymied when they discovered that it was a battle trophy and they could not gain possession without special authority from the Divisional Commander who had classified it thus.

Our M.T. havildar was as thrilled as anyone to have such a unique and sophisticated vehicle under his command. Within 24 hours it was all camouflage painted. What had been shining black and chrome was now dull drab green and brown with a brilliant white star encircled on the bonnet for aircraft recognition. A symbol all our vehicles bore to save us being strafed by our own aircraft.

Though it was I who had discovered this luxurious vehicle and, with Jock's assistance, been instrumental in getting it back to our company lines, my first and last ride in it for a long time to come was the tow back. It did not take long to get the engine going but the privilege of using it was a matter of rank and seniority. It naturally became the OC's personal transport. I was never even offered a seat in it until I eventually took over command of the company a year later, but by that time we were in Bangkok and our life style had changed. I preferred the practicability of my Jeep in Burma and bore no grudge that I was denied the luxury of such a vehicle under conditions that were of little value in realising its potential. On the hot, rutted, dusty tracks of our advance through Burma it was a prestige symbol but in reality a somewhat impractical liability. I was better off in my four-wheel drive Jeep. Though one never realised it at the time it was to come into its own in Bangkok where it became nicknamed by the men as 'the passion oundi' (*oundi* being the Tamil for vehicle).

For the moment there were more absorbing tasks on hand and our 'Battle Trophy' was soon forgotten. We were hell bent on reaching our first major river obstacle, the Chindwin River. Our immediate task was to construct a road to its banks, set up a ferry and get 19th Ind. Div. across. We worked long hours, for in war time everyone is in a hurry to move on, that is, when you appear to be winning. Back at Divisional or Brigade Headquarters they are always planning the next move. Any obstacles to that move must be overcome by the sappers. That's their job. Unfortunately the staff of these headquarters are nearly all infantry except for the CRE. You need a strong character as CRE to convince the other commanders at HQ that you cannot build 28 miles of road rising up to 1000 ft. in a few miles and down again the other side all in a week. You might manage a Jeep track but the heavier and the longer the vehicle that the road had to take, the more earth and rock had to be quarried out of the hillside and the stronger the bridges had to be built.

Most of the rivers that had to be bridged were in fairly deep ravines. Until an approach road was made down the ravine one could not build the bridge and until the bridge was built one could not get the equipment through to build the next section of road. If you built the bridge to take three ton lorries and light artillery, you had to rebuild it or strengthen it if someone then decided that tanks would be sent up the road.

We blasted, bulldozed and built bridges, then replaced the bridges with stronger bridges, blasted more hillside away and bulldozed more earth away to accommodate larger vehicles. We started in late November, 1944, and by mid-December we had reached the Chindwin, the first of the major river barriers of Burma. Here we built ferries and ferried 19th Div. across on their route to Mandalay. It was a great engineering achievement involving a lot of men, machines and equipment, yet at the back of my mind there was always the memory of the burnt out Japanese trucks along the route. They had somehow done the same thing before us in the opposite direction. They had got their transport over the same features without building a motorway to do it. This could not be denied, for their vehicles lay abandoned all along the route. It was not the terrain that had held them up for their vehicles were all facing east. It was the RAF, the monsoon and disease that had overcome them. I felt there must be a lesson to be learnt from this evidence but no one seemed interested in learning it at the time. Possibly we were wasting our resources demanding unnecessarily high standards – who knows.

CHAPTER 11

Down the Kabaw Valley

As I have said, by the time the road was built it was obsolescent, for all the units that were to use it had leaked through during its construction. We had reached the mythical Chindwin and we had crossed it, but only as ferry operators. We were poised to follow through for the assault on Mandalay when orders came to pull out and move south to Tamu again. At first we felt bitterly disappointed but soon rumours of a master plan leaked out. The assault on Mandalay was in fact almost a deception to convince the Japs that the Main IV Corps offensive was coming from the North for the capture of Mandalay. This was in fact the plan until a secret meeting was held of Corps Commanders with General Slim at Advance Tactical Headquarters of IV Corps in the jungle near Sittang, East of Tamu. Here the plan was revealed for IV Corps to drive south down the Kabaw and Gangaw valleys for 300 miles, cross the Irrawaddy at Nyaungu and thence thrust east to capture Meiktila. This would cut off the Japanese armies fighting in North and Central Burma from their bases at Rangoon. In fact the Japanese were deceived into believing that 33 and IV Corps were driving south from Chindwin, crossing at Thonhe where in fact only one division was advancing. The remaining units of these two corps were actually thrusting south down the east bank of the Irrawaddy and IV Corps would cross it in Central Burma at Nyaungu. In order to maintain this deception the advance down the Kabaw Valley could not be headed by units known to belong to IV Corps in case some of them were captured and identified by Japanese Intelligence. The Lushai Brigade headed the advance to Gangaw and were then relieved by the 28th East African Brigade, neither of which could be identified as part of the IV Corps.

History proved it to be a master stroke but at the time it was not so evident. We set off down the Kabaw Valley in the dry season. Both the Kabaw and the Gangaw Valleys had a formidable reputation. In the monsoon they were regarded as death valleys with the highest incident of the worst forms of malaria and almost impassable due to soft, deep muddy tracks intersected by swollen streams at regular intervals. In the dry season we found that their peculiar soil structures turned into deep, soft dust-like face powder under the passage of wheeled vehicles. It rose in smog like clouds that enveloped everything. After a few miles of driving through it we were all coated in the stuff. Helena Rubinstein could have made a fortune out of it. It was that pale terra cotta that women use as foundation make-up, but on our perspiring faces it stuck and caked so that by the end of the day we all had identical make-up. The dark skin of the Indian troops and the fair skin of the British officers was of one homogenous shade.

The raging torrents of the monsoon were now only a series of dry river beds that had to be crossed and frequently they had deep sandy bottoms that sucked vehicles down to their axles.

We spearheaded the road construction just clearing trees and improving dry river crossings. As we progressed further south the track we were up grading to a road became less evident. At this stage we were allocated a number of elephants, the remnants of Bill Williams' "Elephant Bill" Teak Company elephants that had come over to our side. They were fascinating creatures, not quite what the sappers had been trained to use but they were expert at pushing down and clearing the trees that confined our road to a meandering cart track. However, they had their problems: they did not like working with mechanical equipment which frightened them.

Even a Jeep was something to be treated with suspicion, something that stopped work and caused them to lower their heads and blow through their trunks. Left undisturbed on their own they could fell and remove quite a large number of trees, but they turned out to be the origin of all trade unions. They were used to a five-day week and a ten-hour day; when either was exceeded they just ceased to work. Their mahouts could do what they liked but after 5 p.m. they just leant on trees but would not even try to push them over. The war effort meant nothing to them; they stuck to the working hours they had always been used to. You stopped work at 5 p.m. and you did not work weekends. This was fair enough because you do not feed elephants but you turn them loose after the day's work to browse in the jungle. Next morning each mahout knows the characteristic track of his own elephant and follows the trail of his night feeding until he catches up with him, mounts him and brings him back to work. There were complications when your bull elephant was in musk (in season) then he could be difficult or even dangerous. Some elephants were more dangerous than others. Some had the reputation for killing their mahouts by sweeping them off their backs with their trunk and dashing them against the nearest tree. Yet there always seemed to be another mahout ready to take over these fickle rogues. I cannot think why, but it seemed to be a part of the accepted occupational hazards of the profession.

These elephants helped us to push forward with the formation of the road. Behind us came other engineer units to improve it and build it up to the standards of a major highway by laying bitumised hessian on the surface to lay the dust of the dry season, and eventually shed the water of the wet season.

We progressed through country that had never seen more than the occasional bullock cart and now was subjected to the passage of an army corps, not just the fighting troops but that vast tail of ancillary troops that follow in its wake. Our elephants were the pushers down of trees but there was also a corps of more skilled elephants that were used for bridge building. Their skill was incredible. They built elephant bridges across the dry riverbeds with patient skill. They could place great teak trunks within a tolerance of one inch. They seemed to understand the whole principle of bridge building. All we had to do was drive in the dog spikes that held these great teak logs together, and lay and spike the decking boards for a smoother passage over the bridge.

Apart from supervising the road work I also had to push ahead of the work and reconnoitre the country ahead to decide on the most suitable trace to develop for the road. Though we were following the so-called existing road it was little more than a cart track which often split into several parallel cart tracks which were alternative routes created under monsoon conditions in the past. As the passage of carts under rainy season conditions reduced one route to an impassable morass, the cart drivers struck out on another route through the jungle. Sound enough for bullock carts, but if it had to be developed into a main military highway some routes were more suitable than others. It was on one of these occasions when I was walking alternative routes along these tracks with my Jemadar Suri that I suddenly spotted a small herd of animals crossing the path ahead. I had never seen anything like them before; they looked like a cross between wild cattle and deer. They did not seem to have seen or scented us and appeared to be in no hurry. I marked the spot where they had crossed, then borrowed my jemadar's rifle and a clip of five rounds of ·303. I cut the tips off the bullets with my kukri to convert them to dumdum bullets that would expand on impact. Then I set off in pursuit. I reached the point where they had crossed the track. Their large slots were clearly visible on the bare track but when I tried to follow them in the jungle it was not so easy. Occasionally I would find a chance impression on a bit of bare ground, but nothing more was visible amongst the leaves and undergrowth that carpeted most of the ground. As I crept forward I became less and less confident that I was on their trail at all. I was on the point of giving up and retracing my steps when I found a small rise in the ground. At least I had to see what lay beyond so I ventured a little further.

As I reached the top of the rise and peered over I held my breath. There in the small clearing were the five beasts I had been stalking. Their heads were up and they were obviously suspicious and tensed for take-off. I raised my rifle in slow motion and selected a large male that presented a reasonable heart shot with his flank towards me. They were about 75 yards away and I knew I could not afford to hesitate or waver, but the excitement had its effect on my aim. Sweat was streaming down my glasses as I pulled the trigger. The report of the rifle reverberated through the jungle and all five beasts leapt out of the clearing, yet I knew I had hit the one I had aimed at. He leapt in a different way to the others and when I followed the line he had taken I soon found the trail of blood. This I followed for about a hundred yards before I found him in a small depression where I quickly dispatched him with a second shot. I think my first shot had just missed his heart and gone through his lungs. He was a magnificent animal – the body of a large stag, a golden brown with a dark stripe down his back ending in a short tail, not as short as a deer's and not as long as that of cattle. But his horns were shaped like an antelope. When you have been living on tinned meat for months, a big lump of fresh meat is quite a prize.

My jemadar who had heard the two shots had followed up and soon appeared. Together we gazed at our trophy. "Sahib, we have a problem", he said. "With those horns someone will say it is related to the sacred cow and then no one will feel free to eat it. That would be a shame. I think it would be better if we cut off the horns now and then we will call it a deer and without the horns no one will dispute it".

So I drew my kukri and chopped off the horns and we buried them. Then we went back to the camp and sent out a recovery party to bring it back. No one questioned its ancestry. The whole company enjoyed fresh meat for two days and we sent the liver to Div. HQ to keep them happy. The self-styled experts pronounced that it was 'Sang', a rare form of Burmese wild cattle closely related to deer. You can make your own judgment from the photograph. I think the jemadar's idea to remove the horns was very sound advice.

Our progress down the Gangaw Valley was hard work and uneventful, most of the time. However, there was a little light relief over the Theje's daughter. Our head mahout in charge of elephants knew the local headman or Theje. When you have not seen a woman for some months your judgment and reactions become impaired. Up to the present we had not felt very sympathetic towards the Burmese. Rumour had it that when the Japanese were conquering Burma they had been inclined to side with their new masters rather than support the old ones in retreat. They had assisted our exodus with a few deft executions. It only needed a deft swipe with their parangs from the rear at exhausted refugees to claim credit with their new masters – or so rumour had it. There was also the B.N.A. – Burmese National Army, an armed force dressed in uniforms of winceyette pyjama material. Their uniforms and pack were all made from this strange pink and blue material that must have been shipped into Burma in quantities that it could not normally absorb. Once our forces appeared to be on the ascendancy they soon started surrendering in large numbers and the official attitude to the Burmese became more conciliatory.

Hence our party with the local Theje, and every British officer's eye on his attractive daughter. We arrived with a bottle of Haywards Gin which was decanted into a coconut shell and passed around. The chief mahout smiled and took a long draught, smiled at all the company and then brought the lot up over the balcony. I cannot blame him for it was neat gin and he drank it like coconut juice. The headman did the same with the same sickly smile on his face but kept his down. He then passed around some local brew in a coconut shell which we drank and probably produced equally sickly smiles. The Theje's daughter smiled back and eyed us from the shadows of the back of the verandah, but before the formalities were concluded she had completely disappeared into these shadows and by the time that small bunch of British officers returned from their goodwill mission full of a ghastly mixture of Haywards Gin and local arak, she was completely lost in the shadows of unrealistic anticipation. I doubt if the poor girl even realised how the chances of war had made her the unexpected centre of carnal desire for a small group of British officers who had not so much as spoken to a member of her sex for the last six months. Nor were they likely to see another for the next six months.

There was little resistance to our advance until we reached the town of Gangaw. Here the advance Lushai Brigade reported enemy resistance. I do not think it was all that serious but, as so often happens in war, higher command thought this an ideal opportunity to demonstrate its muscle power. Gangaw was chosen as a suitable objective to demonstrate the American strategical air force 'earthquake'. A sort of showpiece for which they had to find a suitable target. Gangaw was selected and the advance was held up until weather conditions allowed this demonstration of power to be affected. In fact, it delayed the advance by some six days until the weather favoured the air strike and the senior officers including the Army Commander, General Slim, could be brought forward to witness this event. Everything stood still until the weather allowed the attack to take place on 10th January, 1945.

Senior officers were in the grandstand and the might of the strategical American air force came over at a great height and released their pay load of bombs on Gangaw. It was an absurd showpiece. The bombers came over and the ground shook with the sheer weight of high explosives that they released, and our artillery fired all they could muster onto the poor little town of Gangaw. Everyone was suitably impressed. That is except the Japs who had obviously vacated their positions while we were waiting for the weather to improve. Certainly there was no resistance when we advanced into Gangaw in its wake. However, this was not because the Japs had been annihilated by the 'earthquake'. They had obviously evacuated the town long before it had taken place. Gangaw had been destroyed but there was not a Jap body to be found amongst the devastation to show that it had been justified. Even the devastation of the town was not very impressive. We felt that a natural earthquake would have made a better job than the American strategic air force equivalent. Fortunately the Japs and the civil population had got tired of waiting, or had got wind of what was being laid on for their benefit. When the Lushai Brigade occupied Gangaw they found two elderly Burmese civilians and four dogs as the sole casualties.

We were glad when this little farce was over as we could then get on with our advance to the Irrawaddy. At this point the Lushai Brigade were relieved by the 28th East African Motorised Brigade who took over the vanguard of our thrust south. They were very different troops from the lean Lushai hill tribes we had been used to.

The East African Brigade was equipped with what seemed like an unlimited supply of brand new vehicles. However, it was soon obvious from the way they handled them that they would not remain new for very long. They drove them with a reckless abandon, with results that were far from wreckless, in fact their wrecked vehicles soon became marker buoys at every obstacle. When negotiating dry sandy riverbeds they had no sense of handling their trucks whatsoever. If the wheels started to spin they just kept their foot on the accelerator until they were dug down to the axles. The next truck tried to drive around the stuck one and repeated the performance until the crossing was completely blocked with bellied vehicles each containing a grinning buck nigger and each complaining that his vehicle was "no damn good". They were more of a hindrance than an aid to the advance as road building machinery had to be diverted to winch them out of these situations when it should have been employed on road construction.

Their discipline was very different to what we were used to in the Indian Army. On one occasion they mutinied and their officers took refuge in our lines until command could be restored. One way and another we were not very impressed by the East African Brigade.

We were at last starting to contact a little Jap resistance to our rapid advance along the west of the Irrawaddy. Past experience in the Arakan and Kohima made us very wary of the potential for a Japanese counter-attack which seemed long overdue. Brigade headquarters were taking no chances and insisted in occupying a good defensive position every time they moved. On one occasion they had found the ideal position only to discover two 500 lb. bombs nestling within their perimeter. They had already dug themselves in and were not anxious to start again but also not keen to spend the night with these bombs in their midst, in case a lucky Jap mortar bomb might detonate one of them. They were, in fact, British bombs that had been dropped on some earlier low level mission and had bounced along the surface without detonating and come to rest in this so-called defensive position for Brigade HQ. The natural reaction was to send for the sappers and I was the nearest sapper!

When I arrived at Brigade HQ they explained the predicament and showed me the bombs. They also explained that there was an RAF Bomb Disposal Officer somewhere back on the L of C who had been summoned, but they had no idea where he was or how soon he could be brought forward. The Brigade Commander's dug out was too close for comfort and he wanted them defused or removed before nightfall. I surveyed the two bombs that were within 30 yards of each other, just sitting on the ground like barrels of beer dropped off a brewer's dray. I know little about bomb disposal, but like all young officers was anxious to please my superiors. If they wanted the bombs made safe I would have a go. Their fuses were obvious at the tail end. A big knurled collar surrounded what was undoubtedly the main fuse. The only hope amongst my tool spectrum was a large pipe wrench whose jaws would just about encompass this collar. We started on the first bomb hoping that it was a right-handed thread. With two men straining on the pipe wrench it moved and we unscrewed the fuse and placed it in the back of my Jeep, but the second fuse we could not budge. The bomb had been lying there for some time and corrosion had seized its thread solid. I reported that its fuse could not be withdrawn and was promptly informed that the Brigade Commander could not tolerate the presence of fused bombs in that location overnight. There was no alternative. We had to remove the bomb which we did with four sappers pushing and heaving to roll it like a barrel out of the area and beyond the perimeter of the Brigade defensive position. By this time it was dark and we made our way back to our own defensive position for the night.

Needless to say it was a quiet night. There was no Japanese counter-attack and next morning we got on with the job of road building. Half way through the morning I received a message that the RAF Bomb Disposal Officer had arrived at Brigade HQ and my presence was required. When I arrived I found a rather white-faced RAF lieutenant. He had been shown the bomb we had failed to defuse and rolled out of the position, and wanted to see the fuse we had extracted from the defused bomb left in the Brigade HQ position. He did not seem very happy. At first I suspected that it was professional pride, but I soon realised that it was more than this. He explained that these bombs were often fitted with anti-withdrawal fuses to prevent the Japs using them should they fail to explode. By rights I should not be here. He explained the very act of unscrewing the fuse should have detonated the bomb, for in this case both were fitted with anti-withdrawal fuses. Not all our bombs were fitted with them, but the code numbers on the fuse identified these two as anti-withdrawal fuses and that fortunately for me the one we had managed to unscrew had failed, probably due to corrosion or faulty manufacture. He solemnly impressed on me that it was essential all British bombs should be left untouched until he had inspected them. After all, that was what he was there for. He need not have bothered. I assured him from henceforth I would leave them all for him, not even the Army Commander would persuade me to have a go.

CHAPTER 12

In Search of the Missing Link

We were now getting nearer to our great objective, the Irrawaddy. It appeared as a broad blue band on the edge of our maps. Sooner or later, somewhere we had to cross it if we were to penetrate the heart of Burma. It was a very broad blue band, anything up to a mile wide. Such a formidable obstacle was bound to be heavily defended by the Japs. An assault crossing of such an obstacle would be the widest assault river crossing of the war and our equipment available probably the most primitive of any wartime river crossing on this scale. It was essential that we trained and rehearsed for this formidable task. The problem was where. There were plenty of rivers on the map but at this time of year most of them were dry. However, there was the Zahaw Chaung. It was not very large but it did have the advantage of actually having water in it, and at one point was almost a hundred yards wide and deep enough to float a folding boat. It was, therefore, naturally chosen as the site for our pre-crossing training.

It did not take long to discover how badly we needed this training. We had spent two years fighting the Japs, but most of it had been in the hills where rivers were generally raging torrents to be bridged. Watermanship had never come into it. Our first week on the Zahaw Chaung left us in no doubt about the extent of the task.

It was chaos at first. It was difficult to believe that many of our men had never seen water, let alone a boat. The sight of a boatload of sappers on an obvious collision course with the jetty became a nightmare when the NCO in charge grabbed the painter and started pulling on it with all his strength in the belief that it would arrest the progress of the boat and diminish the impact.

To start with, our watermanship was the very basic handling of boats that were man-propelled by oars or paddles. It seemed a very foreign medium to many of our sappers, and viewing the chaos that could be achieved by such relatively gentle forms of propulsion we were full of foreboding at the thought of what they would manage to do when propelled by a 22 h.p. outboard motor.

However, we need not have worried, for though their first efforts were deplorable, once they had mastered the basic principles they took the rest in their stride and once under power propulsion there was no looking back. But in the early days it was like teaching chickens to swim. They had been on land too long and water, other than relentless monsoon rain, had become foreign to their way of life. On one occasion in the early training, I remember a sapper falling overboard flat on his face into the water. At first we laughed, then suddenly realised that though he was thrashing wildly about on the surface he was in fact drowning. My first instinct was to dive in to his rescue, something made me change my mind and I jumped instead. Just as well as it turned out, for there was barely a foot of brown water over the rock shelf we had drifted over. I waded across to him without getting my knees wet and picked him out by the scruff of his neck. He was almost unconscious yet he could have stood up and waded ashore himself without any difficulty. The problem was he believed that he had fallen into deep water and knew he could not swim. If he had felt the bottom with his thrashing arms I doubt whether he would have recognised it.

I learnt a lot from this small incident that illustrated just how deadly panic can be. If no one had been there he could have died, not from drowning but from panic. It impressed me very deeply that however desperate the situation may appear to you, your best chance of survival must be to keep calm. The often quoted words of Rudyard Kipling's 'If' seemed to fit the situation perfectly. 'If you can keep your head when all about your are losing theirs......'

The rust flakes were soon scraped off our sappers watermanship. In fact, most of them had been well-trained in the art at Bangalore, and it was only the odd individual who had missed out somewhere along the line in his early training who stood out so severely at the start. Before long the outboard motors were coming out of mothballs and the Zahaw Chaung was enveloped in a haze of blue smoke as a veritable fairground spectacle like a water-born dodgem took over.

Once the sappers had regained their confidence and expertise at handling these temperamental power-driven craft the dress rehearsal for the crossing took place in earnest with the troops who were going to make the initial assault. It was essential that they too were familiar with these craft and their limitations. Not only did they have to know how many men could safely load into a MK III assault boat or a folding boat, they had to know how to take over with paddles if their outboard motor failed. It must be remembered that the outboard motors had travelled several hundred miles up the L of C over rough earth tracks, continuously jolted and subjected to transit stresses for which they were never designed. Not the least of which was a thick coating of red dust.

The I.E.M.E. did their best under very difficult conditions to bring back to life these sensitive outboard motors after their long journey from America to Central Burma, and to sustain life when their numerous carburettor controls had been twisted and turned in every direction by inexperienced operators in a vain attempt to coax back to life the last splutters of over-choked or starved engines.

The 4/15 Punjabis had been chosen as the Infantry Battalion to make the first assault crossing. They had just arrived to start this vital training when I was summoned to report to the CRE at Div. HQ. When I arrived there that evening I did not see the CRE but his adjutant, Bill Baker. He had an unexpected assignment for me. He explained that all was set for the mighty assault across the Irrawaddy by 4 Corps and that as soon as they had established a bridgehead 33 Corps would pass through and strike into Central Burma to capture Meiktila, thus cutting off the Japanese armies in Northern Burma from their bases at Rangoon in the south. To achieve this it was vital that our supporting tanks could be ferried across this great obstacle in the early stages of the crossing. We had the pontoons, the Bailey equipment and the propulsion units necessary to construct the class 40/60 rafts to get the tanks across. But somehow the vital frames with which the propulsion units are attached to the pontoons had been lost on the long L of C from India into Burma. Whether they had been lost or someone had forgotten to order them was not quite clear, but what was clear was that without them we could build the tank rafts but had no means of getting them across to the other side. However, they had managed to locate one propulsion unit frame and this missing link, without which tanks could not cross the Irrawaddy, was to be entrusted to me. I was to be flown out to India with instructions to get 16 more made up by the base workshops and flown back to Burma in time for the crossing, i.e. by $D-3$. We were now $D-8$.

It was a challenge and responsibility to which I felt proud to be entrusted. Here was a job after my own heart. The whole success of the operation depended on it and I felt very honoured that it was entrusted to me, a humble lieutenant; you cannot get much humbler in the chain of command. Next day I was duly presented with my sample of a propulsion unit frame which was loaded into a Lysander light aircraft on the Div. landing strip, which would fly me to the nearest Dakota strip. There I would be flown out to India. This vital propulsion unit frame was not a very impressive piece of equipment, it looked more like a cheap wrought iron bedhead than anything else. It certainly did not look like the missing link that it was, so vital to the ultimate success of the assault crossing and the masterplan for the reconquest of Burma.

The first part of my journey was just what I expected. Everyone was notified of my mission and its importance and a Dakota was held waiting for my arrival by light aircraft as though I had been a VIP. Within minutes the precious frame was transferred and I was airborne for India. We flew up over the extension of the Himalayas that separates India from Burma. It was the first time I had ever flown in an aeroplane. As we descended over the hills to Comilla my ears became more and more painful. No one had told me that in an unpressurised aircraft it was necessary to clear your ears to relieve the pressure changes. Like all young people surrounded by their seniors for travelling companions (and they were all very senior officers) one is reluctant to admit that one is inexperienced and ask for advice. When the pain in my ears became too much I succumbed and asked the senior RAF officer who was sitting next to me if this was normal. I wished I had done it sooner for he could not have been more sympathetic. He quickly taught me how to hold my nose and blow to relieve this pressure. He was even apologetic that he had been too preoccupied with his own thoughts to realise that it was my first time in the air and what I was suffering. He remembered having the same unpleasant experience as a Battle of Britain pilot.

"You must be like me," he said. "It's alright going up, your ears clear themselves, but in a dive you can build up very painful pressures that you have to clear or suffer the consequences. The trick is to hold your nose and blow until you hear your ears pop". I wished I had sought his friendly and helpful advice a little earlier. It took a lot of blowing to clear my ears and when we landed at Comilla I had two very painful ears, having left it too late. But I never forgot his advice and have never let it get that bad again.

Most of the senior officers on my plane got off at Comilla but I remained on board, for my destination was Calcutta and the army base workshops at Barrackpore. Within the hour we were airborne again, and later that evening we landed at Dum Dum Airport outside Calcutta.

Here I was in for a shock. I had presumed that if my mission was that important to the war effort, the staff would have signalled some authority for my mission back to Calcutta. However, when I arrived at Dum Dum no one showed the slightest interest in a scruffy lieutenant clad in jungle green battle dress carrying what looked for all the world like a metal bedhead, and with some unlikely story that it was vital for the success of the Irrawaddy crossing.

Where was my authority? That was what mattered in their world. Without a written authority you could get nowhere. It was late so I settled for the duty truck to the Grand Hotel in Calcutta, where I finally arrived with my strange metal frame.

It was with great difficulty that I managed to sign in there, for without a movement order I was treated with the greatest of suspicion. Back in India no one did anything without a piece of paper authorising them to do it. Nor could anyone believe that a lieutenant could be entrusted with anything of any real importance. So it was quite safe to ignore him and his mad story about some vital piece of equipment without which tanks could not cross the Irrawaddy. Most of them had barely heard of the Irrawaddy anyway. I retired to my room in the Grand Hotel clutching my propulsion unit frame convinced that tomorrow I would be dealing with men who knew what the war was all about and who would be embued with my own enthusiasm to ensure its success.

It was wonderful to sleep in a real bed with all the trappings of civilisation – hot water, electric light, the lot. It did not take me long to fall asleep. Next morning I awoke with a feeling of complete disorientation. The previous night I had been in the jungle ready to wake up to a Jap attack and here I was in a proper bed with nothing more menacing than the early morning noises of Chowringee floating in through the window. Slowly it all came back – just what I was doing there and what I was there for.

I decided I must get transport to take me out to Barrackpore where the Chief Engineer and his staff were located at the Army Group HQ.

I approached the Camp Commandant of the Grand Hotel. This was not all that easy as he was continually beseiged by other officers demanding his attention on such vital matters as reporting the breakdown of the punka (ceiling fan) in their room, or that their hot bath had only been tepid last night, and why was there no room service to bring drinks up to their room etc. etc. Every time I nearly had his attention another officer of rank senior to me would interpose and with a "Just a moment, old boy", he would divert his attention to the newcomer. Most of them seemed to be old friends and I waited seething with impatience as they exchanged reminiscences of other old friends. After about three quarters of an hour there was a momentary lull and I seized the opportunity to explain that I had an important job to do at Barrackpore and must have transport to get myself and my vital piece of equipment there. He eyed me and my piece of equipment with an obvious air of distrust. "Where is your movement order? You really should not be here without a movement order, and I certainly can't produce transport for you without one". I explained that I had been flown out of Burma the previous day and movement orders were not regarded with such reverence on active service there as they were in Calcutta, and no doubt as a major he had powers of discretion to make exceptions on such matters. He looked at me with even deeper distrust. "It's more than my job is worth to start providing anyone with transport just because he has a good story. If your mission is that vital you would have a movement order –

try the MTO." "Where is he to be found?" I asked. "Howrah Station with the RTO, old boy. Failing that I'd take a taxi, that's what most of them do in the end".

It would need a taxi even to get to Howrah Station, so I took his advice and went outside to find one. At least this was no problem. I had wasted an hour trying to get official transport but outside was a splendid black Chevrolet with its turbaned Sikh driver ready and waiting, even a Union Jack pennant mounted on the bonnet. The Sikh driver was delighted that he had found a fare right out to Barrackpore and in no time my strange piece of hardware was strapped onto the luggage carrier and we were off. The Sikh grinning from ear to ear at the thought of the fare he could charge for the journey, and myself apprehensive whether I had the money to pay for it.

The Army Group HQ at Barrackpore was surrounded by a high wire security fence. I hoped that my identity card would be sufficient to gain admittance. I need not have worried. The Gurkha sentry never even asked for it. I shouted through the window, "Which way to the CE?" The sentry sprang to attention and directed the driver to a tree-lined avenue off to the right; as we drove up to it I was impressed by the style of accommodation accorded a CE and even more so when we arrived at the impressive looking mansion. It was built in a Palladian style on top of a large mound with a broad sweep of stone steps where a number of weary looking officers, none below the rank of brigadier, were ascending or descending the steps. To my amazement, as my taxi swept around the gravel forecourt their weary figures looked up, stiffened to attention and saluted. I emerged from my taxi and courteously returned their salute. They remained like statues for a moment and then seemed to collapse. The expression on their faces made it quite clear that this was no welcome to the long awaited courier from Burma with his vital mission for the Irrawaddy crossing. Who the devil did I think I was? was the gist of their opening gambit. How dare I drive up the C in C's residence flying the Union Jack?

Slowly the awful truth dawned on me. I had asked the sentry at the gate for the CE (Chief Engineer) he probably had never heard of the CE but thought I said the C in C (Commander in Chief) and had directed me to the Holy of Holies, the Commander in Chief's residence. Only the C in C is entitled to fly the Union Jack on his car. All the very senior officers visiting or leaving his residence had seen was a black limousine flying the Union Jack and they had reacted accordingly. For a very senior officer to find himself standing stiffly to attention saluting a lieutenant in mistake for the C in C entails a serious loss of face not to be easily forgiven. I apologised and explained that I had been misdirected but this had little impression. What they were really after was the Union Jack which had fooled them in the first place. They insisted that it be removed at once. The poor Sikh taxi driver was equally mystified. He had put it on his taxi to show that he was on the side of the British Raj, after all they were the only ones who could afford his fares. Yet here was the cream of the military Raj demanding that he removed it. How could anyone understand such a perverse race. With a shrug of his shoulders he dutifully removed the flag that had caused the Sahibs to get so angry. He obviously did not understand why and I am not sure that I did, either.

Back to the sentry at the main gate where we made it clear that it was the CE and not the C in C that we were seeking. Fresh directions down a road in the opposite direction soon led us to a large notice, HQRE India Command or some such title fronted a long single story office block with a notice outside enumerating all the staff officers it contained from the Chief Engineer downwards.

Here at last I felt I was home and dry and could afford to pay off my faithful Sikh taxi or at least I hoped I could afford to pay him off. It made a large hole in my cash reserves, but was not unreasonable for the services he had rendered. I thanked him, tipped him all I could afford and staggered into HQRE with my precious Frames Pontoon Propulsion Unit MK I. I was a bit out of my depth when it came to who I should see to execute my mission. The building seemed to contain a bewildering assortment of appointments all titled by equally confusing abbreviations such as D.D.E.W., D.A.D.E.S. or D.A.D.E.E. etc. etc. I told my story to the W.A.A.C.I. (Women's Auxilliary Army Corps India) sergeant behind the window marked enquiries. She seemed equally confused by such an unusual request and appealed to a sapper quartermaster lurking behind a filing cabinet, "Oh Major so and so, in the D.A.D.E.S. office would be able to help you, sir, down the passage and eighth on the left." I parked my propulsion unit frame in his care and proceeded to the door marked D.A.D.E.S. with a feeling that my troubles were nearly over and the action was about to start. On my way down the passage I noted that the first door on the right was marked Chief Engineer.

I knocked on the door marked D.A.D.E.S. There was not a sound. I thought, 'Oh Lord, he's not in. More delay'. I knocked again, this time a tired voice said "Come". I entered and saluted smartly the major who sat writing behind the desk. He looked up briefly and having taken in my appearance and rank continued to write for what seemed like an interminable ten minutes.

While I stood there awaiting his attention I noticed that on the wall of his office was a large scale map of the Irrawaddy with all the deployment of our forces marked up on it, together with the location of all the

The author by the plinth at the base of the Company flagstaff, Bangkok.

Training exercise.
The descent from Pachma

The Battle of Kohima.
(Above) The Approach to Treasury Ridge.
(Below) The Approach to Jail Hill.

(Above) The Battle Trophy.
(Below) Elephant Bill's power units road building.

John Henslow with the de-horned sang he shot.

Gangaw after the USSAF so-called "Earthquake".

(Left) Jemadar Suryanarayana ("Suri")

ht) 421 Ind. Fd. Coy on parade in Bangkok.

(Left) The VCOs of 421 Ind.Fd. Coy. "Suri" in the back row, right.

Irrawaddy crossing. 1/4th Gurkha Rifles landing on B4 Beach, third wave.

Irrawaddy. *(Above)* A tank crossing on a class 60 raft.
(Below) The shuttle-service crossing from A Beach.

(Above) Pagan.
Schwezigon Pagoda built in 1077

(Left) Relaxation on the Irrawaddy.
The author momentarily supportin
'Tigger' Royle.

(Above)
The officers of 421 Ind. Fd. Coy. with the captured staff car and flags at Pagan Camp.
L to R:
Capt. Jock Meldrum, 2nd I/C;
Lt. T.G. Royle;
Major Anthony Dixon, O.C.;
Lt. de Souza, and VCOs.

(Left) The 'tight fit' bridge at Allanmyo.

Nawin Chaung.

(Above)
The jam of teak logs on the river.

(Right)
The buckled Bailey Bridge.

The solution.
(Far right, Above)
Cutting the top cord with oxyacetylene.

(Below)
An explosive charge cut the remaining girders.

Bangkok.
(Above)
Admiral Lord Mountbatten and the King of Thailand at the Victory Parade.
(Below)
A Japanese general bows before the Union Jack at the Surrender Ceremony.

The flood – journey by boat.

(Above) An island where the author spent the night.
(Below) The boat and the passengers.

The flood – journey by rail. *(Above)* The 'propulsion unit' exhibits a captured python.
(Below) The passengers on the bogey.

engineer stores dumps and bridging units. When I thought of the secrecy of all our movements in the last month to deceive the Japs into believing that the main IV Corps attack was being launched on Mandalay and how on our drive down the Kabaw valley no unit that could be traced to IV Corps was allowed to lead the advance for fear of alerting the Japanese Intelligence to the fact that both IV and 33 Corps were advancing down the west bank of the Irrawaddy for a surprise thrust into Central Burma, I was somewhat surprised to find all this vital and secret information displayed on the wall map of the D.A.D.E.S. Particularly as I had obtained access to his office without even being asked for my identity card at the main gates or anywhere else. At this moment the D.A.D.E.S. stopped writing and looked up and spoke. "What did you want? Please be brief as I am very busy".

Aware that he was deeply involved with the whole operation of the surprise assault crossing of the Irrawaddy by the 4th and 33rd Company I knew I was on home ground. I briefly described the reason for my being flown back and then out to Burma within a few days to enable tanks to be ferried across the Irrawaddy to support the master stroke thrust to Maiktila in Central Burma. He listened patiently. Having seen his wall map I realised that he was a key figure at the hub of operations and even if he had not had prior notice of my mission he would immediately grasp the vital necessity of its success. There was a long pause before he spoke. "Look old boy, you may not realise it but I have got to find 50 thousand bricks for a brigadier's mess by Thursday and you come in here expecting me to get you 16 pontoon propulsion unit frames made up without any authority whatsoever. Anyway, this is not a D.A.E.S. responsibility, it would come under the D.D.E.E. If you turn right when you leave this office you will find the D.D.E.E. third door on the right. Please close the door quietly as you leave". I stood for a moment hardly believing my ears. The D.A.D.E.S. never looked up again, but as he continued his writing he said, "Third door on the right". I felt desperate and said "Look here this is vital to the war effort, you must realise its importance." He never looked up but repeated, "Third door on the right". I retired seething and utterly mystified.

Obviously one had to know the staff procedure and I was not very sure of my ground. The third door on the right said D.D.E.E. I knocked and a sergeant opened the door. We saluted each other and he explained that the D.D.E.E. was on leave but he was his Chief Clerk and would do what he could to help. I explained my mission once again. He explained that Captain ..... was the Deputy Assistant to the Deputy Assistant Director of Engineer Equipment but he was sick. However, if I would care to call back on Thursday he would probably be back at work and would be able to advise me.

By now I was fast reaching the end of my tether. I had been flown back from Burma on a vital mission that could mean the success or failure of the main tactical plan for the conquest of Burma but no one was even interested, let alone prepared to help without the magical open sesame of a written authority which seemed to have been overlooked or mislaid by my superiors. A sense of frustration and desperation overwhelmed me.

Desperate situations call for desperate measures. I remembered the door marked Chief Engineer at the start of the passage leading to his assorted staff officers. I felt sure that if no one else was interested in the situation in Burma at least he must be. I also knew that I would not be allowed to get near him if I tried to do so through official channels. My only hope was to burst in on him before anyone could intervene to stop me. As a general he would have an outer office with a worker bee, on duty to prevent the intrusion of other worker bees into his presence. I decided on a surprise assault as my only option left. I gave a quick rap on the door and walked straight in. A charming young captain started the usual slow motion performance of finishing the vital sentence he was writing before even looking up. I took my chance and strode past him to the obvious door to the inner sanctum, gave a quick rap and without waiting for a reply entered and closed it behind me. The office was not very different from any of the others I had been in and out of, but at least it had a general sitting behind the desk. He did not seem outraged at my intrusion, only very slightly surprised. At least he looked up when I entered and did not ignore me while he finished whatever he was doing. I had decided on my approach before I entered. I saluted and said "I apologise for this intrusion, but I have been flown back from Burma and can get no response from any of your staff without written authority which has not been provided by 7th Ind. Division unless it has been signalled direct to you, Sir."

I briefly explained how we were poised to make the assault crossing of the Irrawaddy and how at the eleventh hour it was discovered that we had the Class 40/60 raft equipment and the propulsion units to power them but that the vital frames to fix the propulsion units to the rafts were lost on the L of C, and I had been flown to get duplicates manufactured in time for D day in a few days' time. He was more than understanding, though a little perplexed at the lack of official confirmation of the predicament I had been sent back to solve. But at least he was prepared to assist in any way he could. He wrote out a note to Lt. Col. White at the army base workshops indicating that the manufacture of these duplicate frames was to be given priority and he summoned his charming captain in the outer office to obtain transport for myself and my specimen propulsion unit frame to the army base workshop. He told me to contact the Officer I/C Workshops, Lt. Col. White, and hand him the note he had written. This would make sure that I got what I wanted. I was very impressed by his calm response that I had received by going to the top. He seemed to take it all in, though obviously he had had no notification of my mission. Still needled by the blank wall I had met from his staff, I added one more thing. I pointed out that I had got to his presence without anyone asking to see my identity card and that while waiting for attention in the office of his D.A.D.E.S. I had seen the whole secret deployment of our forces poised for the assault crossing of the Irrawaddy displayed on the wall maps in his office. "We have very strict measures to ensure secrecy up at the front and I find it very disturbing that I can see the whole secret battle order displayed on a wall map without anyone questioning my identity". I am sure the point went home, but he looked at my 6ft. 4ins. and said drily, "I doubt if anyone would suspect you of being a Jap spy".

I had made my point and got what I needed – authority with the C.E.'s signature and transport to the base workshops. Within minutes a 15 cwt. truck arrived. My propulsion unit frame was loaded and I was off to the base workshops. I felt I had at last made the breakthrough and that from now on all would be plain sailing.

We arrived at HQ base workshops just as the O.C., Lt. Col. White, was emerging from his office and about to go home. Full of new found confidence I handed him the authority from the CE and explained my mission. He read the note like Nero with the flames of Rome licking his boots. "Not a hope, old boy. We are on a run of auxilliary bridging equipment and I can't stop the production line on the authority of a note from the CE. Who does he think he is?" My heart fell at his attitude. I tried to explain the situation, but he was unimpressed. "Everyone thinks that their requirement is priority. I decide what is the real priority and you have not a chance". I pointed out the CE's signature. He was still unimpressed. Then he said "Who is your CRE?" "Colonel Wright" I replied. "Not old Tom Wright?" "Yes", I replied. "Oh, that's different. I was at the shop with Tom. O.K. I'll do it but you tell old Tom that Col. White did it as a favour for him".

He shouted something and a Chinese technician appeared. He showed him the frame, discussed a few technicalities of setting a jig for its production and the time it would take for 16 copies to be run off. Eventually it was agreed they would be ready by 1500 hrs. tomorrow. His 2nd I/C would arrange accommodation for me at the mess and would provide transport for the frames to Dum Dum Airport as soon as they were ready. His parting words were, "Don't forget to tell Tom Wright that Col. White did it as a favour for him. I owe him a favour from the past. Goodnight". And he was gone in a cloud of dust. It seemed a funny way to run a war, but at least I was getting somewhere at last.

Next morning I watched the very efficient production line that was producing the frames. It was geared for mass production and once set up could have made a hundred frames in no time at all. True to his word, all was ready by 1500 hrs. except that the paint was still tacky on the frames. A 15 cwt. truck was ready as promised and the frames were loaded and we were on our way to Dum Dum Airport within minutes. I never saw the OC base workshops again after our initial meeting but at least I was now on the home run with my mission successfully completed, or so I thought.

When we arrived at Dum Dum Airport I was once again out of my depth. With no staff training I had no idea who to approach in the RAF for a special plane to fly my precious cargo back into Burma. Nor had the RAF.

In fact, it soon became clear that once again without some written authority no one was able or even interested in providing an aeroplane to fly a scruffy engineer lieutenant with 16 antique bed frames into Burma. The situation was not helped by the fact that it was Saturday and they were all more concerned with getting away for the bright lights of Calcutta for the weekend than listening to some mad story about vital equipment for Burma. After all if it was that vital there would be some special authority or it would be in charge of someone more senior than a sapper lieutenant. I tried everyone but no one would take me seriously. In every case their No. 1 priority was some girl in Calcutta and I was passed from one staff officer to another like a foundling that had just been brought in and nobody wanted to have anything to do with it.

One by one the officers in charge of movements in one form or another slipped away leaving a staff sergeant on duty just in case something brewed up that could not be ignored before Monday morning. It became very clear I was not in that category. In fact I was left in no doubt that without some 'Authority' I would still be ignored on Monday morning.

To have got this far, to have the frames manufactured and ready to load at Dum Dum Airport, only to be faced with this last seemingly insurmountable obstacle was unbearable. I was seething with frustration and pent up emotion at my own inadequacies. I had a feeling that it was my lack of staff training that denied the knowledge of how to handle the situation. I was confused and very bitter at the way I had been sent out to India by my divisional staff without the necessary backing authority that they must have known was essential if I was to have any chance of carrying out such a mission. I was equally bitter at all those staff officers living in their remote and comfortable world where

I thought that they would be focusing all their efforts in supporting the vital war effort and the great assault into Burma. After all that was what they were all there for, yet in reality they did not seem to give it a thought. It was bricks for a brigadier's mess, training equipment and their weekend off in Calcutta that dominated their world. They did not want to be involved with the realities of a war that was 600 miles away, and if I had no authority to command their co-operation so much the better. I could safely be ignored and their date in Calcutta could take priority.

Strangely enough it was a date in Calcutta that proved my salvation. As Dum Dum Airport denuded itself of staff and authority on Saturday night, I wandered around like a lost and desperate soul. In doing so I found another lost and desperate soul. An American pilot who had been stood up by his girl friend in Calcutta. We had a drink together while he told me his troubles and I explained mine. To me it just started as a meeting with someone to whom I could unburden my problems and listen to his extramarital problems.

He was a Yankee pilot who flew Dakota's over the hump with supplies to China. He had a girl friend in Calcutta who for some reason or another had stood him up for this weekend and he was left with 24 hours at a loose end with nothing better to do than lick his wounds, and get sloshed in the bar. Fortunately, I met him before he had got very far in this process. At heart he was a man of action and not that happy with his job. He assured me that very little of the tons of military supplies they flew over the hump into China was ever going to be used to fight our war. Not on our side at any rate. He told me that most of the supplies were rolled away to secret dumps in the hills to build up reserves for their internal conflict with the Communist Kuomin Tang. Another third was actually sold to the Japs to raise funds for their internal conflict and what was left with luck would find its way into the Chinese troops fighting in the North of Burma. As he put it, "Old vinegar Joe (General Joe Stilwell) is a hell of a tough cookie, but he has met his match with those Chinese boys. They supply the minimum of troops to get the maximum of support from Uncle Sam and most of what we fly in will never be used in Burma except by the Japs".

His disillusionment in the realities of his own mission seemed to generate his interest in mine. On his side they were flying in vast quantities of store and equipment with little effect on the reconquest of Burma because of its deceitful misdirection by the Chinese. On my side we were poised to assault into the heart of Burma and the whole operation was in jeopardy because I could not get a few vital pieces of equipment flown in. "Jesus, it just don't make sense", he exploded. "Look Buddy, I've got my Dakota parked outside and no freight order for tomorrow.

If I can shake out Hank, my navigator, you're on Buddy, OK?"

I could not believe my ears. Was he really offering to fly me in without any authority or had I misunderstood what he was saying. Before I could say anything he was on his feet and with a "Wait here Buddy, I'll be back", he was gone in search of his navigator. I waited for half an hour, drinking and wondering if a miracle was about to take place or whether I was the victim of a screwy American practical joke. As time passed I became more convinced that it was the latter. After all if our own air force could not lift a finger to help supply their own forces in Burma without official authority, why the hell should the American air force do it without even greater staff authority. I wondered if I had been a Yank lieutenant seeking help from the RAF to fly a load into China whether they would have done it without the signature of the Supremo. I certainly could not envisage a British flight lieutenant making his own decision to fly me in under similar circumstances. I realised the absurdity of the situation and was about to leave for my bed to think up a last resort strategy for tomorrow when my Yankee pilot returned followed by a very tired and dishevelled Hank, his navigator.

I was introduced to Hank who had obviously been pulled out of his bed and did not share his pilot's enthusiasm for rest day working on odd jobs for their British allies. However, he had a large map under his arm of some unfamiliar scale like 16 miles to the inch, which we spread out on the table. Apparently they wanted me to pinpoint the airstrip that they would have to fly into. As the airstrip which I had been ordered to return to was not completed when I left I only knew that it was somewhere near Myitche on the banks of the Irrawaddy. We eventually found Myitche but I had no idea where the airstrip had been constructed and anyway Myitchie seemed, on that scale of map, almost on the crossing site. However, this did not seem to worry my American friends. They assured me that if it was recently constructed they would have little difficulty in spotting it from the air once they had found the locality. That was no problem. If I would be at the south east corner of the airfield at 7 a.m. tomorrow morning with my load of equipment they would be there and ready to fly it in, and if we all helped load and unload they should be back in Calcutta in time for lunch. It was as simple as that. They would get a few hours' rest in the afternoon before resuming flying stores over the hump into China the next day. I could not grasp how simple it seemed in their eyes for I was used to the tortuous land L of C from Calcutta that would take the best part of a week to negotiate, but to them it was a morning's work, as the crow flies a mere 550 miles. Two hours' flying time and no one would even notice their absence.

Brought up in the strict administration disciplines of the British Army this was like fairyland to me, but under the circumstances only a fairy godmother was going to get these vital propulsion unit frames to the banks of the Irrawaddy in time, and this American pilot was without doubt a fairy godmother. We arranged to meet where his Dakota was parked at 0700 tomorrow. I stood the last round of drinks and found I could not pay for it. My incidental expenses such as a taxi to Barrackpore and a night at the Grand Hotel had devoured the meagre stock of rupees I had brought with me. There was not much need for rupees in Burma and it was fortunate that I had some left over from my last leave in India. I felt very ashamed to have to explain this to my new found American friends. However, it seemed to delight them. "Do you mean to say that your British Army send you back to get vital equipment for the Irrawaddy crossing and expect you to pay your own expenses? Gee, I was told you limeys were tight-fisted, but that beats everything. Say, who is going to pay for the Dak's gas tomorrow if you are skint?" I was about to say that I was sure that it could be adjusted when I got back to my Division but it was obvious from their laughter that the very thought of one ally paying the other for their services to each other in the war effort was the most crazy idea they had heard so far. "OK John, (we were on Christian name terms by now) time to get some shut eye. 7 o'clock on the tarmac tomorrow morning and mind you have a fat roll of rupees with you to pay for the gas".

They retired to their quarters shaking with laughter at this final joke. I retired to the truck lent by the base workshops and squeezed myself and my bedroll in beside the frames in the back. The driver was already asleep across the front seats.

I awoke early next morning. My driver had already found the Indian cookhouse and produced a mug of hot, sweet tea. I told him to be ready to load our cargo at 0700 hours and scuttled off to the mess for a quick breakfast where I thought I might find my Yankee friends, but the place was almost deserted, it was Sunday morning. I began to have doubts. Perhaps it was just a leg-pull on the limeys. I still could not believe that even an American pilot could fly a sortie into Burma as a favour for a friend he had just met in the bar. Certainly not without some clearance from his command structure and some authorisation from above. It just did not make sense, without some control their pilots would be flying all over India at weekends to date up with past girl friends. The more I thought about it the more convinced I became that I had been taken for a ride. That I was young and green must have stuck out a mile. Steve and Hank were probably ground staff with a warped sense of humour. They had probably fallen out of their beds laughing last night at the thought of anyone so naive as to believe that they would hitch a lift to Burma. I was very depressed for I felt I was back at square one and it was Sunday. My chances of getting anyone to listen to me, let alone authorise my flight, were nil before Monday morning. I reckoned it was already about D – 3.

The clock on the mess wall showed ten to seven. I snapped out of my depressing speculations. At least I must make the rendezvous, for to fail to do so and discover later that they were genuine would be unforgiveable. Anyway, apart from making a complete fool of myself I had nothing to lose.

I found my truck and driver ready to go and we set off around the airfield perimeter heading for the south east corner. Airfields do not seem to have corners when you drive around the perimeter at 7 a.m. They just seem to go on and on curving gently one way then the other. Certainly there was no lack of Dakotas. Every bend and bay was occupied by their familiar form but they all stood dead and deserted in the morning light. "Which one, Sahib?" enquired my driver. I wish I had asked Steve for his registration number, but I had not, so I said "Just keep driving on slowly and look out for any signs of life or an open loading door". "Teak hai Sahib" and he immediately started to accelerate. Before I could summon up the Urdu for "I said go slowly", I saw what he had seen, a Dakota with its loading doors open and two figures standing beside it. As we drew up to it there was no mistaking the two figures were Steve and Hank.

"Hi, John, what kept you?" shouted Steve. I was so overwhelmed to discover that my fairy godmother was real and standing there waiting by his Dakota with open door that I leapt out of the truck, rushed over to him and started shaking him warmly by the hand. My overwhelming feeling of relief must have been written all over my face. "Say, John, you didn't think we were going to let you down, did you? Hey, Hank, I reckon John thought we were two-timing him. Well what do you know? That'll be another drink he owes us".

He saw the embarrassment and anxiety in my face. "OK, forget it, just our little joke. Come on, let's get loaded and away. Back her up to the doors, you pass 'em up and we'll load and lash them". We did so and the driver and I passed the frames up to the open loading doors and Steve and Hank took them and stacked them inside. After the sixteen frames were loaded and lashed down Steve turned to me and said, "OK now, let's have this vital equipment you've been talking about". I said "That's it Steve". "What? That load of old iron! Jesus, you boys must be desperate!"

I thanked the driver and dismissed him. We closed the loading doors and while Hank removed various chocks and safety straps Steve took me forward to the cockpit. On the way he stopped opposite a bundle of dirty coloured haversacks. "If things to wrong there's your parachute, but don't jump before I give the word". Next moment we were in the pilot's cabin and Steve's casual air changed dramatically. Switches were tumbling, the engines stumbled into life, and the wireless was crackling. Steve was requesting clearance for take-off. Instructions were coming back on the weather and windspeeds as if the whole operation had been authorised and cleared from the word go. We taxied over to the approach runway and joined the short queue of other aircraft. We were soon at the head of the queue and on the runway with the pretake-off revving of the engines and flapping of controls. Next moment we got the OK from the control tower and surged forward as the brakes were released. A few moments later I realised we were airborne and on our way. My troubles were over, thanks to the U.S. 14th Army Air Corps, or at least two of its members.

To start with, the great Delta of the Ganges with its varied branching waterways passed beneath us. This gave way to open sea, the northern tip of the Bay of Bengal. Then Hank shouted above the engine noise that Chittagong should be coming up somewhere off our port side. Certainly land was coming into view and I realised it must be the Arakan, the scene of 7 Ind. Division's first major encounter with the Japs. I realised that approaching at this angle we must soon fly over Jap held territory. I went over to Hank to get a pinpoint on our position but to my surprise he was not plotting our course but gazing at a large scale map on his knees.

"Hi, John, in half an hour we should spot the Irrawaddy then if you can locate us on this map we'll work our way up or down until we spot Myitche, OK? Better go and join Steve, after all he's steering."

I suddenly realised that apart from setting our original course, navigation was no more than map reading our way in from the air, until we hit the unmistakable Irrawaddy, and I was supposed to recognise our point of contact and direct them in. It was not quite what I understood aircraft navigation to be. When the broad blue band of the Irrawaddy came up on our horizon it was unmistakable, but where we had hit it was far from unmistakable to me. I had never set eyes on it before except as a broad blue band on the edge of our maps. Steve turned to me and shouted "OK, John, do you recognise it, where are we?" I had not the faintest idea but hoped that its distinctive shapes of bends and sandbanks could be matched up with something on their map. However, this was not so easy for the sandbanks change every year and bore no resemblance to anything on the map. Then we spotted a line of trucks with their plumes of dust moving along the west bank below us.

"Could be your boys," said Steve. "Let's take a look". With which we banked steeply and dived down. There was something odd about the trucks. Not being used to aerial views I could not place it at once, then suddenly I realised that they did not have the encircled white star on their bonnets for aircraft recognition that all allied vehicles had to display to avoid being strafed by their own planes. "Look out, they are Japs" I shouted. I need not have bothered for Steve had spotted the difference probably before I had and was pulling out of his dive almost before I had spoken. "Too right they are. Wish we had something to drop on them". We were over them in a flash and climbing again as I spotted some ineffective tracer bullets climbing the sky behind us. "That means we are too far south, you will have to head north until we can recognise some landmark. We should be able to see the Yaw Chaung (a sizeable river joining the west side of the Irrawaddy) and Myitche should be on the next right hand bend". We gazed down at the landscape unfolding beneath us and to my relief the Yaw Chaung, or what I hoped was the Yaw Chaung, came into view. Then out to our right we saw vast pagodas rising out of the dry plain to the east. Even at this height they were huge and impressive, but at that time I had never heard of the ruined city of Pagan. All I wanted was to find the airstrip that had been constructed at Sinthe, just to the west of Myitche. Then I saw the right hand bend in the river that I had been looking for with great sandbanks shining in the morning sun. I shouted to Steve "That looks like the bend we are looking for. Myitche should be almost on the bend and let's hope the airstrip will be somewhere to the west of it".

Steve raised his thumb in reply and altered course to the west. He spotted the strip before I did, and banked first one way and then the other to line up with it. Then the engines throttled back as he came up to it losing height fast. I thought, 'My God, he'll never make it'. He sensed my anxiety. "OK John, I'm not landing, just taking a good look". He flew about a hundred feet down the runway waggling his wings. "There were several Jeeps scurrying about below and various other vehicles driving along the edge of the runway. A bulldozer was still working at one end pushing down palm trees. This time all the vehicles had big white encircled stars on their bonnets. At the end of the runway he opened his throttles and we lifted up over the palm trees. "We'll get down OK, but it's a bit tight for get off", said Steve. "I wouldn't like to lift off with a full load, but we should be OK empty. OK I'm going in this time. Hold tight, it looks a bit rough". We circled round and started to skim over the tree tops as the runway appeared again, dropped fast as the engines throttled right back. It was a bit rough as we hit the ground but with one bounce we were down and braking to a standstill barely halfway down the runway in a cloud of dust. As we came to a halt at the edge of the runway I saw an assortment of vehicles converging on us.

I turned to Steve and Hank. "I doubt if you chaps will ever be properly thanked for what you have done but believe me without your help I would still be tearing my hair out at Dum Dum Airport, and in two days' time a lot of senior officers would be tearing their hair out here. If all goes well with our crossing you will hear it on the news, and know that but for your help it could well have failed". I felt I was sounding a little pompous but in fact it was true, though probably no one would ever know it, and anyway they had saved my bacon for if I had remained stuck in Calcutta and the crossing had failed for lack of tanks, John Henslow would have been a ready-made scapegoat and he knew it.

"Think nothing of it, John", Steve replied. "Hank and I have enjoyed working with you. You're doing a real job and it's a sight better than working for the bastard Chinese. Next time you're back in Calcutta look us up and we'll have a real night out". At this point the engines died as they switched off. We went back and opened the loading doors. There to my surprise was the CRE's Jeep with the CRE and my OC on board. They could not have been warned of our arrival that was for sure, but no doubt they had been inspecting the airstrip construction at the time of our arrival. I clambered down and went over to them.

Saluting the CRE I said with some pride "We have the 16 propulsion unit frames on board but I only managed to get them thanks to these American pilots". I had expected some recognition of what I had been through to be back with my mission completed, but that was not quite the reception I received. All I got was "Good show, what kept you so long?" from the CRE, followed by "Get them off-loaded onto that 15 cwt. truck and sent off to the Field Park Company, who have been waiting for them for the last 24 hours". Next moment they were gone in a cloud of dust.

I would have liked to have pointed out that if they had done their job properly and signalled back the necessary authority I would have had a less frustrating time and would have been back 24 hours earlier. They were lucky to see me or their precious frames at all. In fact, but for Steve and Hank they would still be sitting at Dum Dum Airport. I realised it was pointless to say anything. It was D – 3 and they had plenty on their minds. I had solved one problem for them but there were plenty more yet to be sorted out and this was no time for post-mortems.

After we had off-loaded the frames, I thanked Steve and Hank as best I could. They were less put out than I was at the lack of appreciation that had been accorded them for saving the day. They just said "Think nothing of it, John. It's been a pleasure to work with you boys and the best of luck with your crossing". Then Steve said, "I don't like your runway; can we get onto that road over there?" He pointed to the tarmac road that ran along one side of the runway. 'What's wrong with the runway?" I asked. "It's all right for a supply drop or to land but in this heat if we don't lift fast on take-off there are a lot of trees in our path". I saw what he meant. The bulldozers were still removing them but if anything went wrong on take-off that was it. You either just cleared the palm trees or you did not. Steve decided the road was a better bet. The Dakota taxied down the runway then swung off at the end and on to the road. It was not very wide but at least was clear ahead and straight for a mile. Fortunately, at that moment there was no traffic on it either. He turned the slight bend at that end and having lined himself up opened his engines and surged down the road for lift-off and a moment later he was just a speck in the sky.

CHAPTER 13

The Fatal Change of Plan

I returned to my company position to catch up on what had been happening in my absence. I discovered that everyone thought I had been having a holiday in Calcutta while they had been sweating their guts out on last minute training. "You lucky sod, John, no wonder you took so long. Screwing some WAACI in the Grand Hotel right up to the last moment, I suppose. Some chaps have all the lucky breaks". I could see that I had no receptive audience for the truth here, so I said "Well somebody has got to keep their morale up. It's pretty tough back in Calcutta but I shall need a couple of days excused all duties to recover. You chaps don't know how lucky you are, all this clean healthy living. You've no idea what I've been through for my King and Country". "Kuntry yes, but leave the King out of it" someone shouted.

At that moment Major Tony Dixon, our OC, came in and the conversation became more serious. He explained that he had just attended a briefing at Div. HQ and all was set for the crossing in two days' time. A composite Engineer Assault Company was to be formed consisting of four sections of outboard motor drivers, each of three field companies in the divisions providing one section of OBM drivers together with its officer and jemadar. Tigger Royle would command 421 Company's section, Lt. Steve Goodall would be in charge of 62 Fd. Company's section, Lt. 'Pinky' Murdoch that of 77 Fd. Company and Lt. Lieson that of 331 Field Park Company. Lt. John Henslow would be in overall command of this OBM Assault Company. This latter appointment took me by surprise as I was the one officer who had been withdrawn from the assault craft training at Zahaw to fly back to Calcutta. However, that was the CRE's decision and I had to get on with it. It did not really make much difference. I had seen enough of the training and rehearsals in their early stages to know the limitations of the craft and the outboard motors that had to power them. I had mostly missed the training with the infantry battalion selected to make the initial assault crossing, the 4/15 Punjab Regt. This could have put me at a disadvantage as they were not from my brigade and I did not know the officers very well. However, as it turned out this made little difference on the day due to last minute changes in the order of battle.

The remainder of the company would be involved in building and operating rafts to take over as soon as the initial assault had established a bridgehead and the rafting of vehicles, guns and tanks could commence.

The OC then went on to explain the outline plan for the crossing. The site was by no means ideal. The direct and shortest crossing to Nyaungu could not be used until a firm bridgehead had been established. This was because our west bank approach was over a large expanse of soft sand to the river bank. This would eventually be done and would become the main crossing point known as A beach. On the other bank to the N.E. of Nyaungu just up stream of the town was high ground that formed cliffs at the river bank. These cliffs were intersected with narrow re-entrants with small sand beaches. This had been chosen as the site for the initial assault. Firstly because the high ground on top of these cliffs dominated both Nyaungu and all the river approaches to it and therefore had to be captured before the other crossing sites could be used. Further, the cliffs and the re-entrants afforded some cover for infantry if they were pinned down on the beaches. I am not sure whether it was known at the time, but the cliffs were also riddled with caves that had openings half-way up the cliffs. These afforded perfect machine gun positions for the Japs and commanded a field of fire over most of the river where we would be crossing. This site for the initial assault was named B beach.

The only point where there was a reasonably covered approach to the banks on our side was 1½ miles up stream. This site was chosen as it would enable us to conceal our preparations for the assault crossing to maintain an element of surprise. It was coded C beach and was also chosen as the site for the construction of Class 40/60 pontoon rafts for tanks. The theory being that heavy bridging lorries with Bailey bridging equipment and pontoons could drive up to the river's edge at this point under the cover of darkness. It can be seen from my sketch map of the crossing site that there is also a B beach on our side, directly opposite the B beach on the enemy side.

The plan was that the initial surprise assault would be launched into C beach on our side to B beach on the enemy bank. Having landed the infantry assault troops, the boats would return to B beach on our side to pick up the next wave of assault troops. The reasons for this were that it would take too long to battle up against the river current back to C beach and anyway once the initial assault had taken place the advantage of surprise was over and the shortest route for a quick turnround was the next priority. Finally once the town of Nyaungu was taken and the approach road to A beach completed this would become the main crossing site, though tanks would still cross from C beach where they would not churn up approach roads for vehicles and the strong Irrawaddy current would help their long oblique crossing when fully loaded.

So this was it at last. As we dispersed to get on with organising the task ahead, it was with mixed feelings of excitement and speculation on what sort of a reception we would get in about 40 hours' time.

I went off with Tony Dixon to HQRE for a briefing on the final composition of the OBM assault company and my responsibilities as its commander. The CRE was a very busy man at this stage of the operations. My meeting with him was very brief. He actually smiled and called me by my Christian name. I felt my shares were moving up in the world. "Well, John, you have an important part to play in the assault crossing. Make sure you have it well organised. You will be under command of the assaulting battalion for the actual crossing. Bill Baker, my adjutant, will give you all the details you need to know. You should attend Brigadier Collingwood's special O group briefing at 3 o'clock. Oh, and by the way, it has been decided that the South Lancs will be making the initial assault not the 4/15 Punjabs, you will need to liaise with them. Good luck". And that was it. He departed with Tony Dixon and I was left standing speechless at the bombshell he had so casually dropped at the end.

I turned to Bill Baker who sat smiling behind his desk. Bill Baker was always smiling secretly to himself as though he had just seen the funny side of the worst of situations. He generally had. "Why the hell have they switched to the South Lancs, Bill? Why train for nearly ten days with the 4/15 Punjabs and then change to the South Lancs at the eleventh hour? They haven't even seen the equipment they will be using, let alone had any practice in using it?" "Ah", said Bill, "I gather someone higher up on the staff has had a brilliant idea; prestige. Intelligence does not expect too much opposition and it would be good for morale and papers back home if the initial assault was made by a British battalion. Then someone discovered that the South Lancs made the initial assault on Madagascar so they became the obvious choice. Don't ask me why they did not think of this a fortnight ago. What is more Madagascar was an assault landing, not quite the same as an assault crossing. There they were driven ashore by the Navy in LCTs. They will find things a bit different in a MK III assault boat. However, those are the unalterable facts. Here are the details that concern you".

He then gave me the detailed breakdown of the composite assault company engineers, as it now appeared to be named, also the boats that had been allocated for our use together with the outboard motors. As it happens I still have the notes I made at that briefing 34 years ago. They are pencilled into a little black loose-leaf book that I carried as an aide-memoire. Here they are, exactly as they were written in at the time.

ASSAULT COY ENG.

Coy Cmdr		**Lt. Henslow RE**
Coy Jem		**Jem Suryanarayana**
A Group	Cmdr	**Lt. Goodall RE**
36 Fd. Sdn	1 NCO	12 men
62 Fd. Coy	2 NCO	12 men
421 Fd. Coy	—	6 men
B Group	Cmdr	**Lt. Murdoch RE**
70 Coy	1 NCO	6 men
77 Coy	2 NCO	24 men
C Group	Cmdr	**Lt. Royle RE**
421 Coy	3 NCO	30 men
D Group	Cmdr	**Lt. Lieson RE**
60 Coy	1 NCO	8 men
421 Coy	1 NCO	12 men
331 Coy	1 NCO	10 men

This shows that each group consisted of its officer, 3 NCO's and 30 sappers. However, it also shows that it was even more composite than I had remembered. 62, 77, 421 and 331 were all Fd. Coys in 7 Ind. Div. which leaves 36 Fd. Sqn. 70 + 60 Coys who were also represented and must have come from the engineer units of 17 Ind. Div. who were to assist in the crossing.

On the back of this page in my notebook was recorded the number of boats and OBM's available for the assault crossing.

Assault Bt, Mk. III		30
Folding Boat Equipment		27
	4/	57
		14 + 1
OBM 9.8 hp		49
22 hp	8	
		57

		4 Groups		Asslt Mk III	F.B.E.		
12	9.8 hp	A	8–2 =	6	6	2	22 hp
12	9.8	B	8–2 =	6	6	2	22 hp
12	9.8	C	7–3 =	4	7	2	22 hp
13	9.8	D	7–2 =	5	7	1	22 hp

30 Assault MK III   26 FBE

1 FBE Self + 22 hp OBM

Then came a list of men in my own platoon noted down by their army numbers (we never knew them by name only the last two numbers of their army number).

It was headed by 2 NCO's then the remark   8 best drivers
                                            8 others

Which was then detailed into two columns of their numbers, one headed 1st Drivers the other 2nd Drivers.
Finally I had written

Drivers   Screwdriver
             Adj. Spanner

    I do not remember why under the 4 groups listed of assault boats MK III I had written '8–2 = 6' etc. but suspect this was a later adjustment of the figures when at the last moment a number of these rather delicate canvas-sided assault boats were found to be unserviceable.
    "You will get the final plan of the crossing at Brig. Collingwood's briefing this afternoon but here are the details you need to know from the Engineer's Plan. You must have your assault company formed up here under cover before it gets dark. After dark white tapes will be laid across the open ground to your harbour area near the river's edge. Here the actual assault company can relax while the rest of the troops are carrying forward the boats and motors. They will launch them and fit on the motors and group them under your direction.
    "One company of the South Lancs will be making a silent assault with the paddles, leaving at about midnight and aiming for the high ground to the east of B beach. You will follow with the remainder of the battalion in a powered crossing at 0500 hrs. which has been timed so that you will arrive off the beaches just as it is getting light and you will take the

infantry into whichever beach the infantry company commander indicates. The S.A.S. will have special troops crossing in the dark on floating surf-boards. One of their tasks is to place special shaded lights on the beaches to guide you in. When you start from C beach you have to pass down a fairly narrow channel between our bank and the vast sandbank that you can see on these air photographs. You will have to travel the best part of a mile downstream before you clear this sandbank and can start heading towards enemy B beach. Whatever happens you must avoid running aground on this sandbank but once again the S.A.S. should have placed a shaded red light at the tip. Once you pass that you should be safe to start your approach to the enemy beaches.

"Once you have put the infantry ashore your chaps must turn round and head back as far as you can for B beach on our side. Just here". Bill indicated a spot on the aerial photograph with the tip of his pencil. Apart from the fact that it was just upstream of another sandbank on our side and roughly opposite B beach on the other side, there was not much to mark it. It worried me that with nothing definite to aim for and nearly a mile of open water to cross we could well arrive back at the wrong spot and delay the second wave. I mentioned this possibility to Bill but he just said "You will have to do the best you can. Oh, and I nearly forgot some genius in G plans has arranged for a Harvard to be flying overhead at 05.15 hrs to drown the noise of the approaching outboard motors and ensure that the Japs are taken by surprise". A Harvard was a single radial engined American training plane. As far as I knew its only outstanding merit was that it was about the noisiest aeroplane ever invented. "Oh my God" I said. "All that will do is ensure that every Jap in the area is fully awake and ready to receive us. What could raise their suspicions more than an outdated American trainer wheeling over the Irrawaddy at 05.15 hrs? Whose side are G plans on anyway?" "I know how you feel" said Bill. "But if you are successful in spite of his contribution, he will probably get an O.B.E. and if you fail because of it neither of you will get a mention". I did not guess how prophetic his jest was at the time. "If there is anything more you want to know I'll do my best but I have told you about all I know. You have a lot to organise and not much time to do it in. I would see your group commanders and get all that side of it organised, attend Brig. Collingwood's O Group, then see the South Lancs to button up the organisation for the crossing".

My mind was seething with the thought of what I had to get organised and the short time that I had left to do it in. It was D – 1 and within 15 hours I would be off across that vast expanse of water and only God knew what would be in store at the other side.

"Don't look so worried", said Bill. "I'm sure you will manage very well. If you succeeded against the staff at army group in Barrackpore you should not find the Japs much of a problem". "But what on earth made the CRE choose me to command the assault company?" I said. "I was not even there for most of the training". "Oh, I think he thought the same. If you could succeed against the odds in Calcutta you would have no problem with a little job like this". Bill was smiling enigmatically again. There was no time to say all I would have liked to have said about that so I just said "I hope he will feel the same way at this time tomorrow". And left to have a quick conference with my group commanders.

Though I could not see why I should have been chosen to command the Assault Company, the other officers, at least half of them were senior to me, showed no resentment. We were all pretty close friends, all of the same rank, so it was a friendly and down to earth conference. I explained the details of the crossing plans that concerned them and how they were to organise their group of drivers. They would have two drivers to each boat. Our chief worry was the unreliability of the performance of the outboard motors. We had to make the initial assault over 1½ miles of water in darkness yet had to arrive together at the enemy beaches at first light.

I had devised a plan to minimise the effect of motor failure and the varying performance of the OBM engines, particularly as some were twice the horsepower of others. I explained that the infantry would be instructed to make the crossing in groups of 3 boats and they would hold these boats together by gripping the gunnels of the boat next to them. In this way if one engine faltered or failed it would be sustained by the other two engines until the group was within striking distance of the opposite shore. This way they would at least arrive together and in an organised formation. If they came under fire they could let go and separate and those that had lost power could use their paddles to cover the last 100 yards. This was a technique we had practised with the 4/15 Punjabs but no one was very happy about the last minute switch to the South Lancs. They were even less happy about the idea of having a Harvard flying overhead to drown the noise of our engines.

I left them organising their groups and departed to attend Brigadier Collingwood's final briefing. When I got there, once again I found myself seriously outranked. The brigadier was there with his blackboard and charts surrounded by a group of commanders whose lowest denomination was a major. It may seem strange but your rank was the one thing that distinguished you. It was displayed on your epaulettes for all to see, and it naturally indicated some degree of your importance and responsibility in the operation. With the two pips of a lieutenant on your shoulder no one could accept that you had a very vital part to play and you were treated accordingly. I listened to the exposé of the grand plan for the assault crossing from the back of the circle of officers.

The plan was for one company of the South Lancs Regiment to carry out a silent crossing using paddles, starting from C beach at 3.45 a.m. and occupying B3 and B4 beaches and the high ground between them.

Special boats section and sea reconnaissance unit detachments were to carry out a final reconnaissance of the far bank after dark and report whether the beaches appeared to be occupied. Further detachments were to follow and mark the beaches and the end of the sandbanks with screened lights to guide the powered craft carrying the rest of the South Lancashires, due to arrive on the far bank at 5.30 a.m. He briefly mentioned the Harvard which would be endeavouring to mask the noise of the powered craft. He also explained that the 2nd South Lancs Regiment had been put under command of 33 Brigade for the crossing because of their past experience in combined operations and that they would be making the initial assault. The 4/15 Punjabs would now be assembled at B beach on the home bank ready to follow up on the second wave, pass through the base established by the South Lancs and commence to form the brigade bridgehead.

The rest of the briefing was concerned with the build-up of the bridgehead from B beach and the priorities for vehicles and ammunition etc. that would cross on class 9 rafts to be constructed and operated from B beach until A beach became operative. When it came to any questions there was a short burst of queries from the regimental commanders' mostly concerning communication procedures once they were established on the far side. I was desperately unhappy about the way the actual initial assault seemed to be taken for granted, but while I was wondering how I could chip in to make them aware of the problems that could arise from the combination of antiquated equipment and a last minute switch to assault troops that had had no opportunity to gain experience of the type of equipment they were going to use, I realised that the moment had passed. The brigade commander was launched into his final exhortation of wishing us luck and extolling his confidence in us to uphold the traditions of the 7th Indian Division and add the success of the crossing tomorrow to its Battle Honours.

I looked around for Lt. Col. Mitchell, the CO of the South Lancs, but he had already disappeared. As they were the key to the success of the crossing tomorrow I set off to find where they were encamped.

This was not so easy. When a division has just moved into a new area no one is very sure where anyone is. I kept asking likely informants for their positions and got the usual number of misdirections before I finally located them. Even then in a large area of palm trees, trucks and troops, no one seemed to know where any of the officers could be found at that time. Eventually I found them seated on a fallen palm tree attending their 'O' Group.

I approached and respectfully saluted but though I was tall and the CO was facing me he did not seem to notice me. I stood there awaiting the chance to be recognised and given the opportunity to explain the essential details of which I thought they had no prior experience. They would need to know that each group of assault boats consisted of a mixture of MK III assault boats and folding boats, also just how many men each sort of boat would hold. More important still, that if their organisational groups were to have any chance of arriving at the enemy beaches intact, they must instruct their troops to hold their boats together over the first mile of the crossing or risk being completely dispersed by the vagaries of current, outboard motor performance and navigation of uncharted water in total darkness.

It became obvious that my presence was not going to be recognised by the CO unless I forced it upon him; I stepped through the audience of officers and placed myself between him and his audience announcing who I was and why I was there. At least this interrupted the procedure and for a moment I thought I had a chance of achieving the necessary liaison that was so essential in my mind if we were to succeed tomorrow morning. However, my hopes were short lived. I was informed politely but firmly that they were not concerned with the actual crossing. The organisation for this was in the hands of their beachmaster who was not present. This 'O' Group was only concerned with tactical problems after their arrival on the enemy beaches. If I had any problems about the organisation of the crossing itself I should contact their beachmaster who would be available at C Beach and would sort out any problems that I might have. I would have no difficulty in recognising him, as he had a boil on the back of his neck which necessitated him wearing a white bandage around his neck which would show up well in the dark. If I would now leave them they would be able to continue their deliberation on the problems of capturing and establishing the bridgehead. I felt somewhat rebuffed. It was not what I had expected at all. It was more as if they regarded the engineer assault group as a taxi service for their use on the crossing. I tried once more by pointing out that it would be a bit late to start marching their company strength to our grouping of boats until after it was dark, particularly as two types of craft in use had different troop capacities and what is more there were not enough 22 hp OBM's to power all the heavier folding boats so that some would have a much slower performance when loaded. The CO held up his hand like a policeman stopping the traffic. "Look laddie, I have told you that our beachmaster has all this in hand, if you have any problems he is the chap to see. Now we have a busy day tomorrow and a lot to arrange this evening. Will you kindly let us get on with it".

That was plain enough. I withdrew conscious of the bemused expression on some of his officers' faces. I was not sure what to do next, there were not many hours of daylight left. If I went back to the CRE's office I could only report my failure to achieve any worthwhile liaison with the assaulting infantry. A situation they could do little to alter at that late hour. It seemed that my only hope was their elusive beachmaster. With luck we would be in the forward assembly area for some time before H hour and could sort out the matching of his assault grouping to ours. It struck me that four groups, each under an officer, must have been designed originally to accommodate the infantry assault groups and the infantry must be well aware of how many boats each group contained. Only they could not know the proportion of folding boats and assault craft in each group as I had arranged that myself to give a roughly even distribution between the groups. It would not be impossible to alter the strengths of the groups at the eleventh hour but in the dark a lot of time could be wasted.

Possibly I was worrying unnecessarily. I have forgotten the name of their beachmaster, but he was a major and no doubt had the experience that qualified him for the job. As there was nothing I could do until we met on C Beach in the early hours I decided to concentrate on my own job.

When I got back to my company area I found Captain Wilkins waiting for me. He was the 2nd I/C of one of the other engineer companies and known as Wilkie. He explained that he did not seem to have any allotted task for the crossing and had come along to see if there was anything he could do to help. When time is running out on you it often does not help to have people offering their help as it only distracts you from getting on with the job.

However, there was one niggling anxiety at the back of my mind, and that was our return to the home bank B beach after we landed the South Lancs on the other side. It occurred to me that if Wilkie had nothing better to do he could help us identify the spot we had to home in to on the return journey. "Look Wilkie," I said. "If you can find the right spot on our B Beach where we have to return to to pick up the second assault battalion and wave something that we can see over half a mile of water, it will give us something visible to steer towards, for I fancy at that distance one bit of bank will be indistinguishable from all the rest in the early morning light". We discussed various visual aids. It had to be fairly large to be seen and of a colour we could pick out against the dull green and yellow background. In the end we had to settle for what he could lay his hands on. He owned a large white bathtowel, a strange luxury in the jungle, but his mother had insisted he take it with him, and he used it as an underblanket in his bedroll. Here at last was a justification for having brought it all this way to Burma. So that was settled, when he saw us returning from the far side he would wave his bathtowel as a beacon for us to home in on. He departed, happy that he had some definite part to play in the assault crossing.

I departed to organise the assault company, give them last minute directions (such as the fact that Wilkie's bathtowel would identify our new landing point on the return journey) and get them ready for the move up to the rear assembly area before nightfall.

By the time the shadows were lengthening we were all ready to start the first moves in tomorrow's great adventure. We set off for the rear assembly area where we would rest under cover before the cloak of darkness would allow us to move forward over the open ground that separated us from the water's edge. The rear assembly area was the last area of palm trees, scrub and cover before the expanse of open ground that bordered the Irrawaddy shore. In front of us stretched two or three hundred yards of open, flat, cultivated ground covered in rows of peanuts, so we discovered later. This gave way to a final approach area of sandbank sculptured into shallow dunes that terminated in a long, flat sandy beach. This was C Beach.

When we arrived at the rear assembly area it was like Piccadilly Circus. Troops were converging from every direction – on foot, of course, for vehicles would raise tell-tale dust plumes to give our movements away. The harbour area officer allocated everyone their allotted area where they settled down to await the darkness that would cover the advance to the river bank. Darkness comes quickly in those latitudes but once it was dark we still had to wait for the tape parties to lay the white tapes over the sand that we all had to follow in the dark to arrive at our forward assembly areas.

With nightfall there came a marked drop in temperature and the wind started to increase quite noticeably. Eventually the order came to start the move forward to the advance assembly area. The count down to H hour had started.

We started off, each group of outboard motor drivers led by his officer in a silent single file. Somewhere off to our left we could hear other troops moving forward, just the soft clinking of equipment and the occasional muffled curse. There was no moon but the white tapes showed up clearly and eventually led us on to the soft sands of the sandbank that heralded the approach to the river. Our tapes ended in a large depression in the sand and ahead of us I could just make out the dark line of the water's edge. Here I decided was the right spot to rest up until it was time to board the assault craft. It was in easy reach of the shore and as we had nothing to do until the assault craft were launched, the men could rest slightly sheltered from the wind if they huddled down under the edges of the depression. It was not yet midnight so we had several hours of waiting ahead of us.

Once they had settled in I went forward with the other officers to have a look at the riverbank. The site was ideal, a long straight beach backed by a strip of firm flat sand about twenty yards wide. The drop from this beach to the water was only about two feet. It could not be better except there was no sign of any assault craft. We did however find a small party of sappers from 331 Field Park Company whose job it was to launch the boats when they arrived. We learnt from them that the bridging lorries loaded with the assault craft and the pontoons and Bailey bridging equipment for the tank rafts had gone down to their axles in soft sand three-quarters of a mile back. They were being off-loaded and parties were being organised to carry them forward to the beaches. I explained to the officer in charge of launching the craft the way they should be grouped and hoped this would not require any desperate reorganisation when I checked the grouping requirements with the South Lancs beachmaster. But there was no sign of him at this time. I looked in vain for an officer with a white bandage around his neck but with no success. I wondered whether possibly he had had a penicillin injection and now only sported a piece of sticky plaster on his boil. That would be fatal. I might never find him, thanks to the wonder of modern medicine.

We returned to our forward assembly area to hold a last instruction meeting. The South Lancs were an unknown factor. We had trained with the 4/15 Punjabs who our drivers knew and could at least understand each other in the lingua franca of Urdu. I doubted if many of the South Lancs would know sufficient Urdu to have any worthwhile communication with our drivers. Some of them would understand a little basic English such as left and right, but in the heat of battle would the English soldiers confine their instructions to basic English? I thought they probably would, but not the basic English that my Indians would understand. I reminded them of the importance of holding the gunnels of the craft together until they were across the river and I explained how I had arranged for Capt. Wilkins to be waving a white towel on B Beach as a guide in for our return journey.

We still had several hours to wait before H hour. Activity in the darkness beyond us was mounting as the contents of the bridging lorries were transported forward by manpower. The night became loaded with grunts and hoarse exhortations as carrying parties staggered through the soft sand towards the beach laden with assault craft, motors, pontoons and Bailey panels. Occasionally a piece of human propelled equipment would wander off course and at one moment six grunting and sweating Sikhs practically fell on us as they staggered right through our assembly area with their Bailey bridge panel. It was a wonderful achievement of endurance and muscle power.

When I revisited the beach for the second time it was all activity. Most of the craft were in the water and the men were busy fixing in the outboard motors. Unfortunately, not all the assault craft had survived the journey. The sturdier folding boats were all right, but several of the canvas sided assault boats were already half full of water and were not going to make the 2000 yards crossing that lay ahead. Then I spotted what I was really looking for. A dark figure by the water's edge with a white bandage round his neck. I homed in on the South Lancs beachmaster and introduced myself. He did not have that aura of confidence that I had been led to expect. I told him how the engineer assault company was divided into four equal groups and asked him if this would fit the operational grouping of the assault companies of his battalion. He did not seem very sure about this nor did he know how many there were in each group. He had assumed that when they fell in on the beach we would produce sufficient craft for the requirements of each group. Apart from the first company that would be crossing silently with paddles there would be three other companies making the powered crossing plus the reserve company which included cooks and regimental police for signposting and controlling the bridgehead. He suggested that we would have to adjust the assault craft allocation when his battalion arrived on the beach to embark. He too seemed to have assumed that the Engineer Assault Company was a sort of taxi rank that would produce taxis as required at the time of embarkation. I tried to explain that there was a very limited assortment of craft available and that it needed a combined effort if his battalion was going to arrive at the other side in any semblance of predestined order.

However, his mind was preoccupied at that time with the first silent assault for it was now H – 2 and time for the company that was going to paddle silently across in the night to be preparing to embark. This was his first responsibility and I let him get on with it. He promised to come back to me once they were on their way. About half an hour later I saw the first company of the South Lancs glide by under paddle power. They seemed to be making quite a good pace without much effort with their paddles which showed that there was a strong current running once you got away from the shore. As they were swallowed by the night I could see that they were already having difficulty in keeping together.

There was no sign of the beachmaster but our craft were all in the water with their engines mounted and being fuelled. I found the officer in charge of the launching operation and we checked that the boats were grouped according to the allocation for each assault group. We also checked as far as possible that they were all seaworthy and contained paddles in case their motors failed. Time was getting on and there was still no sign of the beachmaster. I decided that as the boats were ready I would go back and bring forward the assault craft drivers so that they could be allocated to their craft in good time before the infantry came forward. Their long wait huddled up in the dark and cold thinking about what lay ahead was doing their morale no good and they were only too glad to be on their feet and doing something. When we got to the beach I assigned each officer to his group of boats and let them get on with allocating them to their drivers. I was glad to see that the beachmaster had reappeared so I went over to him to continue where we had left off an hour ago.

He still did not seem too clear about the strength of the assault companies but I did my best to impress on him how many man he could get into a MK III assault boat and how many into a folding boat. I also explained that the men should be instructed to hold the boats together in groups of three by gripping the gunnels together with their hands so that if an engine failed on one of the boats it would remain under power from the other two boats until it was within reasonable paddling distance of the enemy beaches. Somehow I sensed that he was not prepared for this shoestring equipment. He had been expecting something rather different. He began to look a very worried man. However, before he had a chance to say what was on his mind his CO appeared with the news that the battalion was moving forward to the beach.

Shadows appeared in the background which resolved into columns of soldiers being fell in along the beach. They were checked, split into groups, hoarse whispers of "Where was Sergeant So and So. Where? Well he ought to be down this end". Suddenly everyone seemed to be asking questions, told to shut up then told where they ought to be and so it went on, and so did the time when we should have been ready to set off. Some boats had to be taken from one group and given to another to adjust to the different strength of the infantry companies. At last the first company were ordered to embark but it was not done in a very orderly manner. Because of the different capacities of the two types of assault craft the beachmaster went down the line counting off 17 men for a folding boat and ten for a MK III assault, whichever the next boat down the line happened to be, and detailed each lot to his respective boat. This in itself was slow enough but worse was to come. The boats were moored in a long line with their stern against the bank. This was done partly because it is easier to embark over the stern and partly so that once their outboards were started they could be released straight out into the river without the confusion of forty odd craft having to turn about in a confined space.

To my horror I saw that the first man over the stern, instead of moving up to the front of the boat, crouched down at the stern and the next man followed his example so that the last man had to laboriously clamber over all his companions and their equipment to reach the last place left in the boat up at the sharp end. I found it hard to believe that even without training they would choose such a cumbersome way to get on board. I picked on one boat filling in this manner and directed the first man in to move right up to the front. I felt their own officers and NCO's should be doing this but it was not easy to identify them in the dark where they all looked alike. Possibly they had removed their badges of rank as it was known that Japs were trained to pick off the officers first if they got the chance. It soon became obvious why they were loading in this manner. The night was filled with muffled curses – "Move up you bastard". "Not 'F' ing likely, you've got a bloody Bren gun. It's your place up front". "Look out where you're putting your bloody feet". "Well budge up then". "Not bloody likely – I'm not going to be the silly fucker up front". And so it went on. To add to the chaos came the cry of "Here, our fucking boat's sinking". And there was no doubt that it was. With the weight of the men on board a slit in the canvas that had been above the waterline had become below the waterline and it was filling fast with water. I had kept my own boat in reserve for such an eventuality and had it worked into position to get them reloaded. All this took time.

CHAPTER 14

Irrawaddy Assault Crossing – Failure and Success

We were still loading the last company when the CRE arrived. He was obviously worried that the crossing had not started for it was now after 0500 hrs. and there was a distinct lightening of the darkness in the east. He made no attempt to contact either myself or the officer commanding the South Lancs, or so it seemed, for the first I was aware of his presence was his voice coming from the right of the line of boats which were all loaded awaiting the signal to be off. "Why have you not started, it's after H hour? Shuru Kirna, Jow, Jow, Jaldi". Such instructions from the CRE were not to be disputed by the sapper drivers. They sprang to life and the next moment engines were spluttering into life and they started to cast off and were away. I do not know whether he spoke to the engineer officer in charge of that group, Lt. 'Pinky' Murdoch, or not, for he did not survive the crossing. I am sure that the CRE was unaware that he had set off the reserve company which comprised regimental police, cooks and the like who now found themselves launched at the head of the assault.

Fortunately, however, he set off a chain-reaction that swept down the line of boats and the last group of boats were loaded with twice the speed of the others. Some engines sprang to life at the first pull of the starting cord and surged out into the stream, others were more reluctant and took several attempts before they spluttered and choked into faltering propulsion.

I shouted at the occupants to hold their boats together by the gunnels, but the South Lancs did not seem to understand, they just squatted in their boats looking grim and determined. I hoped they realised that they were squatting on the paddles which would be their only means of propulsion if their engines failed. I hung back with my own boat to see them all away, confident that with my 22 hp motor I could catch up with the other craft. I was conscious that I had detected the familiar snarl of the Harvard trainer just before the CRE had started off the first assault craft and the darkness was fast giving way to the luminosity of first light. This assault was going to be too late to gain anything from surprise. If the Japs could not hear our outboard motors yet, they certainly must have been alerted by the noise of a lone Harvard whirling overhead.

The stiffish breeze made the water a bit choppy, and as the light increased I could see a long, scattered trail of boats ahead. This was it, we were going in and it had to succeed, but instead of arriving off the enemy shore just as the veil of darkness was lifting in a tight formation we were becoming more and more visible and more and more strung out. I ordered my driver to open up to full throttle and we started to overhaul the boats ahead. Most of them were making steady progress though with a mile of water in front of us at times they hardly seemed to be moving against such a vast background of water. I could see one boat some way ahead of us that was in difficulty, for the driver was repeatedly winding the starting rope and pulling. As I passed the boat astern of it I throttled back and shouted to the driver to run along side it and assist it with a tow until it got its motor restarted. The "Tik hai Sahib" that came back above the noise of our engines assured me that he knew what to do and we opened throttle to try and catch up with the leading formation. Not that there was much formation. Just an endless stream of small craft ahead as far as the light allowed one to see.

My jemadar, Suri, I had kept with me in my command boat for I felt that under the possible stress of battle the lingua franca of Urdu might not get through to some of the drivers and if things became a bit tense and complicated he could shout instructions in Tamil over the noise of the outboards, that would get a quicker response than my limited Urdu to a driver with possibly even more limited Urdu.

By now it was more than first light. The end of the great sand bank that we had to pass before we could start steering east to cross to the other side was easily discernible. I never noticed whether it had a shaded red light on its point for we now needed no such navigational aids. It was daylight and I could just discern the enemy beaches on the far side and our leading assault craft appeared to be opposite the beaches.

As it got lighter I could see a bright orange umbrella on top of the cliffs at the easternmost end of the enemy B beach. With a feeling of elation I knew what this meant. It meant that the first silent assault by the company of the South Lancs had succeeded. They were established on the other side and the orange umbrella was a signal to our own aircraft to avoid them. The increasing light intensity and diminishing distance also made it clearer that our own assault was not going according to plan. Instead of going into the beaches the leading assault craft appeared to be circling in front of them. As I drew closer I could hear the rattle of enemy machine-gun fire and see the line of white plumes of spray as the bullets swept across the water. Some of the boats were within 200 yards of the beaches but instead of moving into the beaches they were circling round in a large arc back into the middle of the river. It seemed madness for they were all such vulnerable targets while they gyrated on the water, small relatively slow moving craft packed tight with men being sprayed with machine-gun fire from the cliffs. I steered into the middle of this vortex to try and find out what had happened. As I came alongside the first boat I yelled "Why aren't you going in? What the hell are you doing?" A row of blank faces stared back at me from below their steel helmets. "Where are your officers?" I yelled. A sergeant raised his hands to indicate he had no idea. I passed on to the next nearest boat and came right alongside it. "Are there any officers aboard?" I enquired. "No sir", came the reply. "Where are they?". They did not know. "Why aren't you going into the beaches?" "We were told to follow the boat in front of us".

    I told my driver to move up to the next boat which seemed to be heading back to the home bank. I could see other boats that had drifted further downstream in the swift current. They would have difficulty in getting back to the beaches against the current. Some of them looked badly shot up and were just drifting down on the current slowly spinning without any sign of propulsion. As I approached the next boat I looked back at the boat we had just left about 50 yards astern. As I did so I saw a line of white splashes arc right through it. It held course for a moment then started to spin slowly and drift downstream. As I came alongside the next boat the answers to my questions were the same. There were no officers aboard. They did not know where they were and they were just following the boat in front. I ordered the driver to head upstream and hold course. I asked the sergeant in charge why he was heading away from the beaches and why he had not gone in when they first approached them. "We are the reserve company, sir. We arrived opposite the beach first so we did a chucka round to let the assault companies catch up but when they came they just followed us round. It's a real 'F' up, sir." How right he was.

    As I looked around it was all confusion. There were still boats quite close to the beaches but because the boat ahead of them had not gone in they had followed it. My heart sank as I looked at the chaos of the great IV Corps assault crossing. If only one boat had had the initiative to go into the beaches the ones behind might have followed instead they were all milling around following the leader, and there was no leader. They were following their tail. The absurdity was that they were a sitting target on the water and their best chance of survival would have been to go straight into the beaches where there was cover from the withering machine-gun fire coming from the top of the cliffs.

    The chaos slowly resolved itself into an assault back to the home beaches. One moment they were circling in mid-stream then the next they were all making for B beach on the home side. The assault crossing had failed beyond redemption. As more and more boats headed back one could see the number of casualties who, for one reason or another, were incapable of going anywhere. They drifted down on the current and became the sole target for the Jap machine-guns. Whether it was just engine failure or whether they had been too badly shot up by the plunging machine-gun fire from the cliffs will never be known. But as they drifted downsteam they came under fire from machine-guns sited on the beaches at Nyaungu; firing across the top of the water their effect was far more deadly than the plunging fire from the cliffs. There were few survivors from these boats when they were recovered later.

With a depressing sense of failure I followed them back to B beach. It seemed incredible that they had been so close to the enemy beaches and had failed to land and now they were making a concerted power assault back onto the home B beach. It was not until some time later at the enquiry held into the failure of the first assault that I learnt the reason for this orderly assault back onto the home beach. While circling around one of the South Lancs had spotted a white flag being waved from the home bank. He immediately took it to be a signal of surrender and headed back to it. The rest of the confused craft were only too keen to follow. I realised that the white flag was Wilkie waving his outsize bath towel as a marker for the returning boats to home in on. He was a bit surprised to see that the returning boats were still full of assault troops. However, at least they came back to the right spot where the second wave of assault troops, the 4/15 Punjabs, were waiting and ready to take over.

As we grounded in shallow water off the shore, I learnt what demoralisation really looked like. The second that their craft beached the occupants rose to their feet, stepped overboard and just walked away. I never heard a word spoken. With their heads hung low they walked up the beach and over the sandbank out of sight. They knew they had failed but did not know why. They might have understood why if they had stopped to watch the second attempt.

As the South Lancs walked up the beach an assortment of officers came pounding down it; my own OC, Tony Dixon, the CRE, I believe was amongst them plus various other staff officers. They all looked pretty grim. This was no time for a post-mortem. My O.C. quickly briefed me that the 4/15 Punjabs were ready and waiting behind the sand dunes. That as soon as we could regroup and be ready we would make a second attempt.

"And this time you bloody well see that you go into the beaches whatever else happend. This time you will have artillery and air support. Just keep going, they will lift the barrage when they see you are off the beaches. How soon can you be ready?" I knew that grounding in the shallows a number of the outboard motors had broken shear pins that would have to be replaced and they would all need refuelling if they were to get there and back. In fact, I could see the RIEME support team were already hard at work doing just this.

At this moment a row of tanks which had appeared over the sand dunes opened up with their guns and their shells and started registering on the far side. Within moments other artillery out of sight began registering on the cliffs where the Jap machine-gun positions were located. Thanks to the efficiency of the RIEME, shear pins were replaced, petrol tanks topped up and even faltering motors were replaced. As soon as all our boats were ready and turned round facing the opposite shore I turned to signal that we were ready, but I need not have bothered. An orderly formation of 4/15 Punjabs were already advancing across the sands towards us. This time there was no question of groups of assault craft each under an officer. Two of my officers, Lt. Murdoch and Lt. Goodall, were missing. I told Lt. Royle and Lt. Lieson that we would load as many men as we could and that I would lead them across to B4 beach which was closest to the ground held by the one company of the South Lancs, whose silent night assault was established on the other side. I impressed on them that at all costs boats must be held together in groups of three until the last moment.

The 4/15 Punjabs marched down like something from a military display, straight into the water and out the twenty yards to the assault craft. They barely broke step to enter the boats and squat down as they had been trained to do. I raised my arm and lowered it forward to point at the enemy beaches. The outboard motors were started and we were off. By now the air was full of the thunder of high explosives being rained down on the opposite shore from tanks and artillery. Then the Mitchells Thunderbolt fighter bomber planes swept in over our heads to deliver all their armament on the opposing beaches.

The effect on our morale cannot be underestimated. Our first assault had failed through lack of organisation, but in the first assault we were like sitting ducks being shot up by an enemy we could not see and with no fire support from our own side. This second attempt was completely different. The cliffs ahead of us were erupting with exploding shells and bombs. The scream of Thunderbolts dive-bombing the enemy position not only gave us confidence, but stimulated our morale for we felt that this time we had the power and support of an army corps behind us where on the first time we had felt isolated and exposed with no apparent support from our own side.

I headed for B4 beach where I could see the orange umbrella on the cliff tops and wondered what that lone isolated company of the South

Sketch Map of
THE IRRAWADDY CROSSING AT NYAUNGU

Silent Night Crossing by one coy of South Lancs ····>····>··
Abortive Powered Assault by remainder South Lancs -->--->--
Successful Assault Crossing by 4/15 Punjabis → ···→ ···→ ··
Main Crossing when bridgehead established A Beach x - x - x - x

Lancs must be thinking. For they must have witnessed the failure of their battalion to land and reinforce them. They must have watched them retreat to the far shore and must have felt pretty isolated in their small company position on the enemy bank after the first assault had failed.

We progressed across the river as planned in groups of 3 boats held together. The bombardment of the beaches did not seem to be lifting as we approached so I steered for the most upstream point where we could land.

Even here shell splinters could be clearly seen cutting the water ahead of us. At least they were random and not aimed as on the previous occasion. In fact I was not conscious of any enemy fire directed at us. We were practically on the beach when we grounded on a hidden sand bar. We were within twenty yards of the beach and stuck. I leapt overboard myself and was joined by the second driver; between us we pushed the boat off the tongue of the submersed sand. Next moment the water was up to our armpits and a moment later we were nose on to the beach and the infantry were off and running up the short sandy beach that formed a re-entrant between the cliffs. The assault craft behind must have seen our grounding and came in below us without difficulty. There was no opposing fire on the beach and we delivered our troops and turned around in a matter of minutes. This time we were heading back for B beach as empty craft for the next wave as planned. We were over the hump and the assault crossing was away at last.

The supporting fire from the artillery and tanks together with the low level bombing by Thunderbolts was moving downstream and concentrating on the town of Nyaungu. Just the sight of all that explosive force being delivered onto the enemy side probably did more for our moral than it did in the way of inflicting damage on the enemy. But when you were out in the middle of no man's land or rather no man's water, feeling like a sitting duck as you approached the enemy side it made a great deal of difference. I could not help wondering if the South Lancs had had that visible support, whether they might not have gone on into the beaches in spite of the inversion of their order of battle.

When we arrived back at B beach the next wave of infantry was waiting on the shore. We cut our engines before we reached the shallows we now knew about, and there was no delay to renew broken shear pins this time. They waded out to us and were aboard with the minimum of delay. Within minutes we were heading back for the beaches. From now on I never saw those threatening little spouts of water arching towards us as they had done in the first assault. Now we knew that the assault crossing we had trained for was going to succeed. All that mattered was to get as many troops across into the bridgehead as was humanly possible before darkness heralded the end of D Day. I even remembered the camera around my neck and photographed the second wave as they moved up the beaches.

I do not remember how many subsequent crossings we made for now it really had become a taxi service and we were soon to be joined by the Class 9 rafts ferrying Jeeps and artillery across. It was gathering momentum at last but we knew that before long the Japs would counter-attack to try and destroy our bridgehead. Everything depended on reinforcing the bridgehead so that it could withstand the inevitable counter-attack that was bound to come.

My immediate task was over. I no longer felt that there was any point in my leading the crossings in for they were now just operating a shuttle service. The second drivers took over and the first drivers got a chance to break off for a cup of tea. I wandered off to inspect the home beach head and the progress towards establishing 'A' beach as the main crossing point.

On my way to 'A' beach a little further down stream I discovered a small re-entrant in the vast sandbar that formed our beach. This re-entrant, like a small forgotten harbour, was full of boats recovered from the initial assault. They were the boats that had drifted downstream while circling off the enemy beaches in the first assault, and had drifted into the Jap machine-gun fire at water level off the Nyaungu beaches. They were a very sad sight for the boats were packed with dead soldiers. No doubt the wounded had been removed and now the dead just lay there forgotten, lying in the boats until the fortunes of battle were decided and time could be found to attend to the dead. It was a pathetic sight. They were mostly South Lancs, but here and there I recognised an OBM driver from my own assault company. Somewhere amongst them must have been the body of Lt. Murdoch but at that time I did not know for sure that he had been killed. I just knew that he and Lt. Goodall were missing.

Later I learnt that Pinky Murdoch had died in the assault and that Lt. Goodall had been shot through the wrist and his craft sunk, but that he and the commander of the South Lancs had managed to swim back to our shore. Steve Goodall was cited for the M.C. by Lt. Col. Mitchell who had been forced to swim back with him. It was as far as I know the only decoration awarded for the assault crossing. (Steve Goodall, on reading this through 30 years later, has corrected me in that one of his OBM drivers was awarded the I.D.S.M.)

At the time I just looked at all the dead bodies in this quiet little harbour and wondered why they had had to die. On the second attempt, with artillery and air support, we had not sustained a single casualty as far as I was aware. In my own mind the fault lay chiefly in the last minute decision to switch the initial assault troops from the 4/15 Punjabs, who had trained with us for the crossing, to the South Lancs who had had no training for this type of operation, and I suspect had never even seen a MK III assault boat before they were ordered to step into one in the dark on C beach.

The reasons for this unfortunate tactical blunder seemed to have been influenced by two misconceived ideas. In the first place someone on the staff had failed to appreciate the difference between an assault landing from the sea in large landing craft (L.C.T.'s) driven from troop ships straight onto the beaches by the Navy, and an assault river crossing in small canvas sided craft only capable of holding a dozen men and their equipment, each independently powered and directed. Once the crossing was under way there could be little communication between the assault craft and its independent command would resolve on the senior man aboard, possibly a lance corporal. Whereas in an assault landing from the sea each LCT would be capable of holding at least a complete company of assault troops with their officers and NCO's formed up and protected by the steel landing ramps until they grounded on the beaches.

It was the fact that the South Lancs had experience of this latter type of assault landing on the beaches of Madagascar, which had been an unopposed landing, that had influenced someone on the staff to make this last minute fateful switch. No wonder the South Lancs CO had regarded the actual crossing as of little concern to him and at his 'O' Group was only occupied with his plans from the moment they landed on the enemy beaches. From his past experience this was when his responsibility started. Even he could not grasp the difference between an assault landing at sea and an assault river crossing. Add to this the daunting fact that this was to be the longest assault river crossing ever made in any theatre of war, and one begins to see the magnitude of this blunder.

There were, I understand, two other factors that influenced this fateful decision. The first was that intelligence reports indicated that there would be little opposition as Nyaungu was mostly garrisoned by INA troops, and secondly there was the natural desire to have this unique crossing made by British rather than Indian troops to enhance interest and reporting in the British press at home. I could understand how both these factors might be considered but they never should have outweighed the facts and allowed such a hazardous crossing to be so unwisely transferred from the troops that had been trained for the task, restricted as that training was, to troops who were not only untrained but whose previous experience would in fact impair their judgment of the difficulties that they would have to be prepared for on the assault crossing.

I wondered what the enemy must have thought about that first attempt, for it must have been pretty confusing for them to be woken up by the noise of an American Harvard trainer plane wheeling overhead in the early hours of first light. Then as the shades of night gave way to morning light they would have seen the great expanse of the Irrawaddy before them speckled with dozens of loaded assault craft set deep in the water under their load of tightly packed infantry. They would now hear the distant burr of the outboard motors and see the haze of blue smoke from their exhausts.

They would suddenly realise that this was their hour. Their quiet sector had without any pre-warning been chosen for an assault crossing by the enemy. They would have seen over fifty assault craft converging towards their beaches. They would have known the inadequacy of their resources to match such a major assault.

There would be no time to rearrange their defences, they would scramble to their machine-gun posts in the cliffs and start firing at this armada of assault craft in the hope that they could inflict the maximum of casualties before it landed on their beaches and gained the natural cover of the many small re-entrants in the cliffs that dominated the water.

They must have been astounded when the leading craft, within 100 yards of the beaches turned back and started to circle round in front of them instead of going into the beaches where they would have soon disappeared from their field of fire and been home and dry for the moment. To the enemy this must have been an inexplicable miracle. For at the moment when all seemed lost, the assault troops had chosen not to land on the beaches but to circle right in front of their field of fire. You do not dispute such gifts you just exploit them, and that is just what the Japs did. It was manna from heaven, for it seemed that having got within easy reach of their machine-guns the assault troops were determined to prolong their vulnerability. Even more extraordinary must have been the sight of this armada changing course and heading back for their own beaches.

To the Japs this must have been the most inexplicable action of all. To their thinking such actions would be inconceivable. They could see only too well what casualties they had inflicted on the approaching assault craft and they could see that they were by no means sufficient to warrant the enemy withdrawing from their attack. They must have thought it strange that we should attempt such an assault without any covering fire. They must have deduced that the whole operation could only be explained as a diversion attack and that the real assault must be taking place elsewhere. What other conclusion could be rationally deduced from such an extraordinary manoeuvre.

I wandered on across the sand bar until I found fresh activity in the form of sappers laying a mixture of army track and P.S.P. to form a road across the sand to what was to become A beach. They were having their own problems in the soft sand. They asked me how the crossing was going and I told them what I knew and left them to struggle on in the sand. Like everyone else they had to work hard to complete their part of the crossing plan on time.

Back at B beach the shadows were getting longer. Now the crossing was really a taxi service. Assault craft, folding boats, and class 9 rafts were everywhere plying back and forth across the Irrawaddy. It looked more like a motorised regatta than an assault crossing. By night fall three battalions had been ferried across plus a large assortment of vehicles, guns and supporting stores. I was relieved to learn that we were not going to continue through the night. The first day's target had been achieved and the risk of night ferrying across such a vast expanse of water was not thought to be worth the risk of losses that could occur through unseen engine failures allowing rafts to carry away downstream.

As the last craft crept back in the first shade of night, I arranged for them to be pulled out of the water and posted sentries to guard against any enemy sabotage parties in the night, or even an unexpected rise in water level that might carry them away in the night. This was all done through the intermediary of Jemadar Suri. He was quick and efficient and full of enthusiasm at the day's eventual success. He called out my driver who was parked under the nearest cover some way off and told him "Sahib, you must take some proper food and a rest. You cannot have slept since yesterday night". I realised that it must have been at least 36 hours since I had slept and was beginning to feel like it. "I don't think you can have done much better yourself, Jemadar Suri", I replied "but I could do with a good meal right now". The jemadar just smiled from ear to ear and said "That will be waiting for everyone as soon as they get back to the company positions".

He was right, for when my Jeep arrived I was soon back with the company and big dishes of steaming rice and curry were moving in every direction. I found officers were already eating and discussing the day's events between mouthfuls. Everyone looked a bit bleary-eyed. The OC gave a quick resumé of tomorrow's tasks and the state of the battle in the bridgehead. Then we all turned in to catch up with our sleep while we had the chance. So ended the most important and the longest day in the campaign to retake Burma.

Next day, D + 1 the ferries started at first light and continued non-stop until nightfall. It gave me a personal sense of satisfaction when early in the morning before the night mist had been burnt off the river by the sun's strengthening rays, I saw the first of the Class 60 tank rafts emerge from the mist on its voyage from C beach under full power of its four propulsion units and home into its landing site on B beach. I thought of the struggle I had had in Calcutta to get those propulsion unit frames made and flown into Burma in time for this great moment. I also wondered what would have happened if I had failed in my mission. I have no doubt they would have got those tanks across somehow for the sappers are great improvisers, but the inevitable delay could have had serious repercussions on the 'masterstroke' thrust to Meiktila.

Later in the day I took a photograph of one of these tank rafts making the crossing. It gives a good illustration of the great width of the Irrawaddy at this crossing point.

On the morning of this second day the South Lancs were ferried across. I wondered what their thoughts were on this second attempt to cross over. They seemed very quiet and subdued this time.

All resistance in the immediate vicinity of the bridgehead was virtually over. A number of Japs had gone to ground in a complex system of catacombs and, as they would not surrender, a party of sappers blew in the entrances to these caves and sealed them in permanently. By nightfall the village of Nyaungu was taken and we got ready to bring A beach into operation the following day.

D + 2 (16th February). This turned out to be one of the busiest days of the crossing. Everyone wanted to get across. The more troops that crossed, the more stores had to be ferried as well to keep them supplied. A beach became like Epsom Downs on Derby Day. A mass of beachmasters and crossing controlling officers had materialised from the staff of two divisions and a corps headquarters. At first it took them a little time to realise that the sappers were operating the ferries and were a law unto themselves. At this stage the corps commander decided to cross 17 Ind. Div. so as not to delay their thrust through the bridgehead to Meiktila. This increased the pressure on the ferries that were now operating from both B and A beaches. The sappers, tired as they were, managed to rise to the demands of the situation and increased their crossing turn round from 45 minutes to 30 minutes.

D + 3. The endless procession of men, vehicles and stores arriving to cross continued all day. It was like cleaning out the Aegian Stables, as fast as you ferried across one lot the next lot were always waiting on your return. The strain was beginning to tell on both men and machines, but the heady spirit of success drove everybody on to a supreme effort to ensure that it was reinforced. We were all very conscious that for some inexplicable reason the Japanese counterattack had not yet materialised. Meanwhile the more troops and supplies we could get over into the bridgehead the less chances of success it would have when it came. After four days of crossing without any visible response from the enemy we had all become a little forgetful of their presence.

That evening as I was making one of many crossings, I was watching an empty tank raft churning its way back upstream to C beach. Further upstream beyond it I could make out one of our Hurricanes flying low over the water coming down river towards us. Then something seemed to fall from the plane as it swept over the raft, and that something exploded. Too late, I realised that this was no Hurricane, but a Jap Zero. Next moment it was overhead and its red roundals clearly visible on its wings. It was followed by another. But this did nothing except follow the leading plane in a steep bank over the cliffs of the crossing site and disappear from view and that was it. The stricken raft seemed to be maintaining course and though we all kept a keen eye on the sky from then on there was no further threat from the sky, though our own fighters suddenly became very busy over the crossing site which gave a few anxious moments for those of us who were none too confident on aircraft recognition. I heard later that one bomb had hit one of the rafts, four pontoons and blown it to matchwood, killing one sapper and wounding two. (Tony Dixon informed me 30 years later that in fact whatever the Zero dropped it did not hit the raft or explode, but fell close to the raft sending up a plume of water. In the confusion one man fell overboard and was never recovered. No one else was hurt nor was the raft damaged. At the time they were in fact experimenting with the use of a DUWK to propel the raft. A nice example of the distortion of the truth which so often happens in wartime).

It was later deduced that these Zero's had been carrying out a mission against one of the crossings higher up the river and had come across our crossing on their return journey quite by chance. But it seems hard to believe that one of the biggest crossings of the lot was still unknown to the Japs after four days of continuous operation!

However, our own failures had not been ignored. Shortly after the success of the crossing was established there was an official enquiry. I was sent for by the G.I. Ops. at Div. HQ. As commander of the Assault Company Engineers I was asked for my opinion on the reasons for the failure of the first assault. I gathered the South Lancs were still putting the blame on the failure and breakdown of many of the outboard motors. This I could not agree to and was very outspoken on all the factors that I saw as being the true reason for failure of the South Lancs to get across. In particular, I pointed out that they could not blame engine failure, for the majority of their boats made a very good powered assault back on to their own side and the same outboard motors had been used for the second attempt by the 4/15 Punjabs, with complete success. I sensed that my outspokeness somewhat embarrassed the G.I. He mumbled something about having to be very careful when the reputation of a British regiment was at stake, thanked me for my evidence and politely dismissed me. I do not know what conclusions his enquiry recorded but Brigadier Collingwood, who had responsibility of command for the assault crossing, was posted back to India two weeks later, which may or may not have been a reflection on his part in deciding to change the initial assault troops at the last moment.

I have always felt that the mistakes and failures of military operations should be properly recorded for military history to avoid them being repeated. You learn more from mistakes than you do from the successes, but at the time no one is anxious to dwell on failures. They are bad for morale and tend to get overlooked in the official war diary.

D + 4 (18th February). The endless ferry continued. All my men looked very weary. Class 9 rafts achieving 100 crossings a day.

D + 5 (19th February). First real counter-attack by Japanese from South of Pagan but too late to make much impression on such a concentration of troops in the ever expanding bridgehead. 17 Division and armour already thrusting out en route to Meiktila. Later we strike north to contact and engage Japs east of Pokoku. By now the bulk of IV Corps are across the Irrawaddy and we have reached the stage when for various administrative reasons a reduced number of troops are crossing back from east to west. The ferries are handed over to corps troops and we set up our company HQ on the east bank in Pagan.

CHAPTER 15

Pagan and King Col

Pagan — what a fantastic place! Pagan was a great centre of civilisation founded in 107 AD. Now only the immense pagodas remain spaced out over a hot dusty plain. Each pagoda is an archaeological wonder in its own right, but there are dozens of them towering up to the sky, in evidence of the power and glory that once flourished on this site. Some are encrusted in gold leaf, others are covered in little statues of Buddhas mounting in tiers up into the relentless blue sky above. Little remains of the great city that covered the ground between them. Its less permanent structures have crumbled and decayed into dust. Only the great pagodas remain as symbols of its past glory. Rumour has it that this great civilisation grew to such immense proportions that its demand for timber caused the surrounding jungle to be felled and cleared for miles around. This was done on such a scale that it eventually altered the climate until it created a desert that could no longer support the civilisation. The rains so essential for the sustenance of life diminished when the forests were cleared, slowly the fertile plains baked dry under the fierce sun and became infertile desert. The civilisation waned and was finally sacked by the Chinese and left incapable of supporting anything but the few village communities that survived, either on the banks of the Irrawaddy or around the few wells that had not dried up.

I do not know whether this is true or not, but certainly Pagan had the ghostly quality of a civilisation that had fallen from greatness for one reason or another. Camped amongst its ruins one could not fail to be affected by its quality of mystery. Even in war when the senses tend to become blunted by the demands of the time, there are rare moments when the war can be eclipsed by the very timeless qualities of one's surroundings.

My own feelings were crudely expressed in the poems that I wrote at that time. They contrast with each other but express the timeless qualities of Pagan in two of them, and in the other the contrasting realities of the war we brought to it for just a brief moment in its history as we dug ourselves in to fight beneath the shadows of its great pagodas.

THE RUINS OF PAGAN

Man made you, yet you were his master;
The Gods sat disdained and cold.
His blood ran, you held your plaster.
He has gone his story untold.

Now cactus stands in the paving
Only the wind brushes the hearth.
In the sun fat lizards are bathing,
No concubines go to their bath.

No peacock struts in the sunshine,
Neath the walls of the Paungi Chaung,
The pagoda bells are long silent
All but their echo is gone.

THE GLORIOUS DEAD

Circling vultures death's pattern weave,
Waiting, waiting.
On plantain leaves blue bottles gloating,
The sands run fast, their bowels are bloating.
What glory do their faces leave?
Gaping, gaping.

PAGAN

Can man have really made the brick
And later the undying bond?
Some architect the walls made thick,
And laid the moat beyond?

And can man have come to plunder,
To breach your walls and crack your face?
Tear your earthen heart asunder,
And kill your craftsman race?

And can, when a thousand years after
Man comes to fight again,
Your aged stones hold back their laughter
Your bricks his might disdain.

Around us the battle ebbed and flowed. Rumours were rife that the Japs were advancing in strength from the south. Certainly there were fierce encounters for various tactical positions but no big strategic battles ensued. The 14th Army had taken a very bold initiative and the Japanese forces, good as they were, had been manoeuvred on a grand scale. My own company had played a major role in the crossing and were now allowed to enjoy a few days' respite before our next operational assignment.

The sappers idea of a rest was to get back into the river to keep cool. Two American power boats had been allotted to us for the river crossing but had arrived a little too late. They were very fast on their own but were too light for the job they were intended for which was propelling pontoons into position in bridging and rafting operations. However, their speed and manoeuverability made them ideal for surf boarding – an early form of water skiing that we developed on the Irrawaddy. The surfboard was half a door that was towed on a long rope, another rope was fixed to the two leading corners of the board and you hung on to this like a pair of reins while standing on the surfboard. Crude, but it worked extremely well. The power boat was extremely manoeuverable as its steering was by a joystick. Pushed forward you went to the left and pulled back to the right so that with one movement of the stick you could change from full left rudder to full right. We soon developed a game whereby the driver did all he could to dislodge the surf rider and the latter had to see how long he could stay on before being ducked. However, we soon discovered that the quickest way to dislodge the surfboard rider was not to make quick swerves from left to right, but to maintain full throttle and full lock in one direction. This had an effect like swinging a weight around on a piece of string and the surfboarder was travelling faster sideways than he was forwards. It took a lot of skill to stay on and when you came off you hit the water at terrifying speed. Another variation was to get two on the surfboard and one to climb on to the other's shoulders. Only Tigger Royle and myself achieved this and there is the photograph to prove it, though I must give full credit to the photographer for we only held it for the length of the exposure, about 1/50th of a second.

Our other relaxation was fishing. Not with conventional tackle but with explosives. Our explosives stock was starting to deteriorate in the heat of central Burma and with the arrival of fresh supplies we were ordered to destroy the old stocks before they became unsafe. The conventional procedure would have been to burn them, for gelignite, guncotton and TNT will burn fiercely if ignited and only explode if detonated. However, this seemed a waste of resources so we decided to detonate them under water and collect the harvest of fresh fish to supplement the rations. With a little experimentation we developed a technique that was so successful that we supplied most of the division with fresh fish. A great treat when you have been living off tinned food for a couple of years.

We set off like a small fishing fleet having selected our site. The gathering boats, MK III assault craft, held back while the demolition boat, loaded with prepared charges each fitted with progressively shorter safety fuse, steered in a wide circle lighting and throwing over its charges, starting with the longest fuse and ending with the shortest. The object was to achieve a simultaneous detonation of a large circle of explosive charges so that any fish within the circle would be stunned by the combined effect and come floating to the surface. The gathering boats moved into the circle as soon as the charges exploded. The sappers loved it and the fierce competition to gather up the most fish became like a fairground dodgem car scene on water. It was not always the first on site that did best for the smallest fish always rise first, the bigger they were the longer they took to surface. On one occasion we thought we had collected the lot and were setting sail for the shore when someone spotted what looked like a Jap miniature submarine surfacing. It turned out to be the most enormous catfish that I have ever seen. With a pole through its gills it was all two men could do to lift it and they could not get its tail off the ground.

While we relaxed, surfing and fishing, the IEME had found their busman's holiday, an Irrawaddy steamer, the M.V. *Ontario,* beached and riddled with bullet holes and rust, but recoverable. They worked on it in spare moments day and night for seven weeks. She was patched, caulked and repainted, her piston engines overhauled. Finally she was relaunched on 25th March at Pagan where she had been beached, but though it was a remarkable achievement for a Divisional IEME workshop I never discovered what use was made of this river steamer or what became of her.

This short respite from the war came to an end for me at any rate when the East African motorised brigade at Letse, some 12 miles to the west of the river, were reported to be taking a hammering from a large Japanese force. Their task had been to push down the road to the west of the river pretending that they were the main corps advance with the object of deceiving the Japanese forces and drawing their attention away from the crossing site. They had achieved this a little too well and found themselves being heavily counter-attacked by superior Jap forces. They had finally been surrounded and boxed up at Letse. Two battalions from my brigade were ordered to go to their assistance together with supporting arms. However, Letse lay on the other side of a barren ridge of hills and there was no road over to them. My platoon, together with two bulldozers from the Field Park, was ordered to construct a road to Letse to enable guns and transport to get there. The only other road to Letse was from the north and would have meant a long journey north to Pauk before one could join the track back south to Letse. Our short cut road over the hills, once constructed, would mean that if the situation demanded further reinforcements and tanks these could more quickly be supplied.

Knowing that the Japs were in some strength in the Letse area we had a screen of infantry forward of our road building operations. It was harsh country, bare mica rocks and the only vegetation was cactus. The heat was terrific so that the rock was almost too hot to handle. We sweated away in that scorching desert for three or four days carving a crude road out of the rock strewn hills. A few days before we had been surrounded by water, now, when we needed it most to replace our copious sweating, it was tightly rationed to one warm water bottle of the precious stuff. By the end of the day our tongues were dry with dust and cracking. The infantry screen ahead reported casual sniping and certainly we knew that the plume of dust our road markings created must have been visible to any enemy for miles around. At last we made the crest of the last ridge and there lay Letse in the sandy plain below. No signs of the village but the East African Brigade's Admin. Box was clearly visible in a small group of palm trees.

From what we had heard of the situation at Letse we had fully expected to be attacked while constructing the road to relieve it. For the moment we could see no sign of the Japs but we could, however, see plenty of signs of the East Africans. As soon as we appeared over the skyline some of them were not waiting any longer, and we could see vehicles moving out of the base and heading back up the track to the north in a stream of dust plumes. They had had enough of Letse and were off.

By the time we had completed the road down to the plain and our guns and transport were moving in it seemed that the major part of the East African Brigade had already left. I thought that we were sent to reinforce them but they seemed to think we were relieving them, or so it appeared at the time. Those that remained were full of stories of the Japs attacking every night and on one occasion had got through their wire defences on one side of the perimeter before being repulsed.

Certainly there was plenty of visible evidence of a battle with empty shell cases and holes everywhere. The sappers were allotted a fair section of the perimeter to defend and we set to work to get prepared for the inevitable night attack. The infantry immediately sent out patrols to try and locate the Jap forward positions as it appeared that the E. Africans had neglected this necessary precaution towards the end of their occupation.

I remember that on my section of the perimeter there was a deep nulla that wound its way right up to our forward positions. It was a dry eroded water course only about five feet wide but with vertical sides just like a trench system and would afford a perfect covered approach for the enemy. It worried me a great deal, for if the enemy came up to it undetected in the dark they could lob grenades into our positions a few yards away and be quite safe from our small arms fire. In the end I sighted a Bren gun to fire on fixed lines down the one length we could see into before it turned across our front. There was no time to set up an elaborate booby trap system but this did seem the ideal situation in which to use that simple grenade in a tin device that had made fools of us all on the jungle warfare course back in India. We set up the trip wire and grenade just after the straight section that our Bren gun covered. It was a bit close to our own positions but we would be well shielded from the blast. If the Japs crept up the nulla in the dark the forward ones would be killed by the grenade when they ran into the tripwire and the Bren gun should get any following up behind them. My only worry was that one of our infantry patrols might get lost and blunder into the trap in the dark. I checked with one of the infantry patrols and was relieved when he told me that if any infantry patrols went out at night they would not be so stupid as to return by any other route than the way they had gone out, and if they got lost they would stay out until daybreak.

We settled down to await the oncome of night and the expected enemy assault. Sentries were posted but we never really slept. Our ears were pricked for the slightest sound that might herald the Japanese attack. It was Kohima all over again. Fear and the knowledge of impending danger tuned one's animal instincts for self-preservation to a very fine pitch. If you dozed off the slightest sound had you instantly awake and alert. The night can be very long but eventually the eastern sky became more luminous and dawn was breaking.

We felt slightly cheated that in spite of our vigilance and preparation there had been no attack. The infantry patrols reported no Japs in the immediate vicinity though they bumped into one or two pockets of Japs a mile to the south.

The next night was the same except that we were all galvanised for action by firing on the side of the box, but it turned out to be nothing more than a trigger-happy sentry who thought he saw something move in the darkness. For the moment it seemed that the Japs had pulled out and we were not sorry to receive orders to return to Pagan where our specialised services could be better employed. In spite of the anticlimax we were relieved to leave Letse. Even without the Japs it was very inhospitable. In fact it later became more active as Japanese forces retreating from the west regarded it as a threat to their escape route from the outflanked areas to the west of Tilin and their last line of escape to eastern Burma.

We returned to Pagan and left the Letse garrison to enjoy its short-lived lull in activity in the sweltering heat of that plain.

Back at Pagan the situation was what military historians term as fluid. The speed of our advance had thrown the enemy into confusion. The result was very satisfying in some respects but it also meant that we had no idea where the enemy concentrations were located. To counter this a fast moving armoured column had been created nicknamed "Puff Coll" after its commander Col. Pugh. It careered about the vast ill-defined no-man's-land seeking out enemy concentrations. When it bumped into any enemy, if they were small groups it engaged them. If they were larger formations it wirelessed back their location and estimated strength and quickly withdrew. They proved a very successful tactical force spreading confusion amongst an already confused enemy and locating any concentration that could pose a threat to our bridgehead. On one occasion the bulk of the staff of the 2nd I.N.A. Division surrendered to it.

In early March the commander of "Puff Coll" took over command of 33rd Brigade from Brigadier Collingwood. Lt. Col. Mainprise-King, known throughout the division as 'Mainspring', took over command of "Puff Coll" which became renamed 'King Col'.

It was about this time that I was ordered to join 'King Col'. My briefing from HQRE was that I was going with them to make a water supply reconnaissance. The countryside between Pagan and the oil field at Yenangyaung was very dry and arid. The CRE wanted me to find out what potential water resources there were in this area over which the divisions would soon be advancing to capture the oil fields. It was quite obvious from maps and aerial photographs that there were no rivers or ponds in the area so that meant village wells. When I questioned my OC Tony Dixon what I was expected to do to assess the potential of village wells while on a highly mobile fighting reconnaissance column, he suggested I use my intelligence and engineering knowledge. "Measure the depth of water and the circumference of the well then empty it and time how long it takes to refill. That will give you the potential capacity of the well". A splendid shop theory but I could not see 'King Col' hanging around at every village well while I emptied it and waited for it to refill. Impractical as the whole idea seemed I had no choice but to duly report to 'King Col'.

Once again it did not appear that anyone had thought of informing

'King Col' of the reason for my joining them. However, they were delighted to be assigned a sapper officer. Just what they needed, I was told, to lead the column in an open armoured car and look out for mines. If I spotted any I was to stop the column and get out and clear them. As the speed of the column was to be 30 or 40 mph I felt this was a pretty tough assignment. I pointed out to 'Mainspring' that when you laid land mines you covered them over so that they could not be seen even at a walking pace, let alone 40 mph, and if there were mines then the first indications they would have of them would be when their leading vehicle blew up with their sapper officer in it, who then would not be available to clear a path through the minefield. I was glad that they saw the sense of this and I was repositioned behind the leading vehicle. However, the primary purpose of my being with them was not appreciated. "Your CRE must be mad. The one thing King Col does not do is hang around. And what do you want water for, there is no shortage in the Irrawaddy?"

They were obviously not going to take my village well reconnaissance very seriously and I really could not blame them as I did not think much of it myself, but supposed I would have to produce something to satisfy my superiors.

We set off at a cracking pace bumping and bouncing out of the deep ruts in the dusty track. I had no idea where we were or where we were going. About midday we approached the first village I had seen. Most of the column deployed and stopped outside, just the leading armoured car, my armoured carrier, and a section of infantry on foot approached it carefully. It seemed very dead and deserted. I held my tommy gun across my knees with my thumb on the safety catch. In the centre of the village there was a small maidan with shady trees and what looked like two Burmese men who ran off at the first sight of us. The armoured car's gun traversed round the houses surrounding the maidan and the infantry deployed to search the buildings. Before long they came back with two very frightened looking Burmese. The commander of the armoured car passed a message on his wireless and a moment later a Jeep joined us carrying the interpreter. The interpreter seemed to know all the necessary questions required. There had been some Jap soldiers in the village but they had left two days ago. There were only a handful of villagers left in the village, all the rest had fled to avoid the fighting. They did not want to be caught between two armies. They thought there were Japanese soldiers still in a village five miles south of here, but they could not be sure. As he came to the end of his interrogation I felt this was my chance to get some information about the water supply so I asked the interpreter to enquire about the village water supply. It appeared there were only two wells, one of which was dry, the other was very low and the water was not very good. I enquired about other villages with wells in the area but he did not seem to know much about them except the village five miles south where he thought the Japs had a good well, but he did not know how good. Perhaps enough for a hundred men, not more as the weather had been dry for a long time. That was as much as I could get for King Col did not hang about. Orders were given to rejoin the column and we were off heading south to check on the next village.

As this was reported to be occupied by the enemy two armoured cars took the lead in front of me. Everyone seemed to have forgotten about mines when there was a loud bang that seemed to come from around the bend in the hill where the leading armoured car was, but out of sight. The next moment we were ourselves around the bend and scattered huts on the outskirts of the village were in view. The leading armoured car had left the track and was streaking across country firing its gun at some unseen target, and the other armoured car was quickly following suit. Then the driver of my carrier shouted "Dushman" which means enemy, and pointed to the nearest huts. Men carrying rifles were scattering out of the huts. This seemed to be my chance to use my tommy gun in earnest, so while the driver sprayed them with his sten gun I emptied my tommy gun at them. How many, if any, were hit I have no idea for they were all of 80 yards away and running off through the long grass. Our fire downed them but they could have been hit or just taking cover from the fire. Other vehicles from our column seemed to be dispersing in every direction, bullets flying everywhere, but as we had no wireless in our carrier I had no idea what was happening or what to do. The battle ahead seemed to be intensifying from the sound of the gunfire. Every now and then I caught a glimpse of armoured cars streaking around in the trees ahead and firing their guns at something, but the dust they raised made it difficult to see what that something was.

I felt a little lost and isolated sitting in my carrier waiting for the fog of war to lift. Then suddenly it seemed to be over. The armoured cars were streaking back towards us. As they shot past a figure appeared from the turret of one of them making obvious signals with his arm and I first caught the shouted order "Wapas jhow" above the whine of the engines. That meant go back. Obviously we were pulling out at speed which could only mean one thing — we had bumped into a larger force than expected. My driver started to turn our carrier around but as he got broadside on in the track his front wheels dropped into one deep rut and his back wheels into the other. Then he stalled the engine. With the fatalist shrug of the shoulders he picked up the starting handle and announced "Battery karab hai Sahib". I suddenly felt very frightened and very vulnerable. Here we were, having just stirred up a hornets' nest of Japs, stuck in full view of them broadside across the road with a dud battery.

The rest of King Col was already a fast disappearing cloud of dust. The driver inserted the starting handle and gave it a few hurried tugs but the engine did not even splutter. The driver looked up apologetically and started to explain how he had told the M.T. havildar this morning that his battery was no good, but he had done nothing about it. It was only started by towing this morning he added. Things began to look very black indeed and I had even blacker thoughts. Being taken prisoner at this stage of the war with the Japanese in retreat would be a fate worse than death. In fact, after what we had just done to them it was very unlikely that they would bother to take a prisoner except for the pleasure of a Japanese officer to make another notch on the hilt of his samurai sword. Cursing the driver and his MT havildar for allowing a vehicle to go out on such a mission with a defunct battery, I leapt out of the carrier and took over the starting handle. I ordered the driver back into the driving seat with an adjoiner that if the damn engine started I would shoot him if he let it stall again. Then cursing Ford of Tatanugga who had made the carrier I summoned all my strengh and swung that handle round and round as though my life depended upon it and, in fact, it probably did. About the tenth revolution it made a cough then a splutter and then died again. The driver and I decided that next time it fired he would pedal the accelerator. I glanced in the direction of the village; there was nothing to be seen except little columns of smoke from fires started by the skirmish. No doubt they were still licking their wounds but it would not be long before somebody spotted us for we must have been very conspicuous, a dark carrier broadside on across a light dusty track. Sweat from the heat and anxiety was streaming down my face. I tried cranking that heavy lifeless engine once again, round and round and round. It seemed as dead as mutton and the exertion was telling on my strength. I felt the revolutions getting slower yet I dared not stop for I would be too exhausted to start again. Just as I felt my strength ebbing from me the engine unexpectedly fired again. The driver plunged his foot down on the accelerator and it roared into life belting clouds of black smoke from the exhaust. He had learnt his lesson and he maintained maximum revs while I pulled out the starting handle and leapt into the carrier, as I did so I heard that strange familiar cracking in the air around us that is made by bullets breaking the sound barrier. We had been spotted but just too late. We leapt out of those ruts like a startled deer and bounded down the track at full throttle raising our own smoke screen of dust to shield us from the enemy fire. I have never felt so relieved in all my life.

CHAPTER 16

The Advance on the Oilfields

I was even more relieved when we caught up with the tail of King Col, sooner than expected for they had realised that the carrier with their sapper was missing and were about to send an armoured car back to the rescue. I was also told that they had bumped into a mixed force of Japs and INA of far greater strength than realised at first, hence the order to pull out. They too were glad that they did not have to go back to try and rescue me, for the enemy had a number of anti-tank guns which could have been sighted down the road by the time they returned. After this the journey back to the bridgehead was an uneventful relief.

That evening I reported the little I had discovered about the water supply east of the river and the futility of trying to do a water supply recce with King Col. Nobody seemed particularly interested in the subject anyway, as our brigade was under orders to move back west of the river. I was not sorry to be relieved of any further expeditions with King Col, for though it was exciting there was little that an engineer officer could do except spectate and risk getting shot for no useful purpose.

Soon we were crossing back from east to west across the river. The ferries were still operating bringing more replacements and stores across, and our men and transport crossed on the return journey, so that the rafts were laden in both directions, but by now they were being operated by corps engineers and our men who now considered themselves experts in watermanship were highly critical of their performance. Which was rather amusing remembering their earlier performance when training on the Zahaw Chaung. To give them their due they had come a long way since then and had every right to consider themselves expert after all the experience they had had.

Having crossed back, there was another of those between periods, so familiar in war while units were re-grouped for the next operation. We occupied some of this time in converting some of the large country craft that sailed the Irrawaddy. Rather the equivalent of Thames barges, they were ideal for transporting the vast quantities of stores that were necessary to keep an army in the field. Ammunition, food and a multitude of other ancillary stores. Our next divisional major operation was to advance south down both sides of the Irrawaddy to recapture the oilfields. The present idea was to convert a number of these country crafts from sail-powered craft using 22 hp outboards. This would enable much of the heavy stores to be shipped down the central axis of our advance rather than tie up dozens of supply vehicles following up on the rough tracks over which the land route of the advance would have to negotiate. Sailing these craft was a very skilled performance that only the local Burmese boatmen could do but they were not regarded as sufficiently reliable and were liable to panic and jump overboard if they came under fire which left an uncontrollable craft gyrating down the Irrawaddy into enemy territories, as we had already experienced in the 1/11 Sikh crossing at Pagan.

To gain practice in manoeuvering these craft under power we decided to use them to ship our engineer stores back across the river.

There was however, one unfortunate incident I remember, when we were in midstream and almost out of control. In the ensuing excitement one of the section havildars fell overboard. The current was very strong at this point and he just seemed to disappear. I dived into the river myself and swam under water trying to locate him, but could see no trace of him. When I surfaced I realised just how strong the current was at that point, for I was already forty yards from the craft and after a second attempt I surfaced so far away I was worried if I could make it back to the craft and I doubt if I could have made any headway towards them against the current. However, they realised the situation and re-started the motors to make a powered sweep down below me where I quickly drifted alongside. Sad to relate the havildar was never seen again. I later learnt that he could not swim at all. Unusual for Madrasis, but even if he could swim, he would have had a difficult time in that strong current. In wartime death is commonplace, even if not a direct result of enemy action. The other sappers in his section were not slow to take advantage of it. From then on every bit of equipment missing from their store was accounted for as being in the possession of the havildar when he fell overboard. The list included two sledgehammers, an axe, a field compass, a tow chain, a crowbar, and several picks and shovels. No wonder the poor chap sank without trace!

Eventually all the divisional units were disengaged from the battles they were fighting and were formed up for the advance on the oilfields. On the east bank, 33 Brigade and 89 Brigade were to advance on Chauk and Yenangyaung and my own 114 Brigade was to advance down the west bank to Seikpyu. The regrouping of scattered formations took time but this was also the occasion for a major regrouping of the higher order of battle at Corps level. 7 Ind. Division was transferred from IV Corps to 33 Corps under General Montagu Stopford, together with the

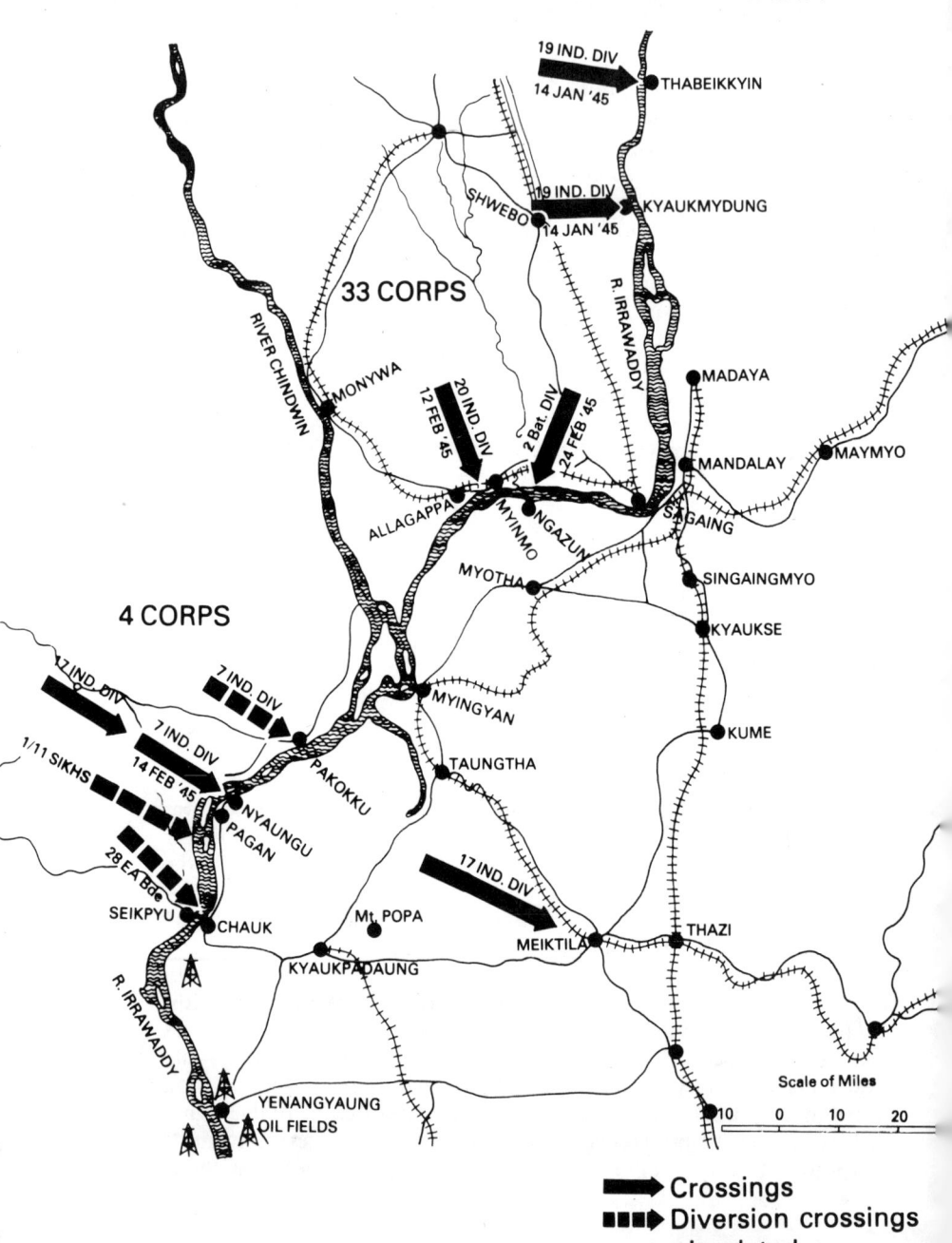

2nd British Division and the 20th Indian Division plus a large assortment of supporting arms such as a regiment of medium artillery and tanks and flame throwers. By now it was early April and everyone was deployed for the next strategic move south down the Irrawaddy.

Our first objective was Seikpyu on the opposite bank to Chauk, the most northerly of the oilfields. Before we could advance on these two towns, 33 Brigade had to take Kyaukpadaung and the 5th Brigade of 2nd British Division, together with 268 Brigade, had to dislodge the Japs from Mount Popa, a volcanic feature that dominated the approach roads to the oilfields on the east bank. Mount Popa was a formidable feature to attack for it rose like a miniature Fujiyama from the dry plains of Central Burma to nearly five thousand feet. It was covered with thick vegetation and apart from the Japs it also had the reputation of being infested with hamadryads, the most deadly of snakes, the king cobra. It is claimed that the king cobra releases sufficient venom in one strike to kill twelve men. When they rear up to strike their head is up to five feet above the ground. In spite of these two daunting opponents our two brigades managed to dislodge the Japs who threatened our advance south and were no doubt happy to leave the hamadryads in sole occupation as soon as this was achieved.

On the west bank however, 114 Brigade was running into very stiff opposition. Most of the sappers' time was spent turning rough tracks into roads fit to enable the trucks and guns to support the advance. Much to everyone's surprise our one brigade on the west bank had to contend with larger Jap forces and far stiffer opposition than the remainder of the divisions found on the east bank. In fact when they attacked Chauk they found that the Japanese forces had withdrawn to the west bank having crossed in the night to Seikpyu.

They captured Chauk on 17 April and we found ourselves confronted with the bulk of Chauk's defenders. The whole of the divisional artillery from both sides of the river concentrated its fire on Seikpyu and inflicted heavy casualties on the Jap formations concentrated there. While we were still struggling to take Seikpyu the rest of the division on the east bank took advantage of the situation and pushed on south towards the main oilfields at Yenangyaung, which they captured on the 22nd April. Here once again to their surprise the Japs withdrew from east to west. Though this time they were prepared to counter such a crossing with night fighters operating by the light of the full moon, the Japs were saved by the weather which suddenly turned to cloud and rain which masked their crossing from night strafing.

On the west bank our advance which was planned as a covering move to protect the flank of the main thrust down the east bank to capture the oilfields turned out to be the major operation where fighting was concerned. Naturally, no one had anticipated that the Japs would withdraw in the opposite direction to their main line of retreat eastwards. Undoubtedly, the speed of our advance had caught them with the major portion of their fighting formations in the hills to the west of the Irrawaddy and they feared their complete annihilation. These formations were withdrawn eastwards and southwards down the west bank of the river and the formations east of the river were crossing back to join them so that my brigade found themselves confronted with opposing enemy forces being reinforced from both west and east.

To combat this situation it was decided to cross our own 89th Brigade from east to west at Kyaukye. This was not the ideal site but with a few mishaps this was achieved so that we now had another brigade plus armour west of the river to match the greater concentration of enemy troops on this side of the river. It had a profound effect on our expected battle for Salin.

The enemy had fought very stubbornly up to this moment but once they realised that their line of retreat was threatened by 89th Brigade they evaporated and we took Salin almost without opposition.

A vast assortment of Japanese equipment lay everywhere. Salin was quite an oasis. We found a large ornamental lake and on its shores there were hundreds of semi-tame domestic duck. Tigger Royle and I set about trying to catch a few. The thought of duck was very tempting. When we drove up to the lake in our Jeep the duck were waddling and quacking all around us. It seemed just too easy to step out and pick a few up, but those duck could waddle quite fast and when we got out of our Jeep they proved expert at maintaining just enough distance to prevent us making a quick grab.

After one or two abortive attempts we got more desperate and so did the ducks, who started to head for the water. There were so many of them they moved en masse on the ground. We just could not grab an individual. As they started to take to the water I saw our roast duck dinner fading and in desperation threw myself headlong at them in a dive like a rugger tackle and managed to smother about five ducks. Even then three of them escaped and I was left with one that I had firmly by the neck and another completely winded beneath me. Tigger just sat on the ground laughing his head off. Two out of about a thousand was not a very creditable performance but it was better than nothing.

Back at the mess that night six hungry officers made short work of two roast duck, but pronounced them as so delicious after weeks of curried bully beef that Tigger and I were ordered to try again and make sure we did better next time. Next day as we arrived at the lake the ducks were thick on the shore, but as they saw our Jeep arrive they swept like a wave into the water and paddled away in great formations to the centre of the lake. They had memories and were not going to be caught that way again. We were stymied.

Then I remembered that we had acquired a lot of abandoned Japanese equipment near Salin, amongst which were some small mortars. This seemed an ideal opportunity to try them out on a worthwhile target. We shot back to our lines and soon returned with two of these mortars and several cases of ammunition. We set them up on the shore and tried a few ranging shots. We soon discovered how the mortars worked, but we also discovered that the duck were now out of range. A quick reconnaissance located two very solid wooden boats moored in the reeds not far away. In these we mounted the mortars and paddled slowly towards the formation of ducks. When we estimated we were well within range we opened up with a ranging shot. This went a little too far but after that we were on target and our H.E. mortar bombs dropped right in the middle of the flotilla of ducks scattering the formation in every direction. After four or five direct hits we moved in to pick up. That night there was enough roast duck for one a piece and we gave a lot away to the neighbouring messes. We heard no complaints about anyone breaking their teeth on mortar splinters so presumed no one suffered.

We would have had another go, but before we could improve our gunnery technique we were on the move again. The immediate object was Pyinbyu then Sagu and Minbu. I have no clear memories of this advance except that it was all go; units leapfrogging each other all the way to Minbu with diminishing opposition from the Japs now in full retreat.

I really only remember Minbu for its strange mud volcanoes. Amazing features that must have been physically connected with the oilfields. Perfect symmetrical little volcanoes about 150 ft. high, you could walk straight up the sides to a little crater on the top. There in the crater liquid mud erupted with great bubbles of gas which would ignite if you threw a lighted rag onto the mud. Every now and then a large bubble would cause the mud to spill over the crater edge and run down the side where the sun soon baked it hard and dry and was presumably the process by which these strange miniature volcanoes were formed.

The other event that recalls Minbu was that our OC Tony Dixon, who had commanded the company since we left the Arakan, was repatriated and Major Selby Pride took over the company. In my naive way I could not understand why he could bear to be repatriated when we were so close to our objective of retaking Burma, the culmination of four years fighting – 30 years later I am not so naive.

Selby Pride I knew had been 2nd I/C of the company at one time in the Arakan. He was a bit older than Tony Dixon and had taken it for granted that he would succeed to the command of company when the OC Major Bewoar was killed in action, which in fact he did at the time but had to step down when Tony was posted in to take command. Whether this was by accident or design I do not know but presumably the CRE would have some say in such matters and the CRE had been killed at about the same time as Major Bewoar, so that possibly the new CRE, Lt. Col. Wright had had little time to assess the situation and had requested a replacement company commander as a matter of course. Whatever the true reasons were the situation was deeply resented by Selby Pride and his resentment was reflected in his relationship towards Tony Dixon. Selby disappeared from the scene and never was seen again until he finally reappeared to take command of the company when Tony left at Minbu.

When their OC left, the VCO's and sappers always rose to the occasion with genuine feeling and gave a farewell party. This always took the form of a Burah Tamasha (big feast) consisting of a super hot curry and extra rum. The departing officer was garlanded with flowers. The subador major would make a speech and the commanding officer was given a great send off. Selby Pride, as far as I remember, did not arrive until Tony had left. There was no handover but, in fact, this was hardly necessary at the time as there was a lull in the operations and Selby knew the men and the VCO's probably better than Tony for he was an ex tea planter and could speak Tamil which gave him a distinct advantage when dealing with the sappers and it was much appreciated by them. I found life a little easier under Selby's command. He was surer of himself and did not resent you querying his instructions as Tony always had, but of course the situation had become less demanding by then. The end of the Burma Campaign was in sight. It was soon to become a mopping up operation and a race for Rangoon.

The other memorable occurrence at Minbu took place thousands of miles away to the west. At breakfast we listened on the wireless to the exciting news that the Germans had offered unconditional surrender to all three allied powers. The war in Europe was over. To us it was more of a feeling of relief than jubilation though we listened to the bells of Bath Abbey and the cheering crowds in Piccadilly more in a spirit of nostalgia than celebration. That evening we sat under the stars drinking and discussing what effect the victory in Europe would have on our lives and came to the inevitable conclusion that it would make little difference in the immediate future. We were too far away and it would take months before the vast resources of equipment in Europe could be shipped out to help our war in the Far East. We also had a sneaking suspicion that Britain would be so involved in restoring its post-war prosperity that we might still remain the forgotten army. My letter home written at the time expresses all these anxieties. We had no inkling of the atomic bomb that was going to solve the problem of our future within two months. To us the imminent retaking of Burma was just the start of a long, hard series of campaigns that lay ahead. Malaya, Siam, French Indo China, Java, Sumatra were but a few of the Japanese held territories that would have to be fought over before we could see an assault on Japan itself. The future held nothing but endless warfare with its inevitable casualties. Secretly each wondered just where his luck would run out.

Our next move was yet another Irrawaddy crossing, this time back to the east bank at Magwe. We were getting very expert at crossing this river by now, and the operation was so routine that I barely remember the crossing itself.

The fighting at Minbu had been pretty hard up to the 8th May when the Japs had become aware that their line of retreat south had been threatened by the advance of the 89 Brigade down the east bank and that they had now crossed back to the west bank and cut off their retreat. The Jap resistance had evaporated over night and they had pulled out once again leaving a mass of vehicles, guns and equipment. At Magwe we were to become the divisional reserve brigade on the next dash to capture Prome, but there were still a lot of Japs further east fighting a desperate rear guard action in Central Burma. Stories were coming through of their latest tank traps where our advancing tanks had found holes in the road hastily covered with brushwood and earth. When they had become suspicious and investigated them they found a little Jap squatting in the hole with a 6 inch howitzer shell between his knees and a brick in his hand ready to bash the fuse when he heard a tank overhead!

Our first task was the bridge at Allanmyo. A steel girder bridge over the river had been blown by the retreating Japs but they had only blown the 120 ft. centre span. It might have been easier if they had blown the lot for the internal clearance between the girders of the existing bridge was only a quarter of an inch more than a Bailey bridge transom and we would have to launch the Bailey centre section through this very confined space. A Bailey bridge is built with a light nose section and launched across the gap to be bridged on special rollers so that you keep building on sections behind the rollers and keep pushing it forward always maintaining the point of balance behind the rollers. The difficulties of building under these confined conditions were considerable. Normally construction on the bank is relatively simple and straightforward. Panels are lifted into position by men standing on either side lifting on a bar placed through the panel. When positioned it is locked in place by a large panel pin jointing it to the next panel top and bottom. The transoms are then slid into place through panels from the side and when positioned are secured with clamps. However in this case, the girders of the existing span barely gave room for men to lift the panels from the outside as they were jammed against the outer girders. The transoms had to be lifted over the panels and lowered first into one side and then back into the other. If the girder of the existing bridge were in the way preventing this then the Bailey span had to be inched forward or backward until it was possible. An alternative would have been to build the Bailey centre section outside the existing bridge and launch it on a series of rollers right through the existing home side span. However, we did not have sufficient launching rollers to do this, nor was it advisable for there was only an eighth of an inch clearance between the end of the transoms and the inside of the existing bridge girders. To have launched the bridge that distance without it moving more than an eighth of an inch either way would have been well nigh impossible, and once a bridge of that weight fouled the outer girders it would have been very difficult to jack it sideways to straighten the launch. With a lot of sweat and careful measurement we inched it forward pushing it with a vehicle, partly because there was no room for men to push it forward and partly because as the officer in charge I only had one man, the driver, to control the launch which was more easily managed with precision than with thirty odd sappers head down and heaving. No one was more surprised than myself when the bridge was safely across the gap without fouling the confining girders of the original bridge. With considerable relief and not a little pride in our achievement it only remained to jack down the bridge onto its bank seats and on with the decking. Within an hour the divisional transport was streaming over yet another obstacle to the advance.

Not long after this, news flashed around the world that Rangoon had fallen to a sea invasion. We did not know whether to feel relieved or cheated of our ultimate objective. However, it made little difference at the time for the bulk of the Japanese forces were hell bent on securing their escape eastwards towards the Pegu Yomas as their last hope of regrouping in Burma. We pressed on south to Prome with the scent of victory in our nostrils, but only too well aware that the Jap forces should never be underestimated in their ability to make a last ditch stand however hard-pressed they were.

As part of the divisional reserve we were motoring south in a vast conglomerate of vehicles all heading for Prome. Our duties were few, for the advance brigade had bridged all the obstacles and we just followed in their wake until we reached the Nawin Chaung at Milestone 185. Here the retreating Jap forces had blown the existing bridge over this tributary of the Irrawaddy and it had been bridged with a Bailey bridge by 62 Fd. Coy. The opening of the monsoon season had produced some heavy downpours though the monsoon proper had not yet fully broken. Nevertheless the opening stanzas had caused a considerable rise in the water level of the local rivers. When I crossed the Bailey bridge over the Nawin Chaung I was fascinated to see the great jam of teak logs above it. Teak is felled during the dry season and the great tree trunks of teak are pulled out of the forests by elephants and left on the river banks. When the monsoon breaks the river level rises and these great baulks of timber float away down to the Irrawaddy where they are herded into great rafts and shepherded down to the saw mills near Rangoon.

However, as I reached the far side of the bridge my fascination was abruptly detracted by the sight of the top chord of the Bailey panels buckled into an S bend. I pulled into the side and walked back to investigate. To my horror I saw what had happened. The mass of teak logs released into the river by the rising water level had been obstructed by the fallen girders of the demolished bridge that barred their onward progress to the Irrawaddy. As more and more teak logs floated off the river banks and came downstream they joined this obstruction to their progress until a massive log jam formed above the bridge. The pressure that such a log jam can exert is very considerable and all this pressure was exerted against the demolished bridge that obstructed their progress. Eventually it had become so great that it was physically forcing this mass of demolished girders downstream. Unfortunately the girders of the old bridge were at one point on the south bank still higher than the Bailey bridge that had replaced them. They had been forced downstream until they came up against the side of the new bridge. Here the force exerted by the log jam had built up until it had started to buckle the Bailey bridge and force it off its bank seats. I could see that the buckle in the top chord of the Bailey panels had already reached a point where the bridge could collapse under the weight of vehicles, yet the Indian Military Policeman on the bridge was cheerfully waving on the traffic over the bridge. Vehicles were crossing almost nose to tail. The buckled top chord was becoming more pronounced as I watched it and the bridge was developing a definite sag.

I leapt at the M.P. and ordered him to stop all traffic approaching the bridge. This was not so easy because he was at the wrong end of the bridge and those at the other end approaching it could see nothing wrong with it. In wartime every officer believes that he is vital to the war effort and should have priority. However, having despatched the MP to the other end of the bridge he did eventually manage to stop the flow of traffic coming across it, and only just in time. By then the heaving, groaning mass had nearly forced the far end of the bridge off its bank seats. There was some delay before my signals back to HQRE brought out my own OC and the CRE. Together we looked at the great mass of logs grinding and groaning under the pressure of pent up water behind them. One thing was obvious. Unless the pressure could be relieved soon the whole bridge would be swept off its seatings.

We even considered trying to break up the log jam with explosives but decided it had gone too far and unless we could sever the girders of the old bridge that were in contact with our replacement Bailey, there would be no bridge left to save. It was decided that the end of the Bailey bridge must be jacked up off the bank seat and the end section dismantled. The field park company would bring in oxyacetylene cutting equipment and cut through the south end of the old bridge girders while we laid explosive cutting charges on these girders where they entered the water. The Bailey bridge was jacked down onto a pier of 12" x 12" baulks built up from the demolished girder bridge to support it while we dismantled the Bailey back to and including the buckled panels. Once this was done, the next step was to cut the top chord of the old bridge where it entered the water. It was essential to calculate the very minimum charge required to cut the remaining girders without damaging any of the Bailey bridge immediately above it.

We had collected a large audience for the operation, for as more and more vehicles were held up by the unexpected closing of the bridge their occupants came forward on foot to see what the hold-up was caused by and they hung around impatiently spectating until movement forward could be restored. One really needed a P.R. Officer to answer all the enquiries from senior officers frustrated by the hold-up who seemed to regard that the whole thing had been engineered by the sappers for their own amusement. When the time came to fire the charge it took even longer to persuade this mass of spectators to get off the bridge. In the end I just waited until my jemadar had forced them back beyond the centre pier then I blew my whistle, waved a red flag and forced down the exploder plunger. There was a splendid bang that sent some of the audience surging back to the other side, and to my relief the offending girders dropped smartly down six feet. So neat was the job, in fact, that the temporary support piers of 12" x 12" timbers never even fell off the girders of the old bridge when it dropped. The end of the Bailey, deprived of its support, sprung up and down as it suddenly became a cantilever and the flexing of the bridge caused by this cleared the remaining reluctant spectators in a rush from the far span. The problem now was how to build back on to the end of the bridge that was some sixty feet off the bank and some fifteen feet above the top of the log jam which was still firmly held by the girders of the old bridge.

Without long boom cranes there was no alternative but to launch out from the bank a new section of Bailey and join up in mid-air. Not the easiest of jobs. It required very accurate siting and launching to meet the panels of the bridge sixty feet out exactly square so that the panel lugs would engage. Having achieved this and pinned the top lugs there was a wide gap between the bottom lugs, for both sections of bridge were still in cantilever. Fortunately the approach to the bank seats was an uphill slope so that by building more tail to our launch section we could lever up the join until the bottom lugs of the joining panels were almost home. The final adjustment was made with somewhat precarious jacking from below and with a sense of relief I saw the lower panel pins go home and from then on it was just a matter of dismantling the launching tail, jacking down and redecking before the traffic was passing over the bridge again.

It would possibly have been easier to have put the whole bridge back on to launching rollers and built on and launched forward from the far side, but the congestion of traffic on the other side would have made it difficult to bring up equipment to that side and the bridge was 250 ft. long with one centre pier. It would have meant building a lot of tail to move it forward by manpower or a bulldozer, and traffic was stacked back for a mile on the other side.

Once the pent-up traffic was over the experts decided that the bridge would have to be strengthened to a higher class so we then had to set about doubling up the panels. The whole job was completed within two days and we were off again on the road towards Prome.

It was about this time, early May 1945, that Jock Meldrum, our 2nd I/C, left the company on repatriation and I found myself promoted to take over his job. It felt good to have the captain's insignia of three pips on my shoulder, but I missed having my own platoon and the challenge of the varied engineering tasks that went with it. This was the work that I had done for the last two years and thoroughly understood. The 2nd in command job is more administrative and I had had little opportunity or inclination to learn this side of army life. However, it was a very necessary side if one had any ambition to future promotion so I had to master the paper side of warfare.

My appearance was a little unconventional for the part. About the time of Letse, the heat, the dust and the lack of water had become so uncomfortable that I had ordered the company barber to shave my head. Partly because the sweat caked red dust in my hair made it itch and partly because I felt that in the immense heat it would be cooler to have no hair. The barber had dutifully shaved my head clean to the scalp except for a small tassle left on the top. He was a Hindu and explained that this was a Choti that Sahib must not cut off. For should

I get killed in battle this tassle would enable the Gods to pull my soul up to heaven. So the Choti was left; times being what they were, I might need it. What is known as a Yul Brynner hair style was a bit before its time and caused a lot of amusement to my brother officers but it was very practical under those conditions. However, as it started to regrow I first had a short stubble bristling over my scalp. The effect when I was wearing my steel rimmed army issue glasses was reminiscent of those caricatures of German officers in the First World War. I remember visiting one of our British battalions and overhearing one of their privates saying "Look at him, mate, he's a "F"ing German. What's a Fritz doing out here?".

By the time I had become 2nd I/C of the company my *en brosse* hair style had developed into a tight mass of curls. Most unexpected for my hair had not been that curly before it was shaved off. As 2nd I/C I had to deal with more senior officers in the division and I was conscious of them eyeing my unusual hair style with a rather old fashioned look, but were most gentlemanly and would not directly comment on it. Those that noticed the Choti were Indian Army officers who knew its significance. I was very sunburnt and could have passed for an Indian but they knew that my height excluded this possibility except for a Pathan, but they were Mohammedan and would not have a Choti. I could see them eyeing me with a look of deep puzzlement, reluctant to enquire unless they offend on religious grounds.

On the 18th May my lucky stars must have been in just the right position. I received the news that my name had been drawn out of the hat for L.I.A.P. I think it stood for Leave in Advance of Python. Python was the code name for the leave due at the end of a long period of overseas service. LIAP was a special leave that those who had been overseas for more than two years could be entitled to. Each division would receive a few vacancies, but for each vacancy there would be many who qualified. The lucky names were drawn from a hat like a raffle ticket. It was the most valuable raffle ticket I have ever won before or since. It entitled me to be flown back to the U.K. for 28 days' leave and then flown back out again. After 2½ years in the Far East, mostly on active service, this surpassed my wildest expectations. As things turned out I had to wait until 10th July before this dream materialised.

In the meantime there was a little more unexpected fighting before we reached Prome. Prome had already been taken by 20 Division, a quick dash down the road, but it soon became apparent that the Jap forces escaping from the Arakan were massing at Kama on the west bank for a breakout across the river, and then make for the Pegu Yomas which now that Rangoon had fallen was their only hope of withdrawal.

At Pegu in south east Burma was the railway line that went south to Mulmein and on to Malaya.

The monsoon was starting with cloud covered skies and occasional heavy downpours. One brigade plus two battalions of the Nepalese Army were attacking the retreating Japanese remnants of 54 Division at Kama on the West Bank. In the night a considerable number of these Japanese had managed to cross the river and establish a bridgehead on the east bank between Kama and Zalon. My brigade, 114th and 33 Brigade, formed two wide cordons around the scattered area of the Japanese bridgehead and there ensued several days of confused fighting as the Japs tried to break out of this cordon. The position was pretty desperate. It says much for the discipline and tenacity of the Japanese Army that in a position where one might have expected to take large numbers of prisoners only seventy-four were taken, though 1396 dead were actually counted at the end of the operation. As we were now back into a thick jungle with all the heat, wet and discomfort that goes with it there must have been many wounded that never survived. However, despite the pounding they were given many small parties must have slipped through the net in the thick jungle at night, for our cordon had to cover an area of 50 sq. miles.

There was not much call for engineer services in this type of fighting and we were sent on to Prome ready for our brigade's next task, clearing the road south to Rangoon.

The approach to Prome I remember best for the abrupt change in vegetation. Central Burma is dry and relatively barren of trees except for the odd village oasis and river banks. As we approached Prome there was what appeared to be a green curtain ahead of us, as we got closer we saw that the dry plain gave way to jungle over quite a short distance. I have recorded how the great civilisation centred around Pagan denuded the surrounding countryside of trees and in doing so had changed the climate. Whether there is any truth in this story I do not know but certainly this change in vegetation marked the reverse. As we passed through the green curtain into the jungle on our approach to Prome it started raining. In the plains the day temperature had been 112° in the shade. The jungle around Prome was like a Turkish bath.

Prome had been one of the largest cities in Burma. It had been heavily bombed by the Japs when they invaded in 1942. There was little evidence that anything had been done to repair the damage under Jap occupation. My first job in Prome was to pull down a number of unsafe buildings one of which was a cinema. Its roof had gone in the 1942 air raids but the four gaunt walls remained more or less intact. In the middle of the building a tall tree grew out of what had once been the stalls. It towered up above the outer walls more than two storeys high. It was incredible to think that that chance seed had grown into such a tall tree in only three years! Such is the growth rate in the heat and moisture of the rain forest.

The demolition of the cinema was no problem. It had large window spaces in two opposite walls and lying inside the building were several large roof girders. It was just a matter of passing the winch cable from one of our bulldozers through the window, fastening it to the mid point of one of the large girders then starting the winch drum. As the girder could not pass through the window it pulled the wall outwards which with a little persuasion swayed and rippled before collapsing in a pile of rubble and dust. It only had to be repeated on the opposite wall and the lot came down in an equally impressive cascade, only the tall tree in the centre remained, and that was a threat to no-one.

My only other memory of Prome was the flying foxes or fruit bats. At times the air would be full of these large bat-like creatures, whirling like rooks overhead and, like rooks, they had a form of rookery for they would favour one or two large trees and return there when their foraging was done. The tree would become weighted down with hundreds of these creatures hanging from the upper branches not unlike strange brown fruits as they hung motionless until something disturbed them.

It was now the end of May and as we moved into June my brigade was assigned to clear any remaining Japs from the country east of the road to Rangoon, while 33 Brigade mopped up west of the road.

There was one strange rather sad incident. When I was visiting 77 Fd. Coy. who had established a ferry across the Irrawaddy in 33 Brigade area. The river was over a mile wide at this point and they had no wireless communication with the opposite bank. The young officer in charge of the operation was standing on the ferry jetty awaiting some prearranged signal from the other shore when he was struck by a bullet in the head and killed. It was just a single shot from the far bank. The shot was barely heard but the position of entry of the bullet left little doubt as to the direction it had come from. No Jap sniper could have possibly achieved such accuracy at such extreme range, for at that distance a man, let alone his head, was barely discernible. It later transpired at the enquiry into the officer's death that the prearranged signal to send over the ferry was a single shot fired from the other side and this was what the officer was waiting for. The enquiry was reluctant to be more specific than record death from a random shot that could have been fired by one of the many small, cut-off groups of Japs seeking to exfiltrate from west of the Irrawaddy. But it seemed far more probable that it was that one signal shot carelessly directed in the air towards the east bank a mile away, plus a million to one chance that had caused its trajectory to pass right through that unfortunate officer's head.

CHAPTER 17

Rangoon, LIAP and the Bomb

Towards the end of June most of the Jap presence immediately west of the 150 miles of road to Rangoon was accounted for. They were either killed or had escaped west to the Pegu Yomas. We arrived in Rangoon at last for a few days' rest before moving on to the last battle east of Pegu on the famous Sittang Bend. It was famous because it commanded positively the last escape route from Burma for the defeated Japanese forces. It was also fought under the most atrocious conditions of pouring monsoon rains in low lying swamps and paddy where the water was mostly waist deep. Stretcher parties carrying out the wounded could not put down their stretchers to rest or the occupant would have been drowned. The only dry land was the railway embankment. The remnants of two Japanese armies, the 28th in the Pegu Yomas and the 33rd East of the Sittang Bridge were making a last determined effort to withdraw their forces from Burma. I did not know how fortunate I was to be spared this last battle. In Rangoon the long awaited order for my return to the U.K. on 28 days' leave finally came through. I was told to remain in Rangoon for the last few days before my flight back to the U.K. on 10th July.

I spent those last few days looking around Rangoon, that magical goal in our minds for the last two years. The mystical symbol of Rangoon was the famous Schwe de Gon Pagoda that towered above the city looking out to sea from whence it was an equally famous landmark for all ex-patriots of Burma.

You approach the pagoda up tiers of steps that ascended the great mount on which the pagoda is built. At the top around the base of the pagoda were a number of ornate stalls selling various religious artefacts to the Buddhist pilgrims, plus a lot of the souvenir junk that I suspect had been hastily manufactured to take advantage of the vast number of sightseeing British and Indian troops. Rangoon itself was incredible for the speed with which its business population had opened up to take advantage of its new occupying forces. I was worried at the time because the mainspring of my watch had broken some weeks back and I had been using an army issue pocket watch from my company stores. I soon found a watchmaker open and in business but, as he politely explained, it had not been possible to get any spares during the last three years of Jap occupation and he had no spare mainsprings suitable for my new watch. However, if I would leave the watch with him for a few hours he would rivet the spring together and this should last me until I could get back to England or India where I could get a replacement spring. The thought of riveting anything so delicate as a watch mainspring so fascinated me that I left it with him to repair. A few hours later I collected my watch repaired and going again. As it turned out his repair lasted for four years and the English watch repairer was astonished when he saw how the mainspring had been repaired and learnt how long it had lasted.

The other shops in Rangoon had a fair assortment of goods they had either hidden away since 1942 or had somehow managed to procure at short notice, but my real fascination was in the shops selling gem stones. In the bigger ones they had trays of rubies, sapphires and other precious stones. They also had trays of imitations that were so good that to the inexpert eye they were indistinguishable from the real thing, except by price. I learnt that these very good imitation stones were imported from France before the war on a regular order. The Magok ruby mines of Burma were world famous and every tourist that stopped off at Rangoon enquired about the famous pigeon blood rubies. Few could afford the real thing but the imitations were so good that they sold readily. Many were sold by the less scrupulous dealers as genuine, knowing that the buyer was a tourist and unlikely to discover his mistake before he left Burma.

Money was a bit of a problem in those early days. There was no Burmese currency other than the Jap occupational money. This the Japs had printed on an as required basis and after the British occupation it had become worthless. However, some of the old Burmese currency hidden away during the occupation started to appear and in the meantime Indian rupees were most acceptable. I did not buy any gemstones, partly because I did not have the money available, but chiefly because I was so impressed by the quality of the imitations that it scared me from attempting to try for the real thing.

On the 10th July I drove out to Rangoon Airfield and boarded the Dakota aircraft assigned to take the lucky LIAP officers back to the U.K. It was one of the Dakotas that had been used for air dropping supplies and was bare inside except for a long strip of canvas seating down either side of the fuselage. Few of us had any clothes other than our jungle green uniform plus a spare set of slacks and bush shirt wrapped up in our bedrolls. I had the luxury of my father's old British warm wrapped in my bedroll. We sat tightly packed facing each other in two rows as the plane took off and headed for Calcutta over the Arakan hills. From the look on everyone's face it was clear they would have been quite happy sitting on the floor as long as they were flying west. I looked out of the small window behind me and saw the city of Rangoon with its tree-lined avenues and the great Schwe de Gon Pagoda pointing its golden finger at the sky. They say that if you look back at the Schew de Gon as your ship leaves Rangoon you will always come back again. I knew that I would be back in 28 days so I was taking no risk of its spell.

The journey home took three days, but stopped overnight at Calcutta and Baghdad and staged at Karachi, Bahrain, Lidda in Palestine and lastly for a meal in Sardinia. This would seem very slow by modern standards but it must be remembered this was all done in a twin-engined service Dakota, sitting on canvas bucket seats and there was no food on board except boiled sweets.

At the overnight stop at Calcutta I spurned the Grand Hotel with its transit camp bedlam and sorted out a bed with Ian Melville Stevens, the Editor of the *Statesman*, a most likeable friend of my father's who had offered me a bed any time I was in Calcutta and with whom I had stayed before. His flat had the rare luxury of being air-conditioned which was worth a dozen ceiling punkas in the Grand Hotel. Further, I was suffering from a recurrence of malaria and though I was stuffing myself with Mepacrine tablets to keep it at bay I was feeling definitely off colour.

Next day was an early rise and off to Dum Dum Airport to continue my flight. We had breakfast at the airport and were away for the long hours of stifling flight across India to Karachi where we stopped for refuelling and a late lunch before flying off on our next leg to Baghdad.

It was night by the time we reached Baghdad. All we could see of that historical city was twinkling lights, a fast drive in a 3 ton lorry to the transit camp where we were warned that the thief of Baghdad was as active today as he was in mythological stories, and that no one would take any responsibility for stolen property during our overnight stay unless it was deposited in the guardroom safe. "Don't put your valuables under your pillow, they will be gone in the morning", the officer in charge warned us. Around the buildings and courtyards of the staging camp every shadow seemed to contain a burly bearded armed guard – or was it a guard. One could not be sure – we all played safe and handed in our wallets for safe keeping in the guardroom safe. Next morning we were awakened before sunrise and after a very quick breakfast, driven through the still shadowed streets of Baghdad to the airport where our plane was ready for take-off. We lifted off fast as the sun was rising. Baghdad still remains a mystery city.

Our next stop after passing over miles of sandy waste then the deep blue of the Persian Gulf was Bahrain Island. In those days a desolate

RAF staging post. The heat was so intense that the runway was lost in a mirage. It looked just like the sea with a heat haze enveloping it. Strange vessels appeared to be sailing on this sea which as they approached under full sail suddenly turned into 3 ton trucks travelling down the runway. Beside the runway was a small prefabricated building to which we were directed. Inside there were tables and chairs and a long counter, but nothing to drink other than warm, brackish water and the only food available was American 'K' rations – a strange little box of survival rations designed to sustain American crewmen if they were shot down in the wilds of nowhere. It consisted of little blocks of concentrated dehydrated substances like oatmeal, compressed, dried apricots and vitamin pills and a very dry and concentrated block of chocolate. It was real hard tack and equally hard to swallow without the warm brackish water in which it had to be softened.

The only sign of life other than miles of super heated sand was a small group of palm trees in the far north west corner of the Island. We were told that this was the Sultan's Palace. Our unspoken fear was that some technical fault might delay our departure from this God-forsaken airport. We cheered with relief when our plane departed on schedule. The RAF tour of duty on Bahrain Island was only four months and we fully understood why. Next stop Lidda Airport in Palestine out in the middle of nowhere, but a much more pleasant nowhere than the previous one. Here we had a few hours while the plane was refuelled and serviced. We were given the choice of a bus trip to Tel Aviv or Jerusalem. At Tel Aviv there would be time for a bathe in the sea. Jerusalem was slightly further and there would be little time for more than a tour of the city by bus. I regret that I chose Tel Aviv when I could have seen Jerusalem on the briefest of visits. Tel Aviv was just another modern block of high rise flats on the shore of the Mediterranean. The quick bathe was achieved after haggling with a Jewish barrow boy selling bathing trunks at exorbitant prices. The inhabitants of Tel Aviv all looked like relatives of Fagin. I was glad when I was back at Lidda Airport.

With mounting excitement we were airborne again with only one more stop before England. It is difficult to imagine our magical expectations of returning to England after 2½ years of active service in the jungles of Burma. An England that we had left suffering under the full deprivation of war, threatened with invasion, yet had survived as the only free nation in Europe. Our homeland where nothing would have changed.

We made our last stop over at Sardinia. Europe at last and all the lights were blazing again. To us it was cool and balmy after the heat we had been used to and it was wonderfully civilised. We dined at the airstrip on a table laid out under the stars. We were given wine and grapes and all those wonderful pasta dishes and salads with sardines that assured us that we were now truly back in Europe. It was so novel and relaxing that we were almost sorry to have to leave and board the plane once again for the final flight to England. The excitement of going home after all this time was a fantasy that one could savour as long as one was travelling. One was almost reluctant to actually arrive.

However, we finally did arrive at about 4 a.m. on the 19th July at the air trooping centre in darkest Wiltshire. Documentation, a long train journey to London to another transportation centre office just off Piccadilly, more documentation, the issue of railway warrants to our homes and finally we were free to make the last lap on our own.

It was a strange feeling that overcame me as I arrived at Fleet Station in my jungle green uniform, and carrying my bedroll on my shoulder. I felt lost and out of place. For two and a half years I had lived in the jungle in the closed society of my own division. We all knew each other, we all bore the same tribal emblem on our shoulder, the Golden Arrow that signified our membership of the 7th Indian Division. Now I was confronted with a mass of other people I knew nothing about. They looked at me with strange curiosity. I longed for the sight of a familiar face but there was not one that I could recognise or speak to, yet this was my home town. There were no taxis but I discovered a bus that was just about to leave and jumped aboard for the last mile from the station to my home, Norway Lodge, at the other end of Fleet. As I turned into the front gate in the tall holly hedge I felt like the prodigal son returning home.

I opened the front door and there was my mother. It was a wonderful moment, full of warmth, joy and suppressed emotion. Only to be repeated when my father appeared with my sister Sue, who was now married but at home as her husband was overseas with his regiment in Europe. It was a wonderful family reunion. They had known that I was on my way home and I believe they had been notified of my arrival in the U.K. but naturally did not know just when I would turn up.

The hall was rather dark so at my mother's bidding we went into the library so that she could get a proper look at me. She had last seen me in December 1942. It was now July 1945. In 2½ years a man can change a lot at that young age. I had also grown a moustache and was tanned to quite a dark brown, but she saw through all this and just said "Aw John, you look so yellow. Are you sure you are alright?"I looked at myself in the mirror and I saw what she meant; I did have a very yellow complexion discernible through the suntan; even the whites of my eyes were yellow. Then I remembered that I was taking Mepacrine regularly to suppress malaria, bright yellow pills that did have the effect of turning your skin slightly yellow. I hastened to explain that it was just a side-effect of taking these pills. A fairly intensive course of them for a month known as blanket treatment to get rid of any residual malaria in the body, and nothing to worry about. She accepted my explanation but did not seem wholly convinced. However, for the moment we had 2½ missing years to catch up on. Tales from both sides that had to be retold. For my part all those places and experiences that could not be mentioned in my letters because of censorship and for their part all those incidents that could not be done justice in the confines of an air-letter card.

The details of my sister's wedding, the flying bomb that went between the two tall lombardy poplars either side of the house and the experiences of my Belgian relations who managed to escape from Brussels just ahead of the German invasion and had arrived unexpectedly on our doorstep in the early days of the war. All had to be retold until my eyelids fell lower and lower over my eyes and I was asleep. It was not late but my travelling had caught up with me. It was the end of the long road and my body knew it. I was awakened and escorted to the luxury of my own bed and linen sheets. I had waited three years for this magic moment but had little time to savour it, for within seconds of slipping between the luxury of sheets I was fast asleep again.

The body and the mind that is tuned to wartime conditions does not succomb that easily. Somewhere in the world outside a car backfired and in an instant I was awake and sitting up in bed wide awake and ready for action. But what action, where was I, was that a Jap attack that had awakened me? The sound of the backfire was still clearly registered in my mind, but I was trying to identify it. Was it a mortar bomb or a machine gun burst of fire? Where were we and where were our positions? As I sat up in bed wide awake and prickling all over I slowly reorientated to reality. I was home. There were no Japs within thousands of miles. The war was the other side of the world. I fell asleep again but my reflexes did not fall asleep so easily and any strange noise had me sitting up and wide awake ready to react. It was a strange sensation. Tired as I was these reflexes could have me wide awake before the echoes of the alarm sound had died. This built-in alarm response remained with me for most of the 28 days' leave.

Next morning I was refreshed by my night's sleep but was still unnaturally yellow. Even I began to doubt that Mepacrine tablets were the full explanation. The doctor was summoned and he confirmed that I had jaundice. My parents had gone to great trouble to produce food for their prodigal son. They had saved their precious meat and butter ration tokens, they had plotted and contrived with the family butcher and Mr. Canes, our grocer, who had both known me since childhood, to ensure that my home-coming should be celebrated with the best that starving Britain could provide from under the counter. My mother being Belgian and a very good cook had it all planned out. Alas, the doctor's edict changed all this. A strict diet was essential for recovery. No butter, no fat, no eggs and at the end of a long list of no's came no alcohol. Apart from the last it did not really worry me for all I wanted to eat was salad with vinegar, the very thought of any other food slightly revolted me.

It was sad for my parents who had gone to such trouble to produce the proverbial fatted calf for my return, only to discover that all I wanted to eat was lettuce. However, being July this was no problem and secretly I was happy not to be depriving them of the luxuries they had saved for me. In fact, my military ration card would actually reinforce their meagre ration of butter, milk, eggs, meat and sugar, all of which were severely rationed in England at that time.

I suppose I could have reported sick to the nearest military hospital at Aldershot where I would have been admitted and eventually my leave would have been extended to cover the period lost recovering from jaundice. I do not remember that the thought ever occurred to me. Having come home after all that time overseas, the last thing I wanted was to go into a military hospital. The only cure seemed to be rest and diet and I could do that at home. I was out of bed within a few days as I could never stand being in bed for very long, but though I tired very easily I knew I was improving as the deep yellow in the whites of my eyes was getting paler every day.

By the end of a fortnight I pronounced myself cured, possibly a little prematurely but with 14 of my precious 28 days already gone, I sensed that I was passing the half-way mark and was entering the count-down period to the day when I would be returning to Burma and the war. A war that must last several more years if the Japanese were to be ousted from all the territories they had over-run. Obviously Malaya would be our next campaign, then Sumatra and Java or possibly Siam and French Indo-China, depending on the grand strategy that the allies decided. Whatever the order of batting was to be it would be a long and bloody business if the Japs defended all his territories with the tenacity that he had displayed in Burma. Of course, we could expect vast reinforcements in men and weapons now that the European war was over, but this would take time, a great deal of time, to reorientate the war effort to the Far East.

On the 7th August the papers and the wireless exploded with the news that the Americans had dropped an atomic bomb on Hiroshima in Japan. At the time it was difficult to grasp the full significance of this news. After all what was an atomic bomb? I remembered vaguely from my schoolboy physics that if the atom could be split it would release enough energy for the Queen Mary to cross the Atlantic on a thimble full of coal. This was all theory. No one had succeeded in splitting the atom, though a scientist called Rutherford was known to be working on the project at Cambridge.

Wartime security had drawn a veil over any progress in this field until suddenly we were confronted with the news that the allies had developed an atomic bomb and had dropped it on a city in Japan. On August 9th news came that we had dropped a second atomic bomb on Nagasaki. By this time we were receiving pictures of the effect of the first bomb on Hiroshima. It was fantastic. Slowly we began to realise that this was no super heavy bomb but was in a class of its own. We were used to the effects of thousands of tons of TNT being rained down on targets in Germany by squadrons of bombers, but here was one aircraft dropping one bomb that seemed to have annihilated a whole city. It was all so sudden, so unexpected, that it was difficult to assimilate its significance for the future. All one saw was that over night this prospect of years of fighting and loss of life was no longer our inevitable future. This wonder weapon had changed everything. By the 14th August the Japanese High Command had accepted unconditional surrender!

To me this was like a fairytale, the impossible had happened over night. A fairy godmother had waved her atomic wand and a future of seemingly endless fighting, death and destruction had been transformed into peace on earth for me at least. In two days' time I was due to fly back to Burma and the prospect of years of war. In the blinding flash of an atomic bomb all this was changed. We all sensed that this was the end of an era but could not at the time see its full significance. Subsequent generations more fully conversant with the potential horrors of the atomic age should not overlook or misunderstand what its birth meant to us at the time. It heralded the end of our conventional warfare and the beginning of a potentially even more horrific style of war. At the time one did not see the future, only an end to the past and that was worth celebrating.

Celebrate we did with V.J.1 and V.J.2. Two national holidays on the 15th and 16th August. Ironically I was scheduled to fly back to Burma on 15th August. While the rest of Britain celebrated victory over Japan on that day, I struggled to report to the trooping centre in Piccadilly Circus. It was all so sudden and unexpected that no one had thought to extend the celebration to those who had been instrumental in the victory.

I had said goodbye to my parents in the euphoric atmosphere of peace rather than extended war but when I reached London and Piccadilly I was unprepared for the wild celebrations that prevailed. Piccadilly Circus was a seething mass of humanity all intent on whooping it up. Their pent up emotions had celebrated V.E. day in May but victory in Europe still left that dark shadow in the East, that could still claim fathers, sons, husbands and loved ones. The sudden and dramatic lifting of that shadow was not just victory over Japan, it was the final end of the war that had encompassed the world. For those at home it was the end of the fear of that dreaded telegram announcing that the War Office regrets to inform them that .... is missing, believed killed.

This was the final celebration of the release from the bondage of war. It was spontaneous as there had been no time for preparations. Piccadilly was the natural focal point of London. The boarded up statue of Eros was symbolic of all that war was not – love, freedom to do your own thing whatever that might be. They milled around Piccadilly shouting and singing. Occasionally fireworks were released among the crowds, often very dangerously but no one seemed to care. I saw a rocket shoot almost horizontally through the crowd passing through the long hair at the back of a girl's neck leaving its trail of sparks glowing in her hair, but all she did was laugh and shake them out.

The crowd was delirious but needed a focal point. Someone produced a blanket and in no time a girl was being tossed high above the heads of the crowd. I was in my jungle green and wearing a bush hat slowly filtering my way towards the entrance of the trooping centre, where I had to report. It was not easy in that crowd which was gyrating around Eros. One had to calculate the spin-off that would get you to the outer circle at the right moment to gain entrance to the trooping office door or be swept around for another circuit. There was no chance of making headway against the circling crowd. However, just as my goal was in sight I found that I had become noticed in my jungle green and bush hat as another expression of V.J. day. Just what the crowd was looking for.

Before I could reach the entrance to the trooping centre I was seized and in a moment was hoisted shoulder high and borne around Piccadilly Circus as their new found symbol of V.J. They must have been strong shoulders for they carried me round the Circus not once but twice. Everyone was cheering and shouting as though I was the conquering hero of the hour. I began to wonder if I would ever make the trooping centre in time. Fortunately my supporters collapsed exhausted on the second lap almost opposite the trooping centre and I was able to slip through its portals. Inside I found that the warrant officer in charge had witnessed the proceedings. "You need not have worried, Sir, we guessed you were on our lists and heading this way. It's not every officer that gets a send-off like that and we held the transport out back until you could get away. Bit hard you flying back with V.J.2. still to come."

CHAPTER 18

Bangkok and the Fruits of Victory

We left the celebrating crowds by the back streets of Piccadilly bound for Southampton where we learnt that we would be boarding a Short Sunderland Flying boat in Southampton Water that would be our transport back to the Far East. We were all elated by the sudden end of the war and delighted to be going back in a flying boat, a rare luxury compared with the Dakota transport that had brought us out.

It was quite an experience – we boarded a launch that took us to the flying boat. Inside it was so spacious and solid. Our seats were like armchairs. There was masses of room to walk around. Take-off was quite different. The roar of engines, then an increasing bow wave that blotted out vision from the port holes, but soon collapsed as we became airborne. The route too was very different. Our first stop was a lake somewhere in Southern France just north of the Pyrenees, then Sardinia. Sometimes we landed on lakes, sometimes on the sea. We spent the night near Tel Aviv in Palestine where we went in search of female company but ended up with some cheerful but over fat tarts.

Next day we flew gracefully off, heading for Karachi. I no longer remember the stops en route to this city, where we spent four days kicking our heels in the heat and dust of the transit camp. The accustomed priorities had changed. In fact, there seemed no priorities. Everyone appeared to be in a state of limbo. I cannot remember whether our plane was just being serviced or whether it was awaiting spare parts or what.

I passed the time by walking around the port of Karachi sightseeing but there seemed very little to see except the local Bazaar and the Zoo. I do not remember much about either except the heat and the dust and the beggars. The latter seemed to favour the Zoo where they almost outnumbered the animals. I do remember one in particular who approached me with a blanket over his head. When he was within feet of me he drew the blanket aside from his face to expose the most horrifying advanced stages of leprosy. His nose was completely eaten away with the disease, just leaving a sunken cavity. His face looked like a skull with skin stretched over it. Next moment a leprositic hand shot out from under the blanket. It had stumps for fingers and groped for my arm. I rebounded just in time to avoid physical contact, threw a handful of small change on the ground, more to delay his following than out of charity, and walked smartly out of the Zoo back down the road to the transit camp without pausing or slackening my pace until I reached the guard room at its entrance, streaming with sweat from this exertion in the heat of the day. I felt quite sickened by what I had seen and the thought of so nearly being touched by this leper.

I am not at all squeamish and was used to seeing bodies badly mutilated in battle but this was different. The thought of the slow insiduous and irreversible destruction of the body by this horrific disease was bad enough, but that lepers should be allowed to roam the streets begging and pawing at people seemed inexcusable. No doubt it was partly fear of catching the disease that had frightened me, coupled with the unexpected manner in which the beggar had exposed himself. One thing was certain, I was not made for missionary service. Today the only clear memory I have of Karachi is that begging leper's face.

After six days of increasing tension and frustration at the apathy of the movement control organisation we were warned to be ready to take off at dawn next day. We would be flying across India to Calcutta where once again we would be in a transit camp awaiting transport to our final destination. Next day more delays and dawn became midday or later before we were at last back on our lovely flying boat ready for take-off.

Our first stop was on a beautiful lake somewhere in the heart of India. Sapphire blue water, green covered hills falling steeply to the water and not a sign of life or habitation anywhere. As we taxied across the lake after landing we spotted a small wooden jetty with a mount of 44 gallon petrol drums beside it and an RAF launch just leaving the jetty. The launch nosed the great flying boat right alongside the jetty and we were lead away up a steep track to a hut where we were to await refuelling. It seemed that this small section of RAF personnel had spent the war isolated in this Shangrila awaiting the occasional visit of a flying boat crossing the continent and in need of refuelling. By the time we were escorted down to the lake again for take-off the shadows of evening were already lengthening. We climbed up and over the hills surrounding the lake and continued our journey across the continent of India in the fast fading light of evening. In the secure comfort of our seats we dozed away the hours into darkness when suddenly our plane banked steeply and we were aware of our pilot walking down the aisle between our seats saying "Wake up, wake up, you can't miss this, look out of the starboard ports and you will see one of the wonders of the world, the Taj Mahal by moonlight".

I suspect that he had purposely reduced altitude to give us this magnificent view. There it was only a few hundred feet below us. A magnificent view of the Taj in brilliant moonlight. It was breathtaking in its cool beauty. A view that one could never forget. I am sure that we should not have been travelling at this low altitude but the pilot had planned it to give us this rare opportunity that could never be repeated. Thirty years later the beauty of this vision is still frozen on my mind. We circled around it spellbound then lifted quietly back into the night sky where we belonged. I do not know what risks that pilot took but I am indebted to him for taking the trouble to give us that unique view.

Hours later we came down in the muddy waters of the Howrah River at Calcutta. We said goodbye to our pilot and were transported to the familiar portals of the Grand Hotel in Chowringee which had become the wartime transport centre for officers awaiting movement orders to Burma. I soon realised that with the cessation of hostilities no one was very interested in moving anyone anywhere. The place was packed to bursting with officers in transit and most were quite happy to remain there drinking until doomsday now that the war was over.

I made various enquiries of my chance to get flown into Rangoon. Priorities had changed. Active service troops were already a thing of the past. Priority was now only for strange members of the civil administration, whatever that might be. I would just have to await my turn.

Depressed I sought refuge in the flat of my friend Ian Melville Stevens. Apart from the air conditioning, he always seemed to have interesting visitors with whom I discussed a wide field of subjects from philosophy to religion. Not just the dogma of the Christian Church but the varied merits of the many religious sects of the Far East.

I was forced to spend ten days in Calcutta and would have been there for a great deal more but for the arrival at Ian's flat of an RAF pilot snatching a day's rest from the Rangoon shuttle. I was in luck once again as he promised he would fly me in as urgent cargo. Within 24 hours I was happily wedged between his mixed cargo flying into Rangoon. We landed at Rangoon in pouring rain for it was now mid-monsoon. I soon located 421 Fd. Coy or rather the rear party, for the rest of the company had flown into Bangkok the previous day as our Brigade, 114th, had been assigned to Bangkok to take over the surrender of the Japanese army group there. The rear party was about to load our transport at the docks to make the journey from Rangoon by sea around Malaya and Singapore and up the Gulf of Siam to Bangkok. I was told they had built a false superstructure around our captured Ford V8 staff car to make it look like a 15 cwt. truck and that was safely on board and Bangkok bound.

While I was waiting my turn for a flight from Rangoon, I shaved off my moustache and my choti, determined to start the days of peace with a clean face. Rumour already abounded that Bangkok was the best of destinations, full of lovely girls and life with a capital 'L'. I could not wait to get there and was just in time to join the very tail of the brigade's move with what was familiarly referred to as the odds and sods. When I got to the airfield I had no difficulty in getting assigned a flight in and discovered that most of the so-called odds and sods were in fact nurses being flown in to look after the POWs released from the infamous Death Railway.

It was September and the monsoon was in full swing. The weather had closed in and it had been pouring rain for the last three days. The flight over the mountains that separate Burma from Siam, an extension of the Himalayas, like a backbone down into Malaya, had become very treacherous under these conditions. Already flight control had reported that the previous plane to take off had crashed somewhere in this mountain chain. When it was our turn for take-off we were silent, wrapped in our own anxieties for the next few hours flying under these conditions. However, we did not get very far; something was wrong with the plane and within half an hour we were landing at Rangoon again. We were quickly directed across the tarmac to another plane and another take-off in pouring rain, but again within half an hour one of its engines failed and faltered and we were back at Rangoon once again. By the time we were being shepherded in pouring rain to yet another plane the nurses were making forced cheerful remarks about being third time lucky, but no one sounded as though they believed it. We were all distinctly scared of both the weather and the state of the planes for they were the same old Dakota's that had been flogged to death on air supply over the last two years.

As it turned out third time was lucky for we made it over the mountains after a terrific buffeting in the clouds; quite suddenly the swirling rain clouds gave way to a wonderful view of the chequer-board of rice fields and sunshine that was our first glimpse of Siam. Soon we were landing on Don Muang Airfield. As we taxied to the airport buildings we were confronted by lorry loads of Jap soldiers with fixed bayonets encompassing the bounds of the airfield. Even more extraordinary to our eyes was the sight of Japanese officers with swords dangling at their sides and wearing lavender coloured cotton gloves. When you have spent two and a half years fighting against a ruthless enemy that you rarely saw except as shadowy figures darting for cover in the jungle or as corpses after the battle was over, it was very strange to find yourself surrounded by them on every side, yet they behaved as though we did not exist. They carried on their normal military functions as though they could not see us.

In these early days of the Japanese unconditional surrender it must have been a pretty traumatic experience for them. They had been defeated in Burma, but this was but a campaign on the periphery of their empire. They still had a powerful well disciplined army that was trained to fight to the last man for every inch of ground. Suddenly our wonder weapon had changed everything. Their Emperor, for whom they were only too willing to die, had ordered them to surrender. It must have taken a lot of adjusting to this dramatic reversal of their fortunes. Possibly the only way of adjusting to such a sudden change in their status was to withdraw into the confines of their disciplinary code and ignore the sudden arrival of the enemy in their midst. Just carry out the orders of their Emperor and try not to see the humiliating presence of their enemy who by some strange and not fully understood advantage was now able to fly into the heart of their military stronghold and take over their High Command.

The drive into Bangkok was memorable. In those days Don Muang Airport was out in the country some miles from the city. As we approached Bangkok the first signs of the bounds of the city was their war memorial to some war outside our historical knowledge. It was an imposing obelisk set in the centre of a roundabout, depicting a soldier, a sailor and an airman standing on its three sides. Later I heard the Siamese joke that these three men were the only three casualties in the war that it commemorated. This was typical of the Thai sense of humour, so close to our own with their ability to laugh at themselves. A rare quality in Asia that few other nations seemed to possess.

Bangkok was the most fascinating city I had yet seen in the Far East. It was known as the Venice of the East, and not without reason, canals abounded everywhere in the city. In the residential quarter the roads were bounded on both sides with canals, pink with the bloom of water lilies. The houses that bordered these roads each had a little bridge spanning the canal that led to its garden and the house beyond. Raja Damnan Avenue, its main shopping centre, was unexpectedly modern with a very modern sculptured monument in the centre of it. Its Government buildings were obviously modelled on the White House in Washington. Its main hotel, the Ratana Cosin, was the epitome of modern design and comfort. It was all a new and exciting world and amongst it all were their own superb temples and pagodas, adorned with roofs of beautiful glazed tiles. I had seen nothing like it before and the memory of those first impressions were indelibly imprinted on my mind.

My first and most important task was to find my own unit, and this was best achieved by finding the CRE at Div. HQ. Our CRE in Burma, Tom Wright, had been replaced in the last stages of the campaign by

Phil Hatch, a very different character and certainly more suited to the life we were to experience in Bangkok.

I found HQRE near part of the imposing White House Government Buildings. I received an unusually warm welcome and was informed that I had been promoted to the post of Adjutant at HQRE. At first I was flattered by the appointment, but I soon discovered that it was not all that I had expected. In fact, it meant that I was confined to an office sorting out a multitude of administrative problems while everyone else roared around having a jolly good time. I hardy ever saw the CRE except racing past my office window with a Jeep full of pretty Siamese girls. I soon realised why I had landed the job of Adjutant. Someone had to hold the administrative fort and who better than John Henslow, after all he had had his 28 days' home leave and was therefore lowest on the list for enjoying the fruits of victory. I could see their point but it did not make it any more bearable. I sat in my office trying to sort out innumerable administrative problems that my training had done little to prepare me for. Every now and then some of my brother officers would call in and recount stories of the wonderful time they were having in the world outside. Then leave me with a list of problems they had no time to sort out and depart to continue the pressing engagements of new found social life.

I began to realise that I had become a military Cinderella with no prospect of rescue by a Prince Charming except at the weekend, when I emerged like a mole from my office blinking at the light of day and wondering where to start catching up on the exploits of my fellow officers. My friend, Tigger Royle, whom I suspect had manoeuvred himself out of the prospect of Div. Adjutant and into my appointment of 2nd I/C of the company, had quickly appreciated the restrictions of the Adjutant appointment. He suggested we went to the races which we could view from the club house of the golf club where we had already made some good contacts.

It was my first real contact with the Siamese and I was more than impressed by the occasion. The balcony of the club house was packed with a vivacious crowd of very charming and cultural Siamese. The women were exceedingly attractive and well dressed, many of the men had that casual assurance so reminiscent of the product of English public schools which I soon discovered was just what many of them were.

At first it was a little confusing because everyone was introduced by their nicknames. Their true names were long and almost unpronounceable. I was introduced to Pong and Toon. Later I learnt that Toon was Prince Amakabara, educated at Eastbourne College and a member of the Thai Royal Family. He owned a splendid car called a Sampson which was a pre-war English product. His wife, Pong, was presumably a Princess by marriage and their both spoke English and French fluently.

The Siamese were in a strange position. When the Japanese invaded their country as a stepping stone to Malaya and Burma they had the sense to realise that they could achieve little by physically opposing the vastly superior Japanese forces other than the slaughter and subjugation of their people, so they entered into an agreement by which they kept their sovereignty but the Japs could use their country as a base. There was no doubt where their sympathies lay, but it was an intelligent compromise that was typical of the Siamese political diplomacy that had enabled them to remain free from foreign domination in the past. It was the astute diplomatic understanding of their King Chulalongkorn that had kept them free from the threat of English, French or Dutch domination in the 19th Century. In those days it was the powers of Europe that sought to subjugate the Kingdoms of the Far East where they were vieing with each other in an era of empire building. King Chulalongkorn realised that Siam would soon be annexed by one of these western powers under the pretext of protecting their trading interests. With great political sagacity he pre-empted such action by inviting each western power to establish its embassy in Bangkok. A very astute move for once they each had an Ambassador or Consulate representation on the spot, no western power felt free to steal a march on the other. They spent most of their energies monitoring the others intentions and aspirations with the result that any potential advances by one of the powers were quickly countered through diplomatic channels by the others. The result was that Siam became one of the few countries in the Far East to remain free from domination by a European power. The word Thai in Siamese means free, hence why they now call their country Thailand.

The last four years of Japanese occupation, co-existence or whatever they chose to call it, had not been to the liking of the Siamese but they had little choice. The Japanese were at war and took life very seriously. Something that the Siamese were incapable of doing and found very foreign to their nature.

They were a very sociable race, they lived for the day without much heed for tomorrow. The reason for this was obvious: they had no need to. There was an abundance of food, rice, fish and fruit, produced in surplus to their requirements. In my year's stay in Bangkok I never saw a beggar, a sharp contrast to the other countries of the Far East I had visited.

I mention all this because it helps to explain our relationship with the Siamese. Technically we were occuping their country to take over the surrender of the Japanese Army Group that was stationed there. Politically, the situation was somewhat obscure for their Government under the Regent Pi Bul had co-operated with the Japanese to the extent that they had allowed the Japs to use their country as a military base for the occupation of Malaya and Burma. Thousands of allied prisoners of war had been used as slave labour on their territory in the construction of the infamous Death Railway connecting Siam with Burma.

Technically I presume we were at war with Siam because we later signed a Peace Treaty with them. However, the feeling was very much that we were both celebrating the downfall of the Japanese and that we were liberators in their eyes rather than occupiers of their country. There was mutual respect and co-operation between our forces and neither put any constraints on the other.

Back at the races that day I did not make any money, but I made a lot of friends. What impressed me most was how different the Siamese were from the other peoples of the Far East. They were very sociable and loved entertaining but above all their sense of humour was very akin to our own for they enjoyed making fun of themselves. No doubt this stemmed from the fact that they had never been subject to European domination and had the easy assurance of meeting us on equal terms. They had no historical cause for an inferiority complex and the fact that so many of their aristocracy had been educated in Europe, meant that we met on very equal terms. In fact, at that time the heirs apparent in the Royal Family, two brothers, were being educated in Switzerland and, as I have said, the country was under the rule of the Regent Pi Bul. As with all Regents, he was suspected of every machiavellian plot imaginable.

From that day at the races I received various invitations. One to a Red Cross Ball at the Officers' Club which was quite an eye opener to the lavish style of Siamese entertainment. I doubt if it could have been matched in England at the time, but here only weeks after the cessation of hostilities it was like a Hollywood set. An open air dance floor surrounded by colonnades and a large dance orchestra playing in a beautifully illuminated pink sea shell. We sat at little tables on the grass around the dance floor and nibbled lotus seeds. The latter sound more exotic than they were in fact, for they were not unlike melon seeds and the kernel was hardly worth the effort of extraction. On this occasion Pong and Toon were our hosts and everyone seemed to know them and come to their table for a chat. Tigger and I were quite confused with the number of introductions that came at the rate of one every few minutes. We were also very impressed by the number of very attractive women and their equally impressive standard of dress. It was hard to believe that there had ever been a war. It was a very romantic evening under the stars with the orchestra playing all the tunes popular at the time, from 'In the Mood' to 'Mood Indigo'. There was also a very Siamese dance called the Rum Wong with a very haunting and unforgettable tune but the dance itself was even more Siamese. Most of it was executed with the hands. It left the Europeans feeling very awkward and clumsy, for the Siamese have most beautiful and delicate hands which they are trained to use at a very early age. The girls long slender fingers seemed to bend backwards in a graceful curve with the forefinger and thumb held together, while the hands enscribed wide encircling movements like temple dancers. Thirty-five years later I can still clearly remember the melody of the Rum Wong.

The real trouble was that there were too many attractive young girls and by the end of the evening we had failed to home in on any one in particular. We had both had innumerable dances with Pong who was obviously enjoying every minute of the evening, for Toon seemed to prefer chatting to other men than dancing with his wife. Had I been more perceptive I might have seen the seeds of estrangement, for a few months later they were divorced.

This taste of the world outside my office made me even more determined to relinquish my appointment as Adjutant to which I was far from suited. I worked on the CRE and on my old OC Selby Pride, and eventually it was agreed that I should return to 2nd I/C of my company to prepare to take over the command of the company when Selby Pride, who had become engaged to an Australian nurse, would be repatriated.

Tigger took over the Adjutant job for which he was far more suited than I and I returnd to my Company with the greater prospects of freedom during the working hours. The change coincided with the move of our Company HQ to a new location. Our officers' mess took over a house previously occupied by the Japanese Naval Attaché who had been recently interned. When we took over his residence it was intact with all his personal possessions. There was a distasteful scramble for loot. Jim Groves, a Lt. Col. attached to Div. HQ, had his eye on a picture, a Japanese silk painting with Fuji Yama in the background and delicate bamboo forests peering through the mists surrounding it. He was very frustrated to find that anyone in the company, which had first call on the contents, had artistic appreciation and similar interest in it. Possession was 9/10ths of the law and I won, but Jim never forgave me. There was a very fine ivory Ma Jong set that someone collected but the only other loot that I remember falling to me was a set of golf clubs. Being 6ft. 4ins. they were not quite made to measure, but I had an invitation to play golf with Pong and Toon and this was a necessary *carte d'entre* if I was to be able to exploit this invitation. I still have the set at home today but no time to use them other than for the village fête!

When all the handy loot had been divided there remained one object, the safe. A large steel safe, locked and no keys, which intrigued speculation regarding its potential contents. The more we looked at it the more speculation there was on what it might contain. Eventually we could stand it no longer and decided to blow it. After all we were sappers and experts in explosives, though not in safe cracking. The heavy safe was moved onto the lawn and I stuffed the lock with gelignite, a detonator and a length of fuse and we all waited for the resultant explosion. Much to our surprise it worked. Our manuals had trained us for bridge demolition but not for this more refined use of explosives. After the explosion we approached the smoking safe with caution, each had his own ideas of the possible fabulous wealth that it might contain. Gemstones, gold, secret diplomatic instructions. . . with a heavy lever I prised open the demolished safe door. . . it was almost empty except for something on the top shelf: a gramophone record that on inspection turned out to be a recording of Arthur Bliss's march from the film 'The Shape of Things to Come'. It meant little to the other expectant safe crackers, but it meant a great deal to me.

Ten years ago or more, before the war, my father had sold 60 acres of woodland to Arthur Bliss, a musician of distinction who was later, after the war, to be knighted and become honoured as Master of the Queen's Music. He built a modern house in the woods, Pen Pitts, together with a music room where he composed in peace and isolation. As a boy of ten he once invited me into the sanctuary of his music studio and played me a recording of his latest composition, the march for 'The Shape of Things to Come'. He then asked for my opinion on his composition. It seemed more than coincidence that this same haunting theme, thirteen years later, should confront me as the sole content of the safe belonging to the Japanese Naval Attaché to the Kingdom of Siam. To my brother officers it was a supreme anti-climax to their expectations, but to me in a strange way it was just the opposite. It was in its own way a perfect climax to a rather bizarre operation. I had not really expected to find anything of value in the safe for if you are about to be interned, and the sequence of events must have given the Naval Attaché ample warning of his fate, the contents of one's safe would be the first priority for disposal. I have often wondered whether it was accident or design that this one record was left behind in the safe.

The house was in a very attractive residential part of the city. The road that led to it was, like so many in Bangkok in those days, lined on either side by a water lily filled canal and the entrance was by a small bridge over the roadside canal, even the drive to the house had a small feeder canal alongside (which proved my downfall later on).

For the moment, life was ideal. Very few military duties but plenty of social ones. We lived in style and enjoyed the fruits of victory as did our resident companions the Siamese cats. Siamese cats really do come from Siam as we soon discovered. The fish food in Siam was out of this world. For breakfast we used to have what were called King Prawns. They were so large that one filled your plate and was a breakfast in itself. However, the resident Siamese cats were equally addicted to this delicacy and appeared from nowhere as soon as the King Prawns were served, their persistent yowling detracting from one's concentration on this wonderful gastronomic delight. To start with we were fascinated by their presence and fed them rather indiscriminately. Too late we realised our mistake. When more and more homed in on this feline haven, word got around and we found ourselves overwhelmed with a seething mass of yowling Siamese cats all intent on cashing in on our misguided generosity. We slung them out of the windows only to find a dozen re-enter on the heels of the mess waiter as he came in from the kitchen with the next course. They soon made life quite intolerable. It was too hot to keep the windows closed and as fast as you threw them out of one window they were back through another.

I am a little ashamed to record that I was the inventor of Siamese roulette. There was a large central ceiling fan in the sitting room and any particularly stubborn cat was placed on the fan which was then switched on. It was not like a modern high speed fan, but had big blades that rotated slowly, stirring the air into a cooling down draught. As the fan slowly gathered speed, the cat clung onto one or other of the three big blades, but eventually centrifugal force overcame its hold on the blade and it was spun off. There were five windows down one side of the room and a door at either end. The third wall was blank. We numbered the windows and doors and betting was taken on which the cat would exit through. I do not remember the actual odds other than you got double you stake money if the cat was shot clearly through your open window without touching the wall. It was not as cruel as it might seem for the cats were very agile and never received any injury, but it had the desired effect of discouraging their re-entry. Our cat problem was soon solved and Saimese roulette died through lack of their support.

The other thing I remember about our mess was the lizards. They lived behind the pictures during the daytime and came out at night. It was current belief in those days that in the height of inebriation people saw sky blue lizards with pink spots. I do not know where the idea started but in Bangkok those lizards were sky blue and they had pink spots. As they only came out at night to creep across the walls it was easy to see how the story could have come into being. However, I checked in the sober light of morning by looking behind the pictures and there they were, still sky blue and with pink and crimson spots.

The evolution of night life in Bangkok was quite incredible. During the Japanese occupation there had been no night life as we know it, but with the sudden influx of the allied forces, night clubs sprang up overnight like mushrooms. Within the first two months of the allied forces arrival, over eighty night clubs had opened in Bangkok. Many of them, built from scratch, but some using existing buildings. Basically they consisted of a dance floor, a raised section for the band and a roof supported on columns open on three sides to the warm tropical night. It still seems incredible that they had the resources to build so many in so short a time; even more that they could muster the musicians to staff over eighty dance bands. In those days the disco was not invented, and I doubt if recorded music would have stood a chance in competition with the variety of live bands that were available. The electric guitar and Hawaian music was very popular at the time, but so was the big band music of Benny Goodman and Glen Miller.

The other prerequisite of these night clubs were the dance hostesses. Bangkok seemed to have an endless supply of attractive young girls to staff these establishments, but this is more understandable for it needed little training and offered remuneration for just dancing and having a good time. Something that most young girls would have been happy to do for nothing and most Siamese girls seemed willing to do more than just dance the night out with their partners. No doubt it gave them the opportunity to have a good time and be paid for it.

As always under these circumstances some of these establishments were more reputable than others. There was big money to be made and there were plenty cashing in on it. Not least were our own military police, who discovered how to turn their authority to profit as well. When a new night club was nearing completion they would drive up with a flourish with a large notice board saying 'Out of bounds to British Troops'. This they would proceed to nail up outside the premises with as much noise as possible. It never failed to attract the attentions of the new proprietor who never failed to offer suitable remuneration for its removal. Having negotiated a price they took it down and moved on to the next establishment and repeated the process.

One of the first tasks of the brigade when it arrived in Siam was to assist the various bodies that had been set up to administer the large numbers of prisoners of war, in particular the thousands who had been employed on the construction and maintenance of the infamous Death Railway into Burma. I myself had little to do with this operation which was carried out very quickly and efficiently by special teams that went by the usual military abbreviations such as RAPWI, which I think stood for Released Allied Prisoners of War and Internees. Most of the British and Indian POWs on the railway were in a very poor state of health and went straight to hospitals back in India or were repatriated. We saw very little of them in Bangkok except for the Dutch. Whether they had survived better than most due to their long acclimatisation in the Dutch East Indies or whether they had no organisation to repatriate them I do not know. Whatever the reason they came back to Bangkok and formed quite a large contingent of officers.

CHAPTER 19

Jap POW's and the Victory Parade

Now that the tables had been turned and we had large numbers of Jap prisoners to contend with, many Dutch officers were appointed to be Commandants of the Jap POWs. As they had first-hand experience of being prisoners under the Japs, who better to put in charge of these POW camps. It was a kind of poetic justice, well deserved after the cruelty they had endured under the Japanese that the tables should be so completely turned.

One of them I came to know very well. Lt. Stan Kanters, who was in charge of the camp of Japanese engineer troops. Most of them had been supervising the construction of the Death Railway where Stan had been their prisoner, so there was no love lost between them. Such is the fate of POWs their promotion gets left behind. However, his age and military experience would have accorded him at least the rank of major had he not been taken prisoner. I had first call on his camp for any engineering work we had to do. We used them as a pioneer corps though they had many very fine artisans amongst them. I was impressed by their ability to work. They were like ants and given spades and other hand tools they could shift earth like a bulldozer.

I had a Japanese interpreter assigned to me. He spoke fluent American, having been educated in California. I later discovered that he had been in the battle for Kohima and more interesting still he had been with the Jap unit directly opposite Jail Hill where I had built those tank platforms in no man's land about 18 months ago. We went through the battle again and it was fascinating to learn what it had been like on the other side and, above all, how the effect of that 55 mm. medium gun firing over open sights at their bunkers from Treasury Ridge had made their positions untenable. It was something they had never expected and was the last straw that had forced them to start their withdrawal, which soon became a retreat back to Ukrul. As long as they held their position at Kohima they believed they could gain our supply bases at Dimapur and their own supply problem would be overcome, but when they were forced to pull back from these positions they realised that this could never be achieved in time and that they were dependent on their own L of C which was fast failing under the onset of the monsoon. It was the turning point of their invasion of India. From then on they became desperately short of both food and ammunition and had to retreat to survive.

It was fascinating to learn at first hand what it had been like for the Japs at the battle of Kohima, not as a broad strategy but on the very sector where I was involved and from someone who had obviously been there, for he remembered the detail of the to and fro battle too well. At first I suspected that he could be making up a good story to impress me. I cross-questioned him on various aspects of the battle and the terrain and his answers convinced me that he must have been there and in the positions that he claimed his unit was occupying. It really was the most extraordinary coincidence that I should meet a member of the Japanese forces that had been directly opposite me in battle and who could speak English well enough to describe the situation in detail. It also gave me great satisfaction to learn that the efforts to get that medium artillery piece into position at Kohima had been so worthwhile.

He was however a very educated Jap, not the type of person we had been educated to believe that the Japanese were. In wartime you are indoctrinated to believe the worst of your enemy. They were depicted as cruel and sub-human. Certainly their treatment of prisoners bore this out. As soldiers we had great respect for them but regarded their fanatical behaviour in battle as suicidal. No doubt their indoctrination regarding their enemy was far more intense than was ours.

It was about this time that I got another insight into the Japanese character. The Japanese engineer troops that I had under command for various engineering projects were subject to our ultimate discipline. To make this possible on an individual basis, every Jap soldier had his name written in Japanese characters on a piece of cloth, safety-pinned to his shirt pocket. If an individual prisoner's behaviour warranted disciplinary action, all you had to do was remove this cloth tag and hand it into the guard room of his camp with the complaint and it would be dealt with.

One day I was returning from construction site and passed a company of Japanese engineer troops on their way back to camp. They were seated beside the road resting, as I passed in my Jeep they stood and saluted. Out of the corner of my eye I saw one Jap soldier saluting with a cigarette in his mouth. I had a pretty sore head at the time, so I jammed my Jeep into reverse and drove back to him. He was I suspect just a simple soldier who had been smoking as I approached and in a moment of confusion had stood up and saluted but had not removed the cigarette from his mouth. As I reversed up to him my jemadar leant out of the Jeep and took the cigarette from his mouth and tore off the cloth name tag pinned to his lapel, handed it to me and then we drove off. That evening I handed it to Stan Kanters at the Jap POW camp, with a brief note on the offence. Stan smiled wryly and said "If you have got a moment to spare come over to the guard room and watch this being dealt with. The working parties should be returning any moment now, it will open your eyes to Jap disciplinary methods".

We sauntered across to the guard room by the entrance gate and sat down on its verandah. We could already see the first of the working parties marching back down the road that lead to the camp, so we had not long to wait. Stan gave some curt order in Japanese to the sergeant of the guard who disappeared and returned with the Japanese orderly officer of the day. He was a tall thin faced officer with extraordinary aquiline features for a Jap. High cheek bones and stern features that expressed nothing but resentment for the position that the Japanese Imperial Army now found themselves in. There was no surrender in his cold eyes. Stan handed him the strip of cloth with the soldier's name on it, explained the offence and told him to deal with the offender. The Jap officer stiffened but his face remained a mask. As each working party arrived opposite the guard room they were halted and turned left to face the guard room. The orderly officer walked slowly down the line scrutinising them while they stood stiffly to attention, no one batted an eyelid. The orderly officer spat a few words of Japanese at them, the sergeant saluted and ordered right turn, quick march and they were away. I got the impression that they all looked a bit scared of their officer.

The same procedure was carried out with the next two squads, but when the fourth squad left turned to face the guard room I spotted my man with the missing name tab in front. He looked very conspicuous without his white name tag and obviously felt it. The orderly officer had spotted him too and was growling something through his teeth. The tone of his voice got higher and louder and finally ended in what sounded like a high pitched bark. The offender took a pace forward, another bark and the men on either side of him stepped forward. The orderly officer stood in front of him with his hands on his hips and shouted at him for half a minute while the soldier stood stiff and motionless. I was beginning to feel sorry for the poor little Jap, when suddenly the Jap officer drew back his clenched fist and struck him a savage blow in the face. The offender reeled as if he was going to fall but the two men on either side seemed prepared and immediately caught hold of his arms and held him upright again.

The officer spat out a few more invectives then delivered another right to the jaw that seemed to put him out cold, for his head went back then fell forward on his chest. He would have fallen in a heap on the ground but for the men gripping him on either side. Next moment there were shouted commands and the three men took a pace backwards into their places in the front rank or rather the two supporters did and the man in the middle went back without his feet touching the ground. As the squad turned right and marched off there was a quick readjustment in the ranks and I saw the offender was still flanked by two men supporting him and he was still out cold, for his feet were trailing on the ground between them.

The orderly officer watched the squad depart then returned to the guard room verandah, saluted and to my surprise spoke in perfect English. "I have identified the man. He will be punished later", saluted and strutted off in the direction of the camp huts.

I turned to Stan Kanters feeling rather horrified; if that was identification what would the punishment be? Stan was grinning from ear to ear. "Well, John, you've seen a bit of Jap discipline. What do you think of it? When you see how they treat their own men you can understand what they kept for their prisoners. Proper bastards, aren't they? Believe me that officer is nothing special. I've seen far worse than him". I suddenly realised why our POWs had been treated so inhumanely. If this was how they treated their own soldiers one could hardly expect that their prisoners would be treated less severely. It was a bit of an eye opener to me.

I asked Stan what the actual punishment would be. Having been a prisoner under the Japs he was not unduly concerned. "Oh, I expect he will spend the next week working up to his neck in water shovelling mud out of the Klong or something like that", he said casually. As I drove back that night to the comfort of our mess I felt grateful that I had not fallen prisoner to the Japanese.

At weekends I frequently found myself at the golf course with Toon and Pong. My short clubs and erratic play did not provide much opposition for Toon and he seemed a bit bored with the game and often chose to stay behind in the club house chatting and drinking with his friends. On these occasions I went round with Pong and generally played much better as I did not try to hit the ball so hard. The course was a very pleasant one, part through trees and part in the open, but like everything in Bangkok it was intersected by canals. These invariably had a magnetic attraction, for my ball in particular, when they were right in front of the tee and I had to drive off over them. Their presence had an unnerving effect on me for fear of landing in them, with the inevitable result that I topped the ball and it landed fair and square in the canal. This was not as severe a problem as it might seem for though golf balls were scarce and difficult to obtain there were plenty of small boys only too willing to dive in and retrieve your ball for a few tickals (Siamese currency).

These boys could also be hired as 'Agi Wallahs' to stand forward and mark the line of your ball so that you did not waste time looking for it if it landed in the rough. I soon discovered there was another hazard which on some days could save the cost of their hire many times over. The crows in that part of the country found golf balls a great attraction and would often swoop down and pick up your ball almost as soon as it had landed. One day I was sitting on the tee looking down the fairway and waiting for the players in front to clear. There was suddenly a flutter of wings behind me and I turned just in time to see a crow making off with my new ball that I had teed up ready to drive off as soon as the course was clear. I shouted and flung my club at the crow but it missed and the bird flapped slowly away in the direction of Watt Benchapon Pritt, a very lovely old temple that lay off the edge of the race course which encircled most of the golf course. I felt particularly cheated as it had taken it literally in reach behind my back and also it was my last good ball that I had only recently purchased that morning. Needless to say Pong shrieked with laughter at the sight of me chasing the crow and hurling my club at it in an attempt to make it drop my precious ball.

At the next tee she insisted in giving me a new ball. As the drive was straight across a wide canal I declined to accept the gift as in my present mood I knew where it would end up. However, she insisted saying it was a very special ball that could not possibly get lost in the canal. Needless to say it was not long before I drove it straight into a canal. I could not think why it was that Pong was so delighted until I spotted it floating on the surface. It was a floater. I have never seen them anywhere else so possibly they were designed for the Bangkok course. This was one problem solved but there were still the crows. I eventually solved this one too for I had begun to realise that they always took the same flight line when they picked up a ball, straight past Watt Benchapon Pritt. As golf balls were getting very scarce I decided to hide myself with my 12 bore at some suitable point on their flight path. It worked a treat. I picked myself a good spot in some bushes near the edge of the course. I did not have long to wait before I spotted a crow coming with something white in its mouth. A careful swing with my gun, bang, and down came the crow and the golf ball. I soon discovered that a near miss did the trick just as well and left no crow to dispose of, also as they were bringing me the balls it seemed imprudent to shoot all the crows and a very cheap way of restocking my supply of balls. I did not mention this exploit to any of my Siamese friends, firstly because they might wish to reclaim any balls they had lost in this way, and secondly because I was not sure how the Siamese, being Buddhists, regarded the taking of a crow's life – these crows in particular as they seemed to be residents of the local temples. I did wonder, however, whether I had short-circuited a nice little side line of the local priest, as golf balls were of considerable value in those immediate post-war days.

It was about this time when I was first asked out to dinner with Toon and Pong. Their house was a pleasant house situated in the outskirts of Bangkok. The house itself was nothing very special with a small garden in front of it. I was introduced to their son, aged about one year and a very chubby product of such a slim parent. However, what I remembered most was the dinner, not the dinner itself, although this was very good, but the manner in which it was served. We sat at a rather low table and a number of servants brought in innumerable small dishes of delicacies. What was unusual to me was the way the servants all came in on their knees, they shuffled across the floor either on their knees or crouching so low that their heads were practically down to the floor, when they had delivered their burden they then retreated backwards out of the door with their heads kept well down the whole time.

Pong, seeing my embarrassment, explained that because Toon was a Prince in the Royal Household the servants had to keep the level of their head below his. They could also not turn their back on him while in the room, hence the rather awkward manner of serving the meal. I also learnt that in Siam you should never touch someone on the head, not even pat a child on the head, nor should you sit with your feet sticking out towards them. The reasons seemed a bit obscure at the time but it was good to learn these things before you unknowingly insulted someone. The Siamese are sensitive about touching each other. They do not shake hands but place their hands together in front of them as though in prayer and bow the head forward slightly saying "Sawadee". This seems to be the universal greeting in Siam.

The official surrender of the Japanese forces had taken place at 0341 GMT on the 12th September, 1945. General Itagaki had deputised for Field Marshal Count Teranchi as the latter was suffering from the effects of a stroke that he had when he heard the news of the fall of Mandalay. The official surrender took place in Singapore where General Itagaki surrendered 738,400 Japanese forces to Lord Louis Mountbatten.

Later came the surrender ceremonies designed to leave no doubt in the minds of the Japanese generals that they had surrendered unconditionally. The main one took place in Singapore where each general had to publicly bow to the Union Jack and hand over his sword to Lord Louis as our Supreme Commander. A similar ceremony was arranged in Bangkok to take in the general staff of the army group there including the generals responsible for the construction of the Death Railway.

Each Japanese general had to have an escorting allied officer. Tigger

Royle and myself found ourselves assigned to this interesting ceremonial duty. The site chosen was an area of grass playing field surrounded by trees. In one corner of the field was a large flagpole flying an even larger Union Jack and in the middle of the far side was a long series of trestle tables where our 7th Ind. Div. Commander, General Evans, was to receive the surrender of the generals' swords.

On the day we reported to the marshalling point just off the edge of the square, there our Japanese generals were already gathered in a barrack like building. While they were being sorted out and assigned to their various escorts I managed to take a few photographs of them before I had to hand over my camera to my Jeep driver and take over my general for escort. We lined up; there were about a dozen generals, but as escorts we only knew the name of the general to which we were assigned, the names meant little to us, only that as engineer officers we were escorting engineering generals, so Tigger and I assumed that we must have a couple of bastards from the Death Railway. We were instructed by GSOI in charge to march our generals out to the middle of the parade ground, halt and turn left to face the saluting base. Then one at a time starting from the right we would march over to the flag staff where our general would take off his hat and bow to the Union Jack. We would then march over to the saluting base where the general would salute, remove his sword and place it on the table in front of General Evans, salute, turn about and march back to his place. Our only duty as escorts was to accompany the general to make sure he did not try and commit hari kari on the way, see that he carried out his instructions to the letter and announce his name when we came to the saluting base.

There was barely an exchange of glances between the generals and their escorts. They all looked stone faced and I noticed that their escorts had all been chosen with attention to their height. Not one of us was under 6ft. We set off in step and the generals were punctilious in keeping in step with their escorts. They must have felt very humiliated but they all had a military pride. We marched out into the middle of the parade ground and turned left to face the saluting base in a long line.

The GSOI (Ops) clutching his clip board gave us the signal off and I set off with my general to the flag staff where he removed his hat and bowed low to the Union Jack. We then marched over to the trestle table where General Evans was waiting with a suitably serious expression on his face. I consulted my piece of paper and announced the name written on it in my best attempt at Japanese pronunciation. The Jap general seemed to recognise it and stepped forward, saluted, removed his sword and laid it carefully on the table in front of General Evans. Evans was not a very imposing figure for such a solemn occasion. He looked a bit like an overgrown schoolboy. In a strange way it must have contributed to the loss of face that was what the ceremony was all about.

The Jap generals and their escorts followed in a somewhat monotonous repetition until it came to Tigger and his general. When they reached the flag pole, Tigger's general took off his hat and gave a perfunctory nod rather than a ceremonial bow. Tigger with great presence of mind reacted as only Tigger could. He took the general by the scruff of the neck and the seat of his pants and forcibly bent him double in obeisance in front of the Union Jack. It took everybody by surprise not least his escorted general who was forcibly bent double twice over in front of the British flag. The loss of face he had tried to evade was in fact compounded to an even greater loss of face by Tigger's prompt initiative though I doubt if it was ever recognised by the British Military Authorities at the time. Certainly the remaining generals performed their "genuflections" to the flag with almost exaggerated expediency. None of them tried to shortcut his humiliation after that.

The next ceremony was the victory parade. This was postponed until both Lord Louis Mountbatten and the King of Siam were available to man the saluting base. The King of Siam and his younger brother had been incarcerated in an educational establishment in Switzerland during the war. The elder had just come of age in time to inherit the throne and the British made the most of the occasion for political reasons. He was shepherded in with ceremony and took his place on the saluting base while various contingents of British, Indian and Dutch forces marched past for a somewhat delayed victory parade. It was in fact a splendid opportunity for the Siamese to welcome back their King with a bit of pomp and ceremony laid on by the allied forces in the guise of a victory parade. The King of Siam was young, bespectacled and not very impressive, but in his splendid white uniform took the salute with Lord Louis Mountbatten standing beside him on the beflagged saluting base.

The King and his brother took up residence at the Royal Palace and we heard or saw little of them for some time. The Siamese seemed pleased but not ecstatic at the restoration of their monarchy. Their Regent Phi Bul was already under a cloud of some sort for co-operating with the Japs and I think had been deposed before the King's return but I forget the details. Their politics were mostly rumours and very second hand to us and we had neither part nor interest in them at the time.

However, some weeks later we were all galvanised by the rumoured news that the King had been assassinated. Later it was announced that he had accidently shot himself. The official version was that he had a fascination for automatic pistols and had accidentally shot himself through the head with an American 45 Colt Automatic. Knowing the safety devices on this pistol it would seem very difficult indeed to accidentally shoot yourself through the front of your head. No one believed the official version of his death, rumours abounded. The Chief of Police whom I knew socially told me that the evidence pointed to an assassin who had entered the Palace over the roofs. Agents of the deposed Regent were suspect but there was no proof. Political expediency decided that it was best to present it as an unfortunate accident though the evidence was far from conclusive for this theory. There was obviously a lot of hushing up. The King's younger brother was still a minor so the return to rule by the Regent became inevitable. Nobody seemed very happy at this outcome but nobody at the time seemed willing or able to challenge it.

CHAPTER 20

Fire and Flood

Shortly before the King's death there was another episode that involved me more directly. The Great Fire of Bangkok. It started in the street of Goldsmiths or nearby. A boiling pan of fat caught fire, it was a day of strong winds and in no time the predominantly wooden buildings of the area were ablaze. Because of the strong wind the fire quickly became out of control and the Siamese Fire Services were unable to contain the blaze. It swept down the Goldsmiths quarter with quite alarming speed. Before long it was realised that the strong winds, and the fact that most of this commercial part of the city was built of wood, had created a situation not unlike the Great Fire of London in 1666. The Siamese Government appealed to the British occupation forces for help and the GSOI (Ops) sent for the sappers with orders to try and create a fire break down wind of the blaze to halt its progress.

I was ordered to take my company to the scene of the fire and create a fire break somehow. I explained to the GSOI that we had no field park coy so we had no mechanical equipment such as bulldozers to call on. The only alternative was to use explosives and blow up a row of houses to create a break and there was no guarantee that even this would work. After a quick consultation with the Siamese Authorities I was given carte blanche to do whatever I considered necessary to stop the progress of the fire.

The CRE who was present at this 'O' Group meeting said jocularly that if I succeeded I would probably be decorated with the Order of the Sacred White Elephant by the Siamese, to which I replied, "You mean the GSOI will, don't you?" and quickly left to get on with the job.

It did not take long to load a 15 cwt. truck with explosives and muster a platoon of sappers with another in reserve with such hand tools as might be necessary. While they were getting prepared and loading I left them under command of the Subadar Major to follow up and set off myself with my own Jemadar Suri to recce the situation. When we got to the scene of the fire things were worse than I had imagined. It was bedlam and chaos, a real Dantes inferno. The only approach road was jammed with Siamese trying to rescue or pilfer the contents of the shops in advance of the flames. There was little evidence of the fire brigade who I gathered were concentrating their efforts in damping down the other side of the street adjacent to the path of the fire. To windward of the fire there was a mile of glowing embers then came the fire itself and just in advance of it were the crowds. As each successive shop caught fire there were people inside dancing around in the flames passing out the jewellery it contained. Whether they were the owners or just looters it was hard to tell but the necklaces and bracelets seemed to be passed back over the heads of the onlookers so possibly it was an organised salvage operation.

What concerned me most was the rate of progress of the fire and where I should attempt to make my fire break. The wind was moving it forward at quite a pace. I timed its progress roughly, reckoned that it would take at least 20 minutes to lay our charges across the width of the block that was ablaze and counted the houses back until I found a cross street wide enough to give us a reasonable chance. By my rough calculation the houses along the side of this cross street would be on fire in about 30 minutes. I sent my jemadar back to bring up the men and explosives. There was of course the usual delay in finding them and getting them through the crowd that was falling back from the advance of the fire. They were valuable minutes wasted for when it comes to demolishing a street of wooden houses with explosives it is in fact more exacting than if they had been built of brick. If you blow out one side of a brick house the weight of the superstructure will bring down the building in a pile of rubble, not so a wooden house which is not only more flexible but its strength is in its framing not its walls. The charges had to be laid not only on the main supports but on all the main cross beams as well. By the time we had all the charges in position and connected up with a ring main of instantaneous fuse the flames were already licking the beams to which the charges were connected. As the last detonators were inserted there was a grave risk that the whole lot could be detonated prematurely.

On the opposite side of the street there was an archway leading to a large courtyard. This seemed the nearest point from which I could safely detonate the charges. It was too close for comfort but if I was tight up against the back of the buildings I would be shielded from any large falling debris. I ordered the electric cables and exploder to be payed out through this archway to the courtyard beyond and with the exploder key in my pocket started to check that all my sappers fixing and connecting the charges were out of the buildings.

It was an alarming sight for many of the beams with charges fixed to them were now alight. It would be touch and go as to who set the charges off first, my hand on the plunger or the flames, for if one slab of guncotton caught fire its detonator would activate the whole ring main and the lot would explode. Having assured myself that all my men were clear of the demolition site, I doubled across through the archway opposite to the courtyard from where I planned to set off the charges. To my horror I found the courtyard packed tight with people.

We blew whistles and shouted 'Take cover, demolition', but it meant nothing to them. The more we shouted the broader they grinned. Whistles and red flags meant nothing to them. They first thought we were getting over excited by the fire and that they had plenty of time to disperse when the flames reached their side of the street. Little did they realise that any moment 12 x 12 timbers could be raining down on them for we had fixed several hundred weight of explosives on the other side of the street.

Then my jemadar in desperation shouted one word that seemed to get through to them – 'BOMBS'. This they understood and within seconds the courtyard was empty. By now the buildings opposite, prepared for demolition, were ablaze. It was a miracle that they had not self-detonated their charges. Feeling that I had no time to lose I fixed the exploder handle, drew it up and put my whole weight on plunging it down. To my relief the ground shook with the resultant explosion, but to my horror the result was like a giant firework exploding, for the fire had reached over the row of houses and the force of the explosion sent burning timbers into the sky trailing sparks like rockets onto the very buildings we were hoping to save.

As soon as the dust had settled I sent my sappers out to extinguish any resultant fires on our side of the fire break. In fact they found little to contend with, the force of the explosion produced sparks but no flames. Within half an hour it was evident that we had succeeded in establishing a fire break. The Siamese fire brigade moved in and damped down the now tangled timber that was all that was left of the houses along one side of the street. Within an hour there was more smoke than flames and the Great Fire of Bangkok, which was even reported in the British press at home, was under control. To windward there was a mile of glowing embers and these were starting to fade.

I could see a faint glow of light in the East heralding another day; I told my weary men to pack up and go back to barracks. I wandered back up the Street of Goldsmiths that was now just glowing embers, the only remaining remnants left standing in the ashes were the large steel safes that were part of their trade. Some of them had their doors open, others stood closed like sentry boxes in the red hot embers. Some were still glowing full red from the heat of the fire. If their contents had not been removed before the fire reached them no doubt by now these would be in a molten heap inside them. Where the heat of the embers had died right down a crowd of hopefuls were already raking among the ashes for the odd gem stone that might have survived. They looked like crows prospecting for seed corn.

I retraced my steps to my Jeep and suddenly feeling very tired, said, "Wapos Jow" to my driver, which means "Go back home". We had done all we were asked to do and as dawn was breaking it was time to snatch a little sleep.

Looking back on the operation we had been very lucky for at one time the risk of premature explosion had been very high but by the Grace of God we had been spared the casualties that might have resulted if this had happened. Probably nobody but myself knew how close to the wind we had sailed. However, if luck had not been with us and we had lost lives by a premature demolition, I knew only too well who would be on the mat in the morning and held responsible. I had no intention of risking my men's lives, it was just that one has to take risks in an emergency and when wind and time overtake you, what do you do? After a life of total war, you are enured to taking these risks. Thirty years later my judgment would be very different, one would have to abort the operation long before the flames were licking the charges you had just laid. Failure to take this precaution would lay you open to charges of risking the lives of the men under your command. At the time this was the normal practice of combat troops and would have passed without question. Especially if the operation had been successful; failure was always subject to an enquiry but with success casualties were more readily accepted.

That was the great fire and later there was the great flood, both were equally sudden and unexpected, to me at any rate, yet I became deeply involved in both of them.

The flood overtook me during a visit to Cambodia. This country that lay between Siam and French Indo-China (now called Vietnam) was annexed by the Siamese, I suspect as part of the deal with the Japanese when they occupied Siam for military purposes. The Japanese forces had established large engineer stores depots in remote places where they were well concealed and unlikely to attract the attention of allied bombers. One of these bases was in the jungles of Cambodia not far from Phnompenh. I was ordered to go and inspect this depot and assess the value of its contents to the allied forces in terms of usable engineer equipment. In planning the long journey I could see from the map that it was within striking distance of Ankor Wat, often described as the eighth wonder of the world. A fantastic temple city long since deserted and being swallowed by the jungle, but an immense monument to a fallen civilisation whose architects had created a temple city of great scale and artistic quality.

I set off with more intention of seeing Ankor Wat than inspecting the engineer stores depot. The latter was the excuse, the former the real object of the exercise.

I had acquired a splendid operational caravan, not quite up to Gen. Montgomery's style, but not far off it. It was a mobile ops room with sleeping accommodation and other luxuries built into a truck body. We set off from Bangkok, I leading in my Jeep, followed by my caravan and two truck loads of sappers. It was the rainy season and most of the time we seemed to be driving through torrential rain. However, occasionally it did let up and we found ourselves driving along a banked roadway above the flood plains. Our operational base was the town of Batam Bang well inside what is now Cambodia.

We made good progress on the high banked roads though it seemed that as we progressed the surrounding countryside became more water than fields. We were making good progress when suddenly a herd of cattle confined by the flooding to the left side of the road embankment, panicked at the unfamiliar sound and sight of our convoy and decided to stampede across the road to the other side of the embankment. One moment the road was clear, the next it was just a mass of stampeding cattle. My driver did his best but there was no room to manoeuvre or take evasive action and we ploughed into them at about 40 mph hitting one cow with a resounding crunch that brought us to a halt. The impact had quite a damaging effect on the cow. The latter had obviously sustained a broken leg and lay in a heap in front of our Jeep.

My first instincts were to put the animal out of its misery and I drew my pistol to do the humane thing. At this moment the owner appeared up the bank for he must have been tending his herd up to the moment that they panicked. I turned to my interpreter who was travelling in the back of the Jeep and said something like "over to you, find out the value of the cow for which we will pay him and put down the poor creature free of charge". Naturally a lot of unintelligible discussion ensued and finally a price of 40 baht for the cow, which seemed very reasonable, was agreed. I paid the owner the 40 baht and drew my Luger pistol to dispatch it from its misery. This produced a volume of protest from the owner. As a Buddhist to take life was a religious offence that he could not tolerate. I was a bit confused, but my interpreter eventually explained that to kill the animal was against his religious beliefs. He would splint the leg and must do what he could to save the animal's life. It was a hind leg well and truly broken but I admired the man's determination to try and heal the sick animal, when he was so far from his village. We pressed on but I suspect that somehow he would succeed in mending that broken leg.

A little later we arrived at an imposing frontier post, the border between Siam and Cambodia, but at the time it had little significance for it was no longer the border, for under the terms of the Japanese invasion, Cambodia had been annexed to Siam. The impressive concrete colonnades at the border were unmanned and of lost significance. We drove through a triumphal arch of concrete pillars marking the frontier unmanned and forgotten at that point of history. We continued our journey into Cambodia unhindered by any formalities.

Eventually we arrived at the small insignificant village that marked the point of departure from the main road to the stores depot we were seeking. It could not have been more insignificant. We turned off and drove down a cart track to seek out the engineers stores depot we had been sent to inspect. To our great surprise it was there, deep in the jungle of Cambodia. No wonder it had never been targeted for the RAF. It was in the middle of nowhere, but its contents were like Aladdin's Cave to an engineer. The Japanese staff were all there carrying on their duties as if nothing had happened to alter their duties except a change of command. The officer in charge respectfully showed me around the maze of store huts containing everything from aeroplane engines to theodolites with the pride of a zoo keeper displaying the animals under his charge. Everything was meticulously catalogued and accounted for. Once again I was struck by the strange variety of unrelated stores that were stacked within the huts in what seemed to be chaotic order. Gunsights next to bags of commercial zircons next to theodolites next to ammeters and volt meters next to pneumatic drills next to slide rules next to electric motors next to picks and shovels. It appeared chaotic yet the staff knew where everything was and just how much of every item they held. I was impressed by the quality of much of the equipment. Volt meters little bigger than a packet of cigarettes that could measure voltage from 5 to 600 volts by stage tappings. Theodolites, binoculars, levels etc. that were beautifully made and half the size of their cumbersome British equivalent.

We started the difficult task of checking their stores lists but eventually gave up and accepted them, for they appeared to be quite genuine and anyway I knew that it was the variety of items more than the quantities that concerned our allied command. I wrote my report stressing the quality of their instruments which had impressed me rather than the quantity which post operations I knew was of little concern. I must admit that I have some of them in my possession, 35 years later and still in use. The mission completed we set off on our return journey. The Japanese stores unit staff grinned and bowed us out. I have a feeling they could still be there today undiscovered and lovingly checking and rechecking their stores lists.

From the time we had left Pursat to our return, it had rained almost non-stop. The countryside had been well saturated when we left but on our return we could see that it had now become super saturated. Everywhere the water was rising and covering the surrounding countryside. We were used to this but when we got back the attitude of officials made us realise that this was more than the normal for the rainy season. The Mekong River had burst its banks and the mayor informed me that road and rail bridges on the route back to Bangkok had been swept away. We were now cut off and it might be a long time before communications were restored. He assured me that he would make my protracted stay at Pursat as comfortable and enjoyable as he could during the ensuing months. Suddenly I realised that I was cut off from my company and the delights of Bangkok. The mayor's greasy smile, and assurance that Pursat was not lacking in attractive young girls whom he could procure to enhance my protracted stay until the flood water subsided, did nothing to assuage my anxiety. The thought of a month or more in Pursat as guest of the mayor was bad enough but I was in command of a company of engineers back in Bangkok and could not exercise my command by wireless from Pursat. I quickly got my wireless operator to contact HQRE in Bangkok, explained the situation and they promised that they would get a light aircraft out to lift me back. They could get a Lysander out to land on the local football pitch and pick me up. The remainder of the reconnaissance party were doomed to stick it out until the floods subsided. I knew they would not be unduly worried by a protracted period of enforced inactivity so it was agreed that within two hours a plane would be out to pick me up.

I quickly made arrangements for the detachment that would have to remain behind, gathered my essential belongings and made for the local football pitch to await the arrival of the Lysander light aircraft. When I got to the football pitch things were not so reassuring. The flood waters were rising fast and water was starting to creep onto the pitch. However, it was not serious at that time; large puddles were forming but nothing that would prevent a little Lysander from landing.

We waited and waited and while we waited more and more of the landing strip became covered with the rising waters. By the time the aircraft finally could be heard droning in, three quarters of the pitch was covered in water. It was not deep but it was now pouring in and it had become touch and go whether it was safe to land. The little Lysander came in low over the field assessing his chances of landing and taking off. He turned and repeated the performance several times. Each time more and more of the strip was under water, for water was now cascading onto the pitch. I waved and he waved back, but I knew he was not going to risk it. He waggled his wings and headed back for

Bangkok. I was furious but when I looked back at the landing ground it was a sheet of water. It was very shallow and if he had tried I am sure he could have landed but no doubt he knew this. It is one thing to land under such circumstances but quite another to take off and he was not going to risk being grounded in Batam Bang for a month when he could be home and dry in Bangkok!

I retired to Pursat with my interpreter to a somewhat seedy hotel feeling frustrated and depressed. To my surprise the hotel bar was fuller than I had ever seen it before. It seemed that the flooding on the countryside had forced a lot of people back to this last refuge seeking consolation just as I was. They were an odd looking lot of various nationalities, all discussing the present predicament of the flood and the prospect of getting out.

My interpreter was as keen as I was not to be marooned in this backwater of life. Eventually he came back to me with a proposition. He had located a party that had organised a country boat to take them over the flooded land to a point where the railway was still operating and where we could catch a train back to Bangkok. He stressed that the journey would not be very comfortable as the boat would be fully loaded but that one of the party would be a Buddhist priest that would assure our safe passage. If I was agreeable we would leave at 6 a.m. tomorrow and he would take me to the rendezvous. As the alternative was a prolonged stay in Pursat I readily agreed. He stressed that luggage or personal belongings would have to be minimal as the craft would be loaded with passengers with little space for luggage.

I packed the minimum bedroll and returned to await his call in the morning. This came as promised at 5.30 a.m. and we set off through the side streets of Pursat. The evening before I had made all necessary arrangements for my men to stay in the town until the floods subsided and they could rejoin the company in Bangkok. We threaded our way to the very outskirts of the town and eventually arrived on the elevated road leading back to Bangkok. It was a causeway with the flood waters lapping its side almost up to road level. Normally it was elevated well above the surrounding countryside. Less than a hundred yards ahead I could see that the road was submerged below the flood water which was still rising. The craft was not very substantial, just a typical country boat with a curved woven bamboo centre section sheltering the centre of the boat. A strange, motley collection of passengers stood around in the damp morning air: I recognised the priest by his saffron robes, a girl with a parrot on her shoulder like a latterday Long John Silver, a Thai official in uniform, and a chubby, cheerful Chinaman with a trilby hat and dark glasses who later turned out to be a gun-runner or arms salesman, as he preferred to be described. There was also a better class Thai lady who was not very communicative regarding the necessity of her journey. The remainder were pretty ordinary locals wanting to get back to their village that had been cut off by the floods. Those who were bound for Bangkok all seemed to be sporting dark glasses for some reason, other than the sun, which was obscured by the rain clouds.

We were all allotted our places on the boat, a few square feet of deck space where each sat cross-legged like Buddhas. I being an officer in the occupation forces was given the VIP location under the bamboo mat awning and next to a large basket of dried fish. My inability to sit cross-legged without getting cramp, plus the suffocating stench of the dried fish was too much for me. I stuck it out as long as I could then staggered outside into the open air and offered my VIP seat to a girl sitting up in the bows. It was raining and they thought I was being gallant, but I insisted, for all I wanted was to be able to stretch my legs and get away from the stench of the dried fish. They could understand neither of these reasons for all Siamese could sit cross-legged for hours without discomfort and they seemed impervious to the smell of dried fish. The rain was steady but under my bush hat and monsoon cape with my legs stretched out into the point of the bows I was far more comfortable than I had been under cover. What is more I could see where we were going which was much more interesting.

Everywhere was a vast expanse of water, but here and there little islands of higher ground dotted the landscape. The boatman in the stern propelled the boat with a long oar which he operated with his leg. Strange but effective, for we kept up a steady pace across the watery landscape.

At midday the motionless figures began to stir. I gathered that we were going to land on one of the small islands to cook up some rice. The boatman headed the craft for a small island that had come into view and I looked forward to being able to walk a few yards on terra firma to relieve my cramp. As we approached the very small island, the boatman's assistant stood in the prow with a rope ready to leap ashore and tie up. He kept up a running commentary with the oarsman, talking us into the best landing point. Suddenly his tone altered and he started gesticulating and shouting to the oarsman. At first I thought it was just part of the display of local watermanship. Then I realised he was expressing a note of alarm. Then as we slowed down within yards of the island I saw the cause of his alarm. The little island was a seething mass of snakes. They were tangled like spaghetti on the ground and they festooned every tree and branch along the shore. I have never seen such a concentration of snakes in my life. There must have been thousands of them on this tiny island. No doubt the rising flood waters had forced them to seek refuge on this last piece of dry land and the snake population of hundreds of acres was now concentrated within its confines. It was a seething mass of cobras, crites, vipers, rattlesnakes and a host of others that I could not identify. To step ashore would have meant instant death and no doubt this was what our boatman was trying to convey to the oarsman at the stern. Everyone was in agreement that we forget lunch and press on to the village where we hoped to spend the night.

We reached the village by evening, the boatman having paddled the stern oar rhythmically all day without any sign of fatigue. The village was typical of villages in those parts. It was built on the highest plot of ground that existed but this did not mean much as the landscape was pretty flat. All the houses were built on stilts and the flood waters were lapping the doorsteps of many of the huts, but there was a small stretch of terra firma on which we could land and the whole village was standing on it eager to greet us and learn what news we had to bring of the extent of the flood. The exchange of news was spirited and quite unintelligible to me. I do not know how they anticipated our arrival but they had a meal prepared which was very welcome, also two of our passengers were from the village and this was the end of their journey, and undoubtedly our priest helped our prestige and welcome, but the rest of us were complete strangers who were accorded equal hospitality. We sat on one small piece of dry land and food was brought and laid before us. Mostly rice and fish but very tasty and very welcome, having missed out lunch on the island of snakes.

The hospitality extended to various rooms for the night in the village. It looked a bit rural and possibly flea ridden. I decided I would spread out my bedroll on the last bit of dry land near the boat as I had a fear of being left behind on this remote island if the boat went off without me. A fate worse than being marooned at Pursat. I spent a fitful night fighting off mosquitos and dreaming of that strange island of writhing snakes. It was quite a relief to be woken by my boat people assembling for our next day's journey. This time cooked rice and other accessories for lunch were taken aboard. As we had dropped two passengers at the village there was a little more room on the boat and no one seemed keen on attempting another island for lunch.

We took up our allotted spaces on the boat; there was a delay for the protracted goodbyes with the village people for whom the priest was held in obvious esteem; then our impassive boatman quietly propelled us away with his leg oar which he continued to do without let up for hours on end. About midday we sighted another boat plying across the flooded country in the opposite direction and as our courses converged we hoved to beside it for a lengthy chat in Siamese. This went on for some time and I awaited until it was over and we were on course again before getting my interpreter to explain what it was all about.

I gathered from his explanation that we would soon be confronted with the railway embankment where we would either have to manhandle our boat over it or end our waterborne journey and await transport along the railway to Battam Bang from which station trains were still running to Bangkok. After two days in a crowded country boat I was all for the latter but failed to enquire what the railway transport to Battam Bang would be. I just took it for granted that trains were running limited sections between demolished bridges and that in no time we would puff our way to Battam, walk across the last damaged bridge and board the express for Bangkok. We really had no alternative because I could not see our passengers capable of manhandling our country boat over the embankment.

After frantic arguments in which I could take no part, it was obvious that all had come to the same conclusion. By late afternoon the railway embankment appeared on our horizon and by evening we moored alongside. We off-loaded, thanked and paid the boatman who set off for home leaving his odd collection of passengers sitting beside the railway line waiting for something to happen. I enquired when the next train was expected and my enquiry was met with hoots of mirth. Eventually I gathered that no trains were operating on this section but a set of bogies operated by the maintenance and inspection gang would be coming this way within the next hour. Because we had a priest in our party they would stop and take us aboard for the last 50 km to Battam. I was not quite sure what to expect from the inspection crew's vehicle, so we waited and waited and eventually bedded down for the night again. By dawn we were still there waiting and wondering whether the inspection wagon was myth or reality, or at least I did. No one else seemed unduly worried. Their faith and sense of time was different to mine. I had been brought up in a world where time meant everything – synchronise your watches, the assault will start at 0600 hrs, you will be at such and such a place by 0800 hrs, report here at 1500 hrs and so on. To them if something did not happen on time you just relaxed and waited. This was just what they were doing and they could not understand my obvious anxiety.

At about 10 o'clock the Siamese official who had his ear to the railway line stood up and announced that the maintenance bogie was coming. I peered down the straight line and could see nothing, possibly because I was looking for something more imposing than what arrived ten minutes later. The track maintenance vehicles turned out to be just twin axle bogies with planks placed on top for seating. As it developed from a spot on the horizon it became evident that it was already loaded to capacity and its sole means of propulsion was one man pushing it with a long bamboo pole. I doubt if it would have stopped but for the saffron robes of our priest which seemed to command universal respect. It stopped and the usual frantic discussion ensued. A slight rearrangement of the planks balanced on the bogies and an allotment of even smaller spaces per person and we were all accommodated, tightly packed and precariously balanced. I being regarded as heavyweight was positioned near the centre, packed tightly between our Chinese gun-runner and the attractive girl with a parrot on her shoulder. The balance was very critical and various adjustments were made before we achieved equilibrium. The propulsion unit was not without experience; somehow he kept up a steady pace for hours and his stride matched perfectly to the gauge of the sleepers. I felt very cramped and very confined on my one foot of allotted space but at least I could dangle my foot over the edge, whereas those in the middle could afford no such luxury. The Chinese gun-runner had a sack on his lap full of various pistols, American ·45's, Belgian FN, Czechoslovakian and British ·38 Revolvers. He had not failed to notice that I had a Dutch Army Luger in my holster. This was highly valued because it used 9mm ammunition, the same as the Sten-gun and this was in plentiful supply having been dropped in vast quantities throughout Siam and Malaya to what was thought to be resistance style units but later turned out to be Chinese guerilla units which were later to become quite a problem in Malaya.

The Chinaman made offers for my Luger at about every 10km of our journey, the sums involved were quite considerable but I had no intention of parting with it even though it was in fact my own private weapon, bought by myself in Calcutta because I had no faith in the services issue ·38 revolver, but he never gave up. However, on my other side I had the added distraction of a pretty girl with a parrot that would insist on nibbling my ear.

At this point our propulsion unit spotted something on the edge of the railway embankment, dropped his bamboo pole and disappeared over the edge in pursuit of his quarry. The shift of interest quickly produced a shift of balance and one of our planks grounded and we came to a sudden halt. Our friend who had disappeared over the edge of the road, equally quickly reappeared holding a young python. Gripped by head and tail he held up the writhing body like a chest expander with his arms at full stretch. Everyone admired it then he let it go grinning from ear to ear. He performed the capture and release of the python as though it was a heaven sent opportunity for a bit of light entertainment to break the otherwise monotonous journey. I was delighted with the opportunity to get off my square foot of plank and restore my circulation at the point of contact. I photographed the man holding up his two yards of python. The planks were rearranged and in no time we were off again, feeling quite refreshed by the incident. Our human propulsion unit settled down to his steady stride metered to the sleepers once again and continued without a break for another 20 km. It was really an extraordinary feat of endurance yet it appeared quite effortless. By the time we reached Battam I calculated that he had pushed us trotting along the sleepers for 50 km almost non-stop. At Battam we stopped short of the last bridge damaged by the flood water. Most of the bridge had been swept away but the railway line still spanned the gap tilted dangerously on one side, on the other side the train to Bangkok stood invitingly, steam jetting from various parts of the engine as though it was impatient to be off. Planks had been laid on the track suspended over the demolished bridge. Water was cascading through the gap where the bridge had been and it was obvious that if we wanted to board the train the suspended track was the only way to get to it.

After our incredible journey across the flooded lands of Cambodia, none of us was daunted by this last obstacle. We thanked our railway propulsion unit and gave him suitable remuneration for his efforts, then crawled across the last obstacle to our final goal, the train to Bangkok.

The crossing was precarious, the suspended track over a rushing torrent of water was a risk that many would have baulked at, but no one hesitated with the sight of the train on the other side impatient to depart. Each with his own urgent reasons for getting back to civilisation scrambled over the last obstacle. Aboard the train we were suddenly in a different world. The bonds that had united us on our journey were broken. I never saw any of them again. The Chinese gun-runner with his sack of weapons, the enigmatic priest with his dark glasses, the girl with her parrot, all were lost in the return to normality. Myself included. I settled back in the comfort of a first-class compartment with thoughts only for the return to my unit and the problems ahead. The past three days were already just a memory of an incredible journey but also they had been just a means to an end for all of us and we had achieved the end. Back in Bangkok that evening we soon picked up the threads of life, but my detachment in Cambodia and my caravan had to wait six weeks before the road bridges were mended and they were able to come back to join their unit.

CHAPTER 21

Social Life and Sea Snakes

Social life dominated much of those days in Bangkok. After five years governed by the rigours of war and active service in the hostile environment of the jungle it was only natural that the pendulum would swing wildly to the other extreme when hostilities came to an end. Nowhere in the Far East could this swing of the pendulum be more inviting than in Bangkok. It seemed geared to take full advantage of the situation and produce overnight all the facilities required by fighting men deprived for years of the fun of life that is so easily taken for granted nowadays.

A rash of nightclubs opened within weeks of our occupation. The Siamese girls were a fun loving breed without equal in the Far East. No doubt they did it for financial game but they did it in a manner that was not obvious. On the whole they just seemed to be happy to enjoy life to the full, irrespective of financial reward. They too had been subjected to the restraints of wartime disciplines and were making the best of their release from bondage.

The establishment however had to assert its authority and those early days of carefree abandonment soon passed. Orders were promulgated forbidding the transport of civilians in Jeeps or other military transport. To start with they were ignored and one saw countless Jeeps moving about the city loaded with a bevy of pretty girls in the back, all laughing and waving. But slowly the orders began to bite. Senior officers obeyed it to set the example, then the next layer of seniority had to follow suit which soon left the more vulnerable layer of officers below field rank as easy targets for the military police to mop up. They moved in with the determination born from their male ego that dictates the attitude, 'If we can't enjoy something that regulations forbid we will go to any lengths to make sure you don't.' At one moment everything was free and easy, the next you had an MP Jeep on your tail the minute you had a civilian on board. Other things apart it was difficult to adjust to the new attitude of restraint.

I myself was well and truly caught out by the new regulations. I was driving a Jeep load of brother officers and Siamese girls back to our mess after an evening out at a night club. Suddenly my passengers were shouting "Look out the MPs are on our tail". We did not have much further to go so I accelerated to increase the distance between us and our tail, then as I saw the entrance to our residence ahead I turned out the lights confident that I could turn in without lights and that the MP Jeep tailing me would lose us in the darkness. I had not allowed for the complexity of small canals (klongs) in Bangkok. The entrance to our residence was a bridge over a canal which I negotiated with ease but after this the drive up to the house was also bordered by a small canal and in the dark I misjudged the bend in the drive and we ended up in this small flanking canal. It was not deep but it was very muddy and we went right in. The military police had not been fooled by our tactics and soon arrived on the scene. Officers in uniform and girls in long evening dresses waded out of the deep mud in the canal. It must have been a comical sight by any standards, but the MPs' faces were impassive as they politely asked for our identity cards. I remember extracting mine from a waterlogged breast pocket and handing the sodden document to the MP. It was a bit like a Whitehall farce. We felt that it was a bit of a lark that could prove embarrassing tomorrow but the MP's were very correct and impersonal. Their faces never cracked into a smile at the absurd situation. After the formalities of being booked were completed the MP withdrew. The Siamese girls in spite of their dresses being ruined with mud just thought it a huge joke. The solemn performance of the MPs conducting their duties under the restraints they had to observe in respect of their superior officers sent them into fits of smothered giggles during this bizarre episode. When it was politely concluded we left the Jeep in the klong to be extricated by the M.T. havaldar tomorrow and returned to the mess to clean up and dry out the girls and ourselves, uninhibited by any further military regulations. The company dhobi had both dresses and uniforms cleaned, pressed, ironed, starched etc. as required by the following morning when they were once again needed.

    The restrictions on carrying civilians in military vehicles eventually eliminated the use of Jeeps but we had our Ford V8 staff car, Passion Wandi, as the men nicknamed it. In this way we were relatively safe for a Jeep is open and its contents too easily identified, but our Ford V8 Deluxe not only shielded the contents but exuded an air of authority that tempered the MPs enthusiasm to challenge the occupants. It was a style of transport that was at that time only the perogative of very senior staff officers of a rank that the most senior military police knew better than to challenge, whatever his suspicions might be. Under this cloak of respectability that our unique vehicle provided I was able to make many sorties with a cargo of contraband civilian personnel (my Siamese girlfriend) unmolested by the military police.

A favourite sortee at weekends was to the beach at Sira Chai about forty miles out of Bangkok along the eastern shores of the Gulf of Siam. In those days it was an idyllic seaside resort, a long palm fringed sandy coastline, with the resort of Sira Chai marked by a scattering of beach bungalows made from bamboo and dotted at discreet distances under the palm trees and rentable for the weekend at a modest sum. The only other feature was the pier built out into the sea and terminating in a swimming pool. The pool was just the sea enclosed by a shark barrier surrounded by a platform with the usual diving boards, changing rooms and little shops selling delicious sea food.

At low tide the pool was empty but one could wander along the long sandy beaches either side of the pier and swim in the shallow warm sea if you did not mind the occasional invasion of jellyfish. They had the habit of suddenly appearing from nowhere. At one moment you were swimming in an azure sea apparently devoid of life, then suddenly the jellyfish would appear from nowhere and you would be surrounded by these fascinating highly coloured medusa trailing their fantastic undercarriage. It was in this beautiful trailing undercarriage that their armoury lay, for it contained their paralysing darts with which they captured their food. The beauty of the structure of some of those medusa was fascinating while suspended in the medium of the water but when it accidently beached on a falling tide it collapsed into a sad gelatinous mess. Their sting was not that serious for there were always old women pushing vast prawning nets off shore and they had to make frequent stops to void their nets of jellyfish. They just picked them out, gripping them by their crowns and flinging them to one side. This way they avoided contact with the stinging part that trailed beneath them.

The shark barrier around the pool at the end of the pier seemed also to prevent the entry of jellyfish but not all sea creatures. I remember one time arriving there to find the place deserted, even the little shops selling sea food were shut up. The tide was in and the pool was full. I and the other officers who had journeyed out with me to this favourite little resort were somewhat puzzled to find it so deserted. It was a little eerie to find it so devoid of life when the weather was so perfect for a day by the sea. Even the shrimp women were not to be seen plying their nets through the shallow sea on either side of the pier. We decided there must be some religious festival that they were all attending back in their villages, hence why the place was so completely deserted.

I was the first to change into my swimming trunks and dive into the pool to refresh from the hot dusty drive. I swam lazily across the pool. About halfway across I noticed a little head with two eyes sticking out of the water in front of me. It looked like a turtle's head. Fascinated I trod water watching it, wondering how it had got into the pool. Then another appeared and another and another. Everywhere around me these little heads with beady eyes seemed to be appearing. I shouted to one of my companions, George Shaw, who was standing on the edge of the pool. "Look George, the pool is full of turtles. I can see their heads sticking out of the water all around me". George was Anglo-Burmese and familiar with the tropics. He turned his attention to the pool in a casual manner then I saw his whole expression change. "My God! They are not turtles, John, they are sea snakes, get out quick and splash as much as you can". Unfortunately, I knew that sea snakes were even more poisonous than their land relatives. Momentarily I was almost paralysed with fear, then force of self preservation took over and I struck out for the edge of the pool thrashing the water into a foam around me to keep them away from me. As I reached the step I shot out of the water like a seal emerging out of the sea onto rocks. I was cold with fear but when we looked back into the pool there was nothing to be seen. For a moment I suspected I was the victim of a practical joke, but I could see from George's expressions that he was equally shaken and that neither he or our other companions would enter the pool that once looked so inviting and innocent.

We chatted and sunbathed while the tide slowly retreated until the pool was almost empty, then we saw only too well why the place was deserted. The bottom of the pool at low tide held less than a foot of water and it was covered with a dense, seething mass of deadly sea snakes. It was their breeding season and this shore was their habitual mating ground. All the locals knew this and left them to it for this critical fortnight, hence why the place was deserted. In a matter of two weeks it would all be over and the snakes would disperse back into the ocean. The locals would return and the shrimp girls would be back plying their nets along the coast. Only we were ignorant of this annual event being strangers on the shore, and no one had thought to warn us of the dangers of swimming at the time of the sea snake breeding invasion. A bite from a sea snake is far more venomous than that of a cobra. We felt we had had a lucky escape, especially myself who had been right in amongst them. An experience I shall not easily forget.

About this time I found myself invited to a Chinese businessman's banquet. I was not sure why I was invited but suspected that it was the usual ploy for a little graft in the future, a preliminary softening up. However as the initial invitation held no strings I accepted for the sake of the experience. I cannot remember just where it was held other than we were seated at a very long table laden with the most incredible assortment of dishes. Apart from birds' nest soup and shark fin soup, there were even more exotic delicacies such as mice and honey. The mice were cooked whole and still bore their tails by which you picked them up and dipped them in a bowl of honey before lowering them into your mouth. If you could forget what you were eating the result was really very tasty. Later the entertainment gathered momentum as scantily clad girls performed intricate gymnastic displays on the table in front of you, skilfully avoiding contact with the complex distribution of dishes. It was a superb performance of erotica within the confines of a gourmet's paradise.

The Siamese businessman who was instrumental in getting me invited to this Chinese banquet was a pretty sharp customer, or so I thought. He frequently hinted that he could get me a good price for any weapons that would not be missed – pistols, rifles, mortars were at a premium. I made it quite clear that I was not a gun-runner and if I knew of anyone trafficking in arms I would have no compunction in passing the information onto the Chief of Police who I knew personally. He tactfully changed the subject but next day he turned up with a magnificent walnut case containing four cut glass decanters and a tray which he offered me at a very modest price. He explained that it was the property of a member of the Siamese Royal Family who had fallen on hard times and had commissioned him to sell them. The little chest of decanters bore the nameplate of Mappin & Webb of Regent Street. I paid the modest price and still have them though they suffered a bit on the final journey home. I also purchased a German silver salver and coffee set and a Nielo silver cigarette box that was inscribed under the lid to the effect that it had been presented to Prince............ on the occasion of his marriage etc.

I was becoming a bit embarrassed by this high pressure wheeler dealer who I felt was sooner or later going to get me involved in a shady deal, and then I would be hooked for deals of deeper involvement and so on down the slippery slope. I had resolved to confront him with a 'This is where the buck stops' pronouncement, but his regular visits stopped and I did not see him again for about a month. Then he suddenly reappeared in saffron robes with his hair shaved off. For a moment I did not recognise him. It was quite a transformation but the change was not just visual. His whole manner and outlook had changed. He had decided to do his novitiate in the Buddhist faith. A course that all Buddhists had to adopt at some time in their lives and he had decided that now was the time for him. He had come to say goodbye to me before spending the next year of his life as a novitiate priest. From henceforth he would have no possessions and would be dependent for his food on what others gave into his begging bowl when he toured his parish each morning. The transformation was so extreme I found it hard to believe; at any moment I expected him to confide in me that he had planned to strip his local parish pagoda of its gold leaf and that for the loan of a Jeep to cart it away he would cut me in for 25%. The offer never came and he humbly said goodbye and departed. I never saw him again but also I have never forgotten the impression of his transformation. It reminded me of one of Christ's Apostles, I think it was Matthew, who transformed from a collector of taxes to a follower of Christ.

There were a lot of other people in Siam who lived like the bad men of American cowboy films. It was still in the age of bandits that western society remembered nostalgically in their western films but was still for real in Siam.

Down in the dockland known as Klong Toi Docks there was a large godown that had belonged to the Japanese Trading Company of Mitsui Bushan Kaishu or some such name. At the end of the war these godowns were stacked full of the most amazingly diverse contents of valuable stores. Sacks of commercial zircons, antimony, bars of silver, ingots of lead and copper interspersed with everything from aircraft engines to picks and shovels. They had been classed as engineer stores, probably because some staff officer recognised the entry of picks and shovels and left it at that. The result was that the sappers found themselves in charge of this Aladdin's cave of valuables and responsible for guarding them. A task that seemed pretty straightforward, but we had reckoned without the Jesse James's of Siam.

The Mitsui godowns were surrounded by a 10ft. high corrugated iron fence with big double gates giving onto the entrance from Commercial Road but the riverside was not fenced as it was considered that the water frontage was sufficient protection from casual intruders. The section of sappers posted as security from petty pilferers was taken by surprise when one day a posse made a full-scale attack on the gates giving on to Commercial Road, with automatic weapons. They were momentarily overwhelmed but to their credit fought back to regained control. It was all very unsuspected but resulted in the guard of these godowns being considerably reinforced, and just as well for the next attack was a waterbound invasion a few days later that evolved into a full-scale battle with the invaders trying to scale the godowns walls with ladders and climbing in under the spacious eaves. The attack was well planned with a diversionary attack on the main gates. While this was drawing the attention of the guards the main force made the waterborne landing within the cover of a banana grove that stretched from the waters edge right up to the outer godown walls. The grove was within the godown compound. Their attack was not discovered until the guards within the godown suddenly found themselves under fire from people entering under the eaves of the building. There was a lot of noise and a lot of ammunition expended before they gave up and withdrew, with but relatively few casualties on either side: about half a dozen dacoits killed and no doubt a number wounded that got away. I think we had one killed and 7 or 8 wounded. It made us realise the potential and audacity of the Siamese dacoits. From then on our defences and guards were considerably increased which deterred any further attacks.

Life in Siam was now pretty settled. On 12th January 1946, we had an international athletics meeting in their very impressive Olympic stadium. It was classed as international because British, Dutch, Siamese and Indian troops were competing. We took it very seriously at the time for it was part of the necessary conversion to peace time competitive activities. In the past, war was the competitive game, and the rules were slightly different, one now had to re-educate our troops into the idea that you just did you best and that failure to win was no disgrace. I still have a lovely medal embossed with the Olympic symbol for first prize in throwing the discus and inscribed as a record throw for the stadium of 32m 75cm. Not quite a gold but a silver plated copper. I suspect that this distance would not even qualify for a modern athletics event.

By now the occupying forces in Siam were being thinned out. There was talk of concluding a peace treaty to normalise diplomatic relations with a country that had not officially opposed the Japanese even though it was quite obvious where their sympathy lay. More and more units were drafted out. Most of 7 Ind. Div. moved out to Malaya. To my joy our company remained after all the other divisional engineers had gone, but the writing was on the wall and I knew it was just a matter of time before the break had to come. It came in June 1946 when we got our orders to prepare to move to Kelantan on the NE coast of Malaya.

CHAPTER 22

Goodbye to Bangkok

We had been in Bangkok for about a year and had made many friends who had become part of our lives. Certainly I had not only very close friends such as Pong and Toon, but a Siamese girl called Prani who was much more than just a friend, for we had been living together for most of my stay in Bangkok. This was the emotional break that was hardest to accept and hardest to explain to the other partner. However, all good times have their end and ours was in sight. I soon found myself totally immersed in the administration of our impending move from Siam to Malaya. I also soon discovered that many senior staff officers had their eye on our Ford Deluxe car that I had found in Northern Burma and was still our prized possession. Fortunately our divisional commander at the time had been General Sir Frank Messervy and he was now GOC Malaya Command. We had frequent orders to return the staff car to such and such a vehicle depot for the use of General X or Brigadier Y and each time replied informing them that this was a battle trophy and not a CEV (captured enemy vehicle) and that it would only be surrendered under the authority of the GOC Malaya Command. Various senior officers on the Q staff telephoned to explain why it was essential that the car be surrendered. They started off in a friendly and patronising tone, when this did not work they became aggressive pulling their rank and shouting that it was a direct order from the Divisional Commander which I knew it was not, so I politely did nothing, and nothing more happened until the next attempt when we went through the whole rigmarole again. As long as General Messervy remained as GOC Malaya Command I knew we were safe. For we had the divisional order awarding it as a battle trophy to our company with his signature on it. However, if he should ever be posted to some other command our staff car days would be numbered. Too many envious eyes were on it in Bangkok where such forms of transport were very limited. It was obviously very galling for a senior staff officer bumbling along in an old Jeep to be passed by a smart staff car with a young sapper officer reclining in comfort on the back seat. As its dust settled on the staff officer he made a mental note to get that position reversed as soon as he got back to

238

HQ, but they never succeeded, for at the end of June 1946 in the early hours of the morning my company entrained for Malaya. Fortunately it was a special military train and I was OC train. The staff car was quickly loaded in an open truck and sheeted over with a tarpaulin to look like company stores. Once we were out of Bangkok the sheet came off and I and my 2nd I/C travelled in it. It made a splendid observation car and its comfortably upholstered seats were a great improvement on the hard wooden benches that were the only alternative on the train. The journey took four days with one day spent ferrying the train across the river at Nakon Si Thamalat where the railway bridge had been demolished by the RAF during the war and was not yet rebuilt. They had devised a complex system of sidings to different levels whereby each coach was shunted down to the water's edge and on to a large ferry that took it across the water and another little engine took it off on the other side and shunted to and fro over a series of inclines to join the main line on the other side. It was slow and laborious but it worked. By evening the whole train had been ferried across and was ready to proceed again.

On the afternoon of the fourth day we passed through Yala, the last town before crossing the border into Malaya. As we were a military train there was no delay at the border and before long we arrived at our destination, Kotabaru, in the state of Kalantan.

I was most impressed by the clean and businesslike atmosphere in Kotabaru, particularly how smart and helpful the local police force turned out to be. The police had British officers who had presumably been interned during the Japanese occupation but were now back at their job looking as though nothing had happened to disturb the quiet order of their lives. I remember how my father, when I was still at school, had suggested that I might consider the Malay Police as a career when the time came. He had introduced me to a friend of his who had some senior appointment with them who explained what the life and prospects were like. It sounded pretty good but not entirely what I was looking for as I thought it probably lacked excitement. However, when Malaya was captured by the Japanese I felt I had made the right decision even if it was for the wrong reason.

At this time I was somewhat disenchanted by the prospect of a career in the regular army as well. When a Labour government had come to power after the war they had made an ex-coal miner Minister of War. Not that there was anything wrong with an ex- coal miner, except that his knowledge of the forces was likely to be very limited. The papers at the time pointed out that the only record in Hansard of him speaking in the House of Commons prior to his appointment was to ask for a window to be closed.

His appointment was a typical political gesture to let everybody know that with the war over and peace declared with a Labour Government at the helm, a Minister of War was no longer of significance. He made a tour of India soon after his appointment. The result of which was that all officers attached to the Indian Army were put on British rates of pay and income tax. For me this meant that I took a severe cut in my salary and was paid less than my second in command, who was an Anglo-Indian. This may have saved the Government a bit of money but it was very demoralising for officers to be treated this way within a year of our victory in Burma. It was a bad omen for a future career in the regular army. Added to this I had been informed that my regular commission would date for seniority from my 21st birthday. This occasion in my life was celebrated during the Battle of Kohima and I resented the fact that my service for 1½ years before this counted for nought in the army. If I was old enough to command men on active service before my 21st birthday why should it be discounted from my seniority as a regular officer. I felt this to be a very unfair handicap imposed at the start of my career.

I decided that if this was a foretaste of the treatment I could expect in the regular army I had better get out while I still could. I wrote through the Chief Engineer Malaya Command an official letter to the effect that I was no longer desirous of being gazetted as a regular officer. At the time of being selected by the War Office Board for a regular commission we were told that before we were gazetted we would be contacted and given the opportunity to turn it down should we have changed our minds in the meantime. I decided that I had changed my mind and would take my chance in some civilian career, but what career I was not at all sure. The pressures of war had deprived me of the opportunity to acquire any qualifications for a civilian career and at the ripe old age of 23 I felt it was too late to start studying again to acquire them. I could neither afford the time nor the money to do this.

At least I found I was by no means alone on this issue, for I met several other officers who had passed their War Office Selection Board but had become disenchanted and decided not to take it up as a career. Their decision had been made for much the same reasons as mine. The new Labour Government's Minister for War had been the last straw for them too.

At Kotabaru we had a pleasant camp site about two miles out of the town and just on the edge of the jungle. Our task was to start making a Jeep track from the east across to the west of Malaya. I do not think anyone had made a proper recce of the route for I soon discovered that there was a very good reason why no E – W roads existed in that part of the country. The first fifteen or twenty miles was no problem, light jungle and plenty of open cultivated land with a scattering of small villages. After that the jungle became more dense and the gradients more formidable as one approached the mountainous backbone of Malaya. I suspected that we had been given the task just to keep us occupied, for once we reached the mountainous section the resources in earth moving machinery, explosives and bridging equipment would be out of all proportion to the value of any E – W track in that area. We completed the easy part in no time and the locals were delighted to have what they regarded as an excellent bullock track made for them to get their wares into Kotabaru, whereas they had to carry it along footpaths before we made the Jeep track.

I decided to go and consult the CRE before getting involved in the next stage. The CRE was at Alorstar on the west side of Malaya. There seemed to be only two ways of getting there. One was by train going up north through Siam to Patani where there was a railway crossing to the west of Malaya and then back down south again to Alorstar. Two very long sides of a triangle to get to a point that was almost due west of us. The other way was to go back up to Yala just over the border and from there there was a very minor earth road that my friends in the police said should be negotiable in a Jeep and went through the hills to the frontier station of Kroh in Malaya. From there on there was a good tarmac road down to Alorstar. They told me that it was mostly used by smugglers and the like before the war. I decided to give it a try and set off with my driver early in the morning. When we reached Yala it was not difficult to find the road; there were not many roads leaving Yala and only one going west. At this stage it was quite a good road as roads go in that part of Siam, and was metalled as far as the westernmost village marked on the map. After that it was only marked as a dotted line, the symbol normally used for a cart track. However, it was better than I had been led to expect, it was more than a Jeep track and I could see little difficulty for a 30cwt vehicle. Quite a lot of it had been stoned and gritted to form a crude water bound macadam. I had a feeling that the Japs might have improved it for their own use during the war. It wound its way up and up, sometimes through dense bamboo thickets sometimes through primary jungle, with towering trees festooned in creeper. There were several bridges over small rivers but nothing very formidable. I got out and inspected any dubious ones but apart from a few rotten decking planks they were sound enough for the weight of my Jeep. Only one gave me any real anxiety as it seemed to bend noticeably as I went over but that was all and it proved to be the last bridge. After that the road went up and up and one could feel the air getting noticeably cooler, the vegetation changed to scrub and grass patches looking surprisingly green, then suddenly the road widened and became tarmac. We guessed that we must have crossed the frontier but the change in road surface was all that could be seen to mark it. A little further on we came into a wide grass area with a group of administration wooden huts at the other end, but there seemed to be no one about so we just drove on and reached Alorstar that afternoon.

I was rather pleased at finding such a quick and relatively easy way through to the west. What surprised me was that we met no one at all on the way, not even a solitary villager; where our Jeep left tracks on the surface they were the only tracks visible.

At HQRE the CRE was away, life seemed fairly quiet. I was welcomed back to the fold and everyone seemed envious at my protracted stay in Bangkok. They seemed anxious to impress on me that life had been pretty busy in Malaya but it was difficult to find out what had kept them so busy other than the flood of new orders and directives of the peace time administration. As the adjutant wearily put it, things are different now John, if you want to knock a nail in you need to convene a siting board of at least two Brigadiers and a Lt. Col. before you raise a hammer. He then handed me a massive pile of orders and directives covering such exciting subjects as conversions to peace time stores accounting and educational directives for preparing Indian Army personnel for their return to India and partition. When I glanced at them my heart sank and I asked how long before I could expect repatriation. The reply was the usual guarded one; it should not be too long but they were so desperately short of officers: they were leaving faster than they were being replaced and the replacements were not up to much, so you will have to hang on for a bit until we can find your replacement. Already there were few officers either at HQ or in the other field companies that I knew from our Burma days, nearly all had been repatriated so I knew that if I insisted they would have to let me go. Anyway, my 2nd in command, David de Souza, was quite capable of taking over command of my company. For the time being I just made it clear that if the division was ordered back to India I would insist on my right to be repatriated before it returned. In no way was I going back to India to be embroiled in what I knew would be the unhappy process of partition.

The CRE, I gathered, would not be back until late the next day as he was visiting 62 Coy. near K.L. I decided to take the opportunity to visit Penang and have a swim in the sea. Penang is on an island just off the coast and you get there over a fairly busy little ferry. It was an attractive old fort town with colonial style houses and waving palm trees. Most people I had met raved about the beauty of Penang. I was a little disappointed after all I had been led to expect but I suppose if you have spent months of sweating within the green monotony of a rubber plantation Penang, with its brilliant light and cool sea breezes, must have seemed like an escape to paradise, for believe me a rubber plantation is the most depressing landscape in which to be imprisoned.

There are an awful lot of rubber plantations in Malaya. To live on one is like being in an open prison. There is no real light and shade just an eternal dappled green of filtered sunlight. In every direction stretch the regimental rows of the trunks of the rubber trees all aligned in geometrical monotony like prison bars stretching in every direction as far as the eye can see. No wonder the planters exaggerated about the beauties of Penang.

Next day I returned to HQRE to meet our CRE, Phil Hatch. He looked very tired and much older than the man I had known a few months ago in Bangkok. Perhaps the return to peace time accountancy was getting him down as well. We chatted about the 'Good old days' in Bangkok. I explained why I was turning down my regular commission and we discussed my company's present task on the E – W Jeep track across Malaya. On this latter subject he seemed well aware of the impossibility of the task without adequate resources which were unlikely to be made available. He admitted that the real problem was to find something useful to keep the men occupied. He hinted that we would probably be moved shortly anyway, in all probability to Kroh. This came as an unexpected pleasant surprise. I immediately told him how I had just motored up from Yala to Kroh over a road that could easily be improved with a little bridge strengthening to take the company through that way rather than rail them hundreds of miles around the northern end of Malaya. I suggested that it would not only save time and money but that it would be a very worthwhile exercise for the men. The CRE agreed, but the move through Siam by road would have to be cleared by the G staff at Div. HQ but otherwise there were no problems.

I pointed out that most of our heavy transport had been handed in before we left Bangkok and that we now had far more engineering stores than available transport to carry them. However, I could see no real problems as we could form a stores dump at Yala, and send an advance party through to Kroh then ferry all our equipment and stores through by my little road. It would take about four return trips or possibly five to complete the move. We would move the majority of the men the first trip then leave a rear party to guard the stores dump at Yala until the operation was complete. As Kroh was on top of the mountain ridge we would have good wireless communication with our rear party at Yala. Nothing seemed easier. Far easier than the long rail journey around the north of Malaya when we would still have to ferry all our equipment up from the rail head on the west.

Next day I drove back down our little road to Yala making a more detailed reconnaissance of any necessary works and strengthening of bridges required. Again it was surprisingly deserted not a soul did we see until we came across a girl and some goats well down the descent in Siam. It was near a small bridge just short of a branch track that went off to the north. When I stopped my Jeep the girl lifted her skirts and ran away down the branch track leaving her goats behind her. I was rather surprised, for generally the Siamese are easy going and always ready for a friendly chat, but not this one. I thought little of it at the time, but the impression for some strange reason remained filed on my memory bank.

That evening I arrived back at Kotabaru and informed my officers and VCO's of our impending move, dependent on clearance from someone in G ops agreeing to our using the Yala – Kroh track. This clearance came through a few days later but clearance was given dependent on my personally accepting responsibility for any loss of vehicle using this route. I knew what this meant. It was just the G staff covering themselves should any of the bridges fail and write off a truck. None of the bridges were over deep ravines so I was quite sure that even if a bridge did fail we would be quite capable of salvaging the vehicles crossing it at the time.

There had been a fairly rapid turnover of officers in the company of late, only myself and my 2nd I/C David de Souza had been with the company on active service. The platoon commanders were young, inexperienced, and spent a lot of time moaning about conditions that were to us luxurious compared with what we had in Burma. None of them had seen any active service and seemed to have spent the war in depots and training establishments. In my letter home I described them as very poor officer material and very poor company. Their only interest was when they would be released to go home. However, our Indian Viceroy's commissioned officers had been with the company all through the war and were excellent. I really ran the company through them and the one British CSM who was in charge of transport.

We first set up our stores dump at Yala with a rear party in charge. I then moved with Coy HQ and an advance party all in Jeeps to prepare our new site while a platoon was detailed to follow up with stores and equipment to repair and strengthen the bridges to take fully laden 30 cwt. trucks. When they arrived at Kroh the rest of the company would move up bar the rear party at the stores dump and we would then start ferrying the stores and equipment. Twelve empty trucks would go down one day and return laden the next. I estimated that about four return trips would clear all the stores and the rear party would return with the last convoy.

Kroh turned out to be an ideal camp site with a Dak bungalow that we took over for the officers' mess. There were other wooden huts for company officers and the men's lines. It must have been built for a large police detachment or possibly a military detachment as a frontier station but at the moment there was just a Malay police sergeant and two men manning the rather vague frontier post. Being so high the air was fresh and cool, in fact at night we had to sleep under blankets, something we had not done since the days of Kohima. The men were full of enthusiasm for the site and even our moaning subalterns approved.

We seemed to be alone on top of the world but we were not quite alone. We discovered we had neighbours about a mile up a little side road. There was a tin mine of all things. Tin in Malaya is usually dredged in man-made lagoons in the lowlands of Malaya, but this site was unique, being right on top in the highlands. There was a staff of about eight Europeans in charge. The place was very self contained with its own bungalows, coolie lines, administrative buildings, and a large house that accommodated most of the Europeans. It was a bit like a club house with a large dining room and card rooms, and fully staffed.

Much of the mine machinery had been damaged or removed during the Jap occupation but they were in the process of getting the place going again. Strictly speaking it was not a mine as there were no underground workings; they simply blasted the tin bearing soil out of the side of a quarry with powerful water canons. A lot of water is used in the extraction of tin and they seemed to have a very good supply even though they were on top of the world.

They too were delighted to find they had neighbours, a few new faces in their isolated world on top of the hills. They invited me over for dinner in a few days' time, when we had had a chance to settle in.

Next day the bridge repair party arrived, the job completed and we were all ready to start ferrying up the stores and equipment. Wireless communication with our rear party at Yala was excellent so I told them to start loading and bring up the other two platoons plus any additional stores they could manage after which they would be loading up a convoy of stores every other day. They were quite happy having found a few seedy bars in Yala which were equally happy to have their unexpected windfall of custom. The rest of the company arrived the next evening and we settled down to a routine of empty trucks going down to Yala one day and returning laden with engineer equipment, stores and explosives the next day. This routine was only broken by the rather odd celebration of August Bank Holiday. The Indians had their festive days of Dasra and the like, but the British Raj still insisted on their August Bank Holiday. Even in the highlands of Malaya the British still took the day off on the first Monday in August. It seems incredible but it was so and no doubt our Indian troops thought it was a great British religious festival equivalent to their Dasra. Be that as it may, they all enjoyed our holiday, it was a day off, no convoy went down to Yala and I went off to dine and celebrate with the tin miners.

At the tin mine when I arrived they too had the day off and all was prepared for a sumptuous meal. We started with drinks; they seemed to have no shortage of whisky and poured very generous portions. I sensed that we went on drinking because we were waiting for someone. This someone was their Scots engineer who they explained was a bit eccentric. Eventually they gave up waiting and we sat down to soup. The dining room windows looked onto a large lawn surrounded by a high cupressus hedge. Halfway through the soup course a car burst through the cupressus hedge and came to a shuddering halt in the middle of the lawn. The car disgorged a small figure dressed in American naval uniform complete with medals and the American naval ratings hat. It staggered towards us followed by a Malay servant in impeccable white livery. This was, I gathered, their Scots engineer. He made a splendid entry to the dining room. Staggering to the empty place at the dining table he declared that he had parked his battleship on the lawn and the review of the fleet could now commence. He was the life and soul of the party until the meat course arrived then suddenly he fell forward, his head thumping down into the plate of meat that had been put in front of him. His servant who had been hovering dutifully behind his chair just picked him up and carried him out to the car on the lawn, got in and drove him away.

Our hosts explained that this was his usual entrance and exit, but he was a very good engineer and knew all that there was to know about the unique problems of the engineering complexities of this particular tin mine. But he did drink rather heavily. However, his servant managed him very well and when he was sober he was a first class- engineer.

By the time the evening was over and it included a session of bridge after dinner – with more whisky – I was more than ready for my bed, in fact I was well onto being level with their engineer. However, when he had collapsed into his meat course his American naval hat had rolled off onto my plate and thirty years later I find I still have it as a souvenir of that very strange August Bank Holiday celebration.

CHAPTER 23

The unexpected ambush

The next morning I was due to travel down with the empty trucks to visit the rear party at Yala. I was feeling very delicate after my night out with the tin miners, so instead of leading the convoy down, I told my CSM to lead the convoy and I would follow when their dust had died down. This I did, having given them an hour's lead I started off in my Jeep. The convoy was organised to travel in blocks of four vehicles with ten minute intervals between them. On the more major roads this prevented congestion but on this road it was a mere formality, however, it served its purpose as convoy discipline.

I set off at eight o'clock on the 110 mile journey to Yala. The convoy having departed at 7 a.m. After half an hour's drive I was surprised to meet one of our 15 cwt. trucks returning up the road. The driver dismounted and came up to me in great excitement. He informed me that the convoy had been ambushed and that he was coming back for help. I found it difficult to take in but he himself was obviously wounded. He had been at the rear of the convoy block and had managed to reverse out of it. The second block had halted when they heard the attack and, being only armed with rifles, had formed a defensive position on this side of the ambush. I decided that the best course was to return to the company at once and muster a fighting patrol armed with automatic weapons and hope that we might catch up with the ambush party. The 15 cwt. truck driver had already told me that all the other drivers were dead, but he thought he had seen the CSM's Jeep that was leading the convoy drive on but he was not sure. Back at the camp nearly everyone was out on a training exercise and I had difficulty in making Subador Major believe what had happened, but when he saw that the driver of the 15 cwt. truck was wounded it slowly dawned on him that a year after the war had ended there was someone in the jungle who had the weapons and the will to fight on. The driver described this latest enemy as being dressed in green uniform with a cap like a Japanese soldier but with a red star on the front of the cap. Whoever they were they had killed some of our men and we had to be after them. Bristling with automatic weapons we set off for the scene of the ambush. After about

25 miles we came upon the second block of the convoy parked by the side of the road. The drivers had left their trucks and taken up a position on a spur above the road where they could see the site of the ambush about three miles below them. They could see little of the road or the ambushed vehicles but they had heard the grenades and automatic fire and they had met the 15 cwt. truck driver who had managed to reverse out of the ambush to turn round and come back. They were only drivers and did not know what to do in such circumstances. The 15 cwt. truck driver had told them that he thought the other drivers had been killed, so they just stayed put, hidden under the cover of the spur and waited for the next move, either by the enemy or ourselves. The whole situation was a bit beyond me. I told them to stay where they were in case they were needed and continued on down the road. Two bends further on I spotted one of our sappers lying beside the road. I screeched my Jeep to a halt beside him. The noise seemed to awaken him for as I jumped out and approached him he propped himself up on his elbow and saluted. He had obviously been in the ambush for his uniform was soaked in blood and he looked pretty badly wounded. In spite of his condition he gave me a wonderfully concise description of what had happened. I cannot do better than quote from the letter I wrote to my father on the evening of the same day on 6th August, 1946.

"The first sign of the ambush was one of the drivers lying by the roadside where he had dropped, weak from exhaustion and loss of blood. He had a bad grenade wound in his side and a bullet wound through the small of his back. He had managed to escape and had walked and finally crawled two and a half miles to try and get help. Even in the state he was in when I came up he raised himself a bit from the ground and saluted. He then told me quite clearly and concisely what had happened and said that I would find the trucks about two miles further on, but was afraid that all the other drivers must have been killed. He then asked for a drink of water and sank back unconscious."

A very brave man, as emerged from the full story of his experiences which I learnt when I visited him in hospital later on. At the time, as his bleeding was stopped, I got him moved back to the second block of trucks with instructions that he was to be taken straight to hospital.

Two miles further on we finally came to the scene of the ambush. Thick jungle towered on both sides; you could not see more than a few feet into the wall of bamboo on either side. The trucks were stopped in a zig-zag fashion on the track. All was deathly still but as we got out the familiar sickly smell left by the grenade detonations still hung in the air. The first truck was empty but with a bullet lodged in the windscreen: it had only penetrated but not passed through and was held in absurd suspended animation halfway through the windscreen.

The next three trucks were an eerie sight. Each had its driver and co-driver in it slumped forward against the dashboard and riddled with bullets. They could have had little time to realise what was happening before they were dead. There was no sign of the CSM's Jeep that was leading the convoy except for some wheel marks that suggested he had accelerated out of trouble. There was also a stick sharpened at one end and that looked as though it had been stuck in the middle of the road with an old tin can lying beside it. It had little significance at the time but fitted in with my CSM's story later.

Spent cartridge cases and tracks indicated that the ambush party had approached from the south. We soon found a well trampled track down which they had retreated but before long this split in two so I too split my fighting patrol in two to follow up both tracks, however these tracks soon divided again and again until they were so faint that they were barely discernible. It was evident that the enemy had dispersed their line of retreat to make follow up virtually impossible. After a while we had to give up because there was virtually no track left to follow. Whoever they were they knew a thing or two about jungle warfare. We had penetrated about a mile into the jungle but without a trail to follow we were at a disadvantage. They obviously knew this area of jungle as their own territory. I sensed that to follow up blindly might well lead us into a second ambush so I gave the order to pull out. Half an hour later we were back on the road again. The trucks had had their burst tyres changed and been turned round. There was nothing we could do but drive back to Kroh with our dead. Feeling very frustrated, a sense of shock had descended on all of us. That evening I wrote a letter to my father decribing all that had happened.

I also reported the incident to the CRE and Div. HQ. The latter summoned me to report in person the next day. This I did and was rather shocked at their attitude. Gen. Evans, the Divisional Commander, saw me in person and hauled me over the coals for taking a fighting patrol into Siam after the peace treaty had been signed. This seemed to be his chief concern. That we had been ambushed by an unidentified force and had six dead and two wounded did not seem to concern him as much as the prospect of our causing an international situation that might rebound on him personally. No one seemed concerned in identifying who the aggressors might be. Strange when in retrospect we know just how important a factor these Chinese Communist guerilla forces turned out to be. Not many months later they were holding down large forces of British troops that had taken part in the operations against these guerillas. However, that was nearly two years later after the long stalemate in the campaign when our failure to contain their activities was relieved by the more imaginative command of General

Templar who was sent out to Malaya to take command of all land forces operating against the guerillas and bring their reign of terror to a successful conclusion.

The existence of these guerilla forces was not unknown at the time. They had been there in the days of the Japanese occupation and we had supplied them with arms and ammunition in the hopes that they would form an internal resistance force to harass the Japanese. With the unexpectedly early end to the war after the atomic bombs were dropped on Japan, the existence of these Chinese guerilla forces in Malaya seemed to have been conveniently forgotten. Up to now they had carefully avoided any contact with British Forces. They confined themselves to the remote mountainous jungle of Central Malay where the only signs of their existence was from occasional reports of remote Malay villages being terrorised by them and being forced to supply them with food. Even these reports were seldom substantiated for those guerilla forces made it quite clear to the headman of these remote villages that if they failed to co-operate they would all be shot. Occasionally this threat had been carried out so that the locals lived in terror of them, and as they saw little signs of the British administration in these remote parts they co-operated to the extent that they not only supplied them with food they could ill afford, but the were also too frightened to report their existence to the authorities. No doubt the guerillas operated equally freely in S. Siam and probably had bases there. It would certainly account for the lack of use of the Yala – Kroh track by any locals and also why the lone girl I had met on the track had run away so fast. We were dressed in green uniform too and she was not going to stop to make a more positive identification. We could have her goats but we were not going to have her as well if she could help it.

I believe that this remote track went right through guerilla controlled territory. They had observed our going one way empty and returning laden with stores and ammunition the next day. Though it was their present policy not to engage any military forces at that time, this was just too tempting for they were undoubtedly in need of both weapons and ammunition. They had decided to stage a quick ambush, leave no survivors to identify them; if they were successful they would have plenty of time to carry off all that they required for it would be a long time before news of the ambush would get back to Kroh or Yala. However, there was one thing that they had not reckoned with. The strange and unheard of British Festival of August Bank Holiday on the first Monday in August, even in this remote corner of the Empire. But, for this event, the trucks would have gone down to Yala empty on Monday and be returning laden on Tuesday, the day of the ambush. It is only conjecture but I suspect their commander planned and ordered the ambush, then sent a section of men to execute the task together with enough men to carry back the booty. They had stuck a stick up in the middle of the track with a tin can on top of it. The ambush party was deployed and waiting in good time and they were all instructed to open fire as soon as the leading vehicle drove over the can topped stick. The fact that the convoy came from the opposite direction to that expected must have taken them by surprise but the men had their orders and the falling can triggered off the ambush before it could be stopped. The leading Jeep with my CSM escaped by accelerating out of it. He was lucky, for neither he nor his co-driver were hit though a bullet had severed the front of his gaiter in two without touching his ankle. One tyre was shredded by gunfire but he had a spare and once out of the firing zone he had stopped and while his co-driver changed the wheel he climbed up the bank to where he could see the ambush vehicles. The site was swarming with uniformed soldiers that he took to be Japs. He decided there was nothing he could do with a .38 revolver and a rifle between the two of them and drove on down to Yala where they had wireless communication with the company HQ at Kroh. I think he did the most sensible thing under the circumstances but I remember his action was criticised at Div. HQ for not going back to reconnoitre the scene more closely.

The day following the ambush we restarted the convoy but this time it went with an armed escort bristling with LMG's and grenades in spite of General Evans' anxieties. I was determined to complete the move before Div. HQ woke up to the situation and started issuing directives that would leave the company split between Yala and Kroh. By the time they issued orders for the remainder of the company at Yala to be sent by rail around N. Malaya, the move was completed without further incident and I was able to inform them that the company move was completed before their orders were received. They were in fact received on the day that the last of the stores and the rear party were due to set off from Yala so I had no conscience in ignoring them until the rear party confirmed they were moving out of Yala. I left them on the table in my in tray and went off to visit the brave sapper driver who had played possum and survived the ambush to start back up the track to warn the company of the incident. I found him in the Military Hospital looking well and smiling. They had removed all the grenade splinters, neither the bullet fired into his back or the bayonet wound had damaged anything vital. He was sufficiently recovered to give me a more detailed account of his experience.

He was in the first truck behind the leading Jeep when the ambush was sprung. The first burst of grenades badly splintered his side and seeing that he was surrounded he fell forward against the dashboard and played possum. He reckoned that about thirty men came out of the jungle and jumped on the trucks. One man came up to him and bayoneted him twice and then fired a round into him at close range and did the same to the dead body of the driver. Through all this he continued to play possum. Before they left they came back to him, evidently not quite convinced that he was dead. They dragged him out onto the road and one man stamped his boots into his back. He held his breath and managed to get away with it. He just lay there for the next half an hour. When he felt sure that they had all gone he got up and started to walk back up the track to make his way up to the company lines 30 miles away. After about two miles he said he started to feel faint and that he did not remember much more until he saw me standing over him.

When I got back to the company I wrote a recommendation that he be awarded the I.M.M. for his courage and devotion to duty. I am glad that this was eventually approved. It was certainly well-deserved.

This, as far as we were concerned, was the end of the affair but not for Malay and the British Forces. They had plenty more to come but for the moment they were happy to live on in a fool's paradise. For myself the end had come to my services in the Far East. I finally received my repatriation orders. I was due to board the S.S. *Arundel Castle* at Singapore in a fortnight's time.

CHAPTER 24

Farewell to the Far East

When I got back to my unit at Kroh the sands of time were running out. The crate I had ordered from the company carpenter was delivered. It was made of teak and looked like an outsize coffin. It took six men to carry it empty to my office. I explained that it was far too large and heavy for my baggage allowance and would have to be modified to more acceptable proportions. The modified version was produced just in time for my departure but before this there was the customary departure ceremony for all O.C. Sahibs, the Burrah Tamasha.

I had been with the company a long time since I joined them as a lieutenant in the Arakan. We had covered a lot of ground together. From the Arakan right through Assam to the Naga Hills, Manipur and down practically the whole length of Burma to Rangoon, then Siam and finally down to Malaya. We had been through some good times and some very difficult times together. A very strong bond had grown up between us all and I felt very sad that this was now about to be broken forever.

I gave the whole company the day off from duties and the men arranged their own display of their native sports and competitions. There were various displays of local talent such as juggling and balancing acts and one man I remember who had two stout sticks about 5 feet long which he spun like a propeller on either side so fast that you could throw stones at him and the sticks knocked them away deflecting them from his body every time. He did a form of dance twisting and turning within the shield of his rotating sticks. There were many other talents within our ranks that I had not realised existed.

In the evening we had the Burrah Tamasha, a sort of grand feast of super hot curry with the officers, VCO's and senior non-commissioned rank seated around a long series of tressle tables in the open air under the stars. At the conclusion the Subador Major Poiti Naidu made a very touching address on behalf of the VCO's and men of the company saying how sad they were to see me leave the company and how they had much enjoyed serving under my command etc., etc. They then presented me with a gold signet ring inscribed V.C.O.s 421. It was a very touching gesture. I also felt they had misjudged the size of my finger. However, I did not want to let them down on this occasion so I tried very hard to get it past my knuckle but the edge of the shield bearing the inscription was a bit sharp and dug in. I could see the worried look on my VCOs' faces, they had bought the O.C. Sahib a ring that he would never wear. It was too small for his finger. I made a quick grab for the butter, greased my knuckle with it, a bit more persuasion and to everyone's relief the ring was on. Once past my knuckle it was quite comfortable but a very snug fit. Everyone's faces wreathed in smiles again.

I made a suitable speech in reply thanking them for all the support they had given me over the years and reminded them of some of the anxious times and some of the more rewarding times we had had together. I had a very special mention for Jemadar Suri who had been my platoon VCO when I had first joined the company. I could not have asked for a better VCO to be my right hand. He was smart, always enthusiastic and never at a loss for ideas in the most difficult situations and was always there when I needed his assistance. If I had to go through another war I could wish for no better man to be at my side.

It was a very nostalgic evening and the tears in my eyes were not entirely from the very hot chilli laden curry. Next day I left finally for Singapore and the boat home but not before I had shaken hands and said goodbye to every NCO in the company, and one or two very special sappers like my orderly and the mess cook. I was garlanded with flowers which they had produced from nowhere and finally left in our wonderful Ford V8 Deluxe staff car.

I had to leave through a guard of honour consisting of the whole company lining the road waving and cheering as I drove through. It was very traumatic, a bit like being elevated to Royalty for my final exit, but I shall never forget the farewell nor the men I was leaving for another world.

The drive down to Singapore on the excellent laterite roads of Malaya was some 600 miles, but uninspiring. Endless rubber estates, each one more gloomy than the next. The journey was uneventful except for one moment when there was a bang and our windscreen was suddenly obliterated. We could see nothing, then equally suddenly it cleared again. As we ground to a halt the solution became apparent. The bonnet catch had not been fully locked and the slip stream had lifted the bonnet from its mountings and swept if over the car leaving vision restored. We walked back a hundred yards and retrieved our bonnet and it was soon firmly back in place with no real damage done. Next day just as the sun was setting, we arrived in Singapore, that incredible city so full of life. The last few miles over the causeway to the island left me thinking and wondering about the fall of Singapore when the Japs came down from the north by the same route as we were travelling and how easily they had taken the city with all its defences facing out to sea from whence they were so convinced the threat must come. The incredible lack of imagination in the British High Command reminded me poignantly of my recent experience with the ambush by Chinese guerillas, whose existence the British High Command seemed equally reluctant to face up to. History records the price they had to pay for their complacency over the defences of Singapore.

Singapore was full of life it was also very humid. I found the various movement control officers that governed my repatriation. I was directed to a staging camp where all the prospective passengers for the *Arundel Castle* liner were awaiting their ship back home.

I was one of the last arrivals for we were due to board next day. I deposited all my luggage with the M.F.O. (Military Forwarding Officer) and asked him to ensure that it was all loaded on the *Arundel Castle* and not left to go by other freight shipping. My staff car obviously impressed all these officials for they felt that anyone with such superior transport must have pull in the higher echelons and should be given special treatment. All my excess baggage was marked to accompany me on the liner.

The other officers awaiting shipment had been waiting in Singapore for some days and knew their way around. They recommended a visit to the New World Amusement Centre, a Chinese complexity of dance hall and amusement arcade, followed by supper in Hokian Street. The New World was a noisy extravagance of a clip joint with a variety of side line entertainment lavishly stocked with dance hostesses, the polite name for girls of easy virtue.

The noise at the New World was a bit overpowering and as we were sailing next day I suggested that it was a bit late to get involved with the dance hostesses if you did not want to miss the boat. So we moved on to Hokian Street. Here a busy street by daytime was closed to traffic and the restaurants on either side laid out their tables in the street. Here you could sit out in the relative cool of the evening and enjoy the most superb food. It probably does not exist today but in 1946 it was a gem of a place to dine out under the stars on the most exotic dishes you could wish for.

Next morning we all staggered aboard the *Arundel Castle* and so started our last journey back to the U.K. My driver drove me to the dockside in that splendid vehicle. It was quite an achievement to have held onto it all this time. Certainly when I found it in a thicket near Thonan, I never guessed that it would deliver me in state to the dockside in Singapore for repatriation. I said goodbye to my driver and he set off back to the company at Kroh. I often wonder what the final outcome of that staff car was to be. It had become a part of the insignia of 421 Field Company.

Next day we were at sea on the long voyage home. I remember little about this voyage except that I had a number of strings of cultured pearls that were a drug on the market in the early days in Bangkok. The Japanese had nowhere to export their cultured pearls and had overloaded the Bangkok market. When we arrived in Bangkok a string of these pearls could be bought for about 10 shillings. I had bought quite a number but obviously not enough. Some of my fellow officers had failed to get to Bangkok and were desperate to return with a string of pearls to the U.K. where they were still fashionable. They discovered that I was well supplied and put endless pressure on me to part with some of those I possessed.

In the end I agreed to swap a string of pearls for a case of whisky. As the pearls had cost me ten shillings it was not a bad exchange, however, I found that the possession of a case of whisky attracted a multiplicity of friends that I never knew I had, all intent on helping drink the contents. By Port Said the lot was gone. Some of them were very heavy drinkers but as they were not really my choice of friends I was quite glad when the whisky was all gone for their visits to our cabin finished when the whisky finished and we were now left in peace.

Our ship stopped at Columbo in Ceylon but only for a brief pick up of more time-expired soldiers. I would have liked to have had time to visit Kandy in the interior but had to content myself with a visit to the famous Gores Head Hotel for a quick drink and a little shopping then back to the ship to continue our journey. Our next stop was Aden for a similar pick up and an equally brief stop. Aden looked uninvitingly barren. There had been a little local hostility in Aden and only a limited number were allowed ashore and they were warned not to go beyond the main shopping centre for their own safety. I did not bother to go ashore as there was a big scramble for the limited number of shore passes. The apparent attraction was that one could buy Harris Tweed very cheaply in Aden. The very thought of Harris Tweed in that insufferably hot spot brought me out in a sweat. However, in two weeks we would be back in England and it would be October. In England clothes were rationed, hence the great attraction to go ashore at Aden and buy Harris Tweed. Some smart businessman must have obtained a licence to export the cloth to Aden so that it could be sold to returning servicemen who brought it straight back to England in suit lengths. It was practically unobtainable in England at the time; this seemed a rather dubious form of export and someone in the Ministry of Trade must have been half asleep when he granted the export licence. When the shore leave party arrived back a few hours later each was carrying his parcel of Harris Tweed under his arm. It was like a comic opera.

This time there was no long journey round the Cape so we steamed up the Red Sea to the Suez Canal. When we left Singapore there were rumours that we would be sailing around the Cape because the Suez Canal was closed for dredging. Fortunately, like most rumours, it was unfounded for here at last we were passing through that incredible waterway to the Mediterranean. Once in the Med we made a last brief stop at Port Said. No one went ashore as we just dropped anchor offshore, the usual flotilla of bum boats came homing in on us laden with leather poofs for a brisk and noisy barter with the troops on the lower decks. Long lines were thrown up to the lower deck and poofs and other leather goods hauled up and the money lowered down, not always the right amount I fear for there were some very heated exchanges right up to the moment that we raised anchor and went under way leaving a scattering of small boats with their proprietors still waving their arms and gesticulating.

As we sailed on through the Mediterranean we really felt we were on our way home. The first days of October saw our last landfall through the Straits of Gibraltar. The weather was still fine but distinctly cooler air greeted us from the Atlantic. At this point we were allowed to cable our impending arrival to next of kin at home. The ship's radio officer had a great volume containing the codes for all the towns and villages throughout the Empire. When it came to my turn to cable my parents I doubted very much that he would find the village of Zeals, Wiltshire in his book. He smiled and said if it has a Post Office it will be there. Sure enough, he was right, sandwiched between Zea in Greece and Zeara in British Somaliland, was Zeals, Wilts., England, with its own code letters. I was overjoyed, not that it made any difference other than to shorten the cable but it was good to know that my little home village of Zeals was in the code book carried on all ships at sea. I cabled my parents giving my expected date of arrival home so that they could kill the fatted calf. Not that there would be much fatted calf, for food rationing was still in full operation at home, but at least I would not walk in unexpectedly.

There were endless administrative orders on our last days at sea but far better to do it all at sea than waste time at Southampton delaying our return home. The whole business of returning time-expired soldiers was by now very well organised. We were even issued with rail warrants for our return home, as I was treating myself as an emergency commissioned officer, I was issued with a mass of instructions about demobilisation including which centre I would report to and was told they would write to me confirming the day and the time I should report to be demobilised. We were also issued with ration cards and clothing coupons, all essential necessities in post-war Britain. There would be the minimum of formalities when we landed, just customs for our hand luggage. We had already filled in customs declarations forms for heavy baggage in the hold that would be forwarded on to us by the MFO. We were due in Southampton next morning.

We awoke to the nostalgic sight of the Isle of Wight and the Solent ahead. After three and a half years in the Far East I just leant on the rail and feasted my eyes. I was luckier than most for I had been home for a fortnight on LIAP but I had also spent more time abroad than most of them, also my LIAP was somewhat dulled by my spending it recovering from jaundice. This was the real home-coming unmarred by the shadow of war.

I remember little of my arrival at the docks other than that customs were a mere formality and I was soon aboard a train to Salisbury, then on the little side line to Gillingham puffing its way through Tisbury, Hinton, Dinton, station names that evoked childhood memories. When I reached Gillingham the same old taxi driver was there waiting in the October sun for the chance fare to arrive. As I walked over to him, with my suitcase and valise, wrapped around old warrilow, following on the porter's trolley, he quietly folded the *Western Gazette* he was reading and got out of his ancient taxi. To my surprise and pleasure he still recognised me. "Hello Master John, you be back from the wars I see". He had known me since the days when I used to arrive with my Nanny en route for Castle, he always had a flower in his button hole and a bunch of flowers in his cab held in a little silver vase fixed above the dashboard. In the Spring they were always primroses with their sweet smell of the countryside greeting you as you entered the cab. Now it was October and cornflowers had taken their turn.

"I hear the Colonel had moved to Ashfield. You'll be wanting to go there I reckon". Nothing had changed in his small world or so it seemed. His clientele could go halfway across the world to fight in foreign places but it was no concern of his. It was the goings on in his little corner of Wiltshire and Dorset that were his world and it was refreshing to discover that it had not changed very much.

The luggage safely strapped on, I tipped the porter, and we set off for a quiet bumble along the country roads to Zeals and then to Ashfield on the edge of the Stour Valley. As we pulled into the side of the road opposite our new home at Ashfield, my parents who had been keeping an ear cocked for my arrival, appeared out of the front door. It was a wonderful reunion. They both looked wonderfully well and my father appeared as fit as ever. Little could I guess that he would be dead inside six months. For the moment it was just joy and reminiscing on our separate pasts until all the threads were knitted in to fill the gaps and reunite the pattern for the future. So started what was coded by the army as PYTHON, the letters may have stood for something though I believe it was just the code name for repatriation and the leave entitlement of one week for every year spent overseas. This gave me five weeks of paid leave before I had to face the realities of post war Britain. For the moment I could just relax and enjoy the wonders of being home again.

A little later I received my final instructions for demob. The centre I had to report to and the date and time. There was nothing more to do but relax and await that all important demob day after which I would have to start thinking seriously about my civilian future.

I do not remember now that the exact appointed day for my demob but I do remember only too well that the day before I had to report a telegram arrived from the War Office. It read 'Do not understand how regular officer can be demobbed. Report immediately Room 312 Hobart House, The War Office'.

It was a bit of a bombshell for me. Next morning instead of travelling to the demob centre I went up to London and reported to the War Office. Here I was politely informed that I had been gazetted as a regular officer last January when I was still in Bangkok. With the sudden end of the war, the War Office had found it impracticable to contact all the officers who had been selected for regular commissions by the War Office Selection Board to find if they were still desirous of receiving a regular commission.

They had therefore issued an army order informing them that they would be automatically commissioned within two months if they did not inform the War Office to the contrary. Such orders were generally six months out of date by the time they reached Siam. Like it or not, I was a regular officer and would remain so at his Majesty's pleasure until my resignation was accepted.

My war was over but not my military career. However, I often wonder what would have happened if that telegram had arrived a day later after I had been demobbed!

GLOSSARY OF ABBREVIATIONS

ADS	Advance Dressing Station
BNA	Burmese National Army
CE	Chief Engineer
CEV	Captured Enemy Vehicle
C in C	Commander in Chief
CO	Commanding Officer
CRE	Commander Royal Engineers
DADEE	Deputy Assistant Director Engineer Equipment
DADES	Deputy Assistant Director Engineer Stores
DDEE	Deputy Director Engineer Equipment
DDES	Deputy Director Engineer Stores
GSO1	General Staff Officer 1
HQ	Headquarters
IEME	Indian Electrical and Mechanical Engineers
IMM	Indian Military Medal
INA	Indian National Army
L of C	Lines of Communication
LCT	Landing Craft Troops
MFO	Military Forwarding Officer
MTO	Military Transport Officer

OBM	Outboard Motor
OC	Officer Commanding
OCTU	Officer Cadet Training Unit
PR	Public Relations
RTO	Rail Transport Officer
SAS	Special Air Services
VCO	Viceroy's Commissioned Officer
WAACI	Women's Auxiliary Army Corps India
WOSB	War Office Selection Board
Subadar	VCO
Jemadar	VCO
Havildar	Sergeant
Naik	Corporal
Lance Naik	Lance Corporal